MySpace™ For Dummies

Cheat Sheet

Tips to Go from MySpace Newbie to MySpace Pro

It's tough being a MySpace newcomer with an empty Web page and one friend while others have fancy pages and thousands of friends. Take a few steps to make your page tell the world that you're a MySpace veteran:

- **Get signed up:** You need a computer with access to the Internet and an e-mail address. See Chapter 2 for details.

- **Fill in your profile:** Add information to your page that tells a little about yourself. Chapter 2 tells you how.

- **Add a profile photo:** Put your smiling face on your MySpace profile page. You'll find instructions in Chapter 10.

- **Add a profile song:** Search MySpace for your favorite artist and share a song on your page. More about adding music in Chapter 11.

- **Fill up your Friends List:** Search for friends and invite them to your profile. Chapter 4 has the details.

- **Launch your blog:** Share a thought with the world or with just a few friends. You'll find details in Chapter 6.

- **Keep in contact with your friends:** Send mail messages to individual friends — or post a bulletin for all your friends to see. More on messages in Chapter 5.

- **Post an event and invite friends:** Are you throwing a party or going to a show? Set up an event for the world to see, or just let your friends to know about, and send invitations. Get started with events in Chapter 8.

- **Customize your page:** Dress up your drab MySpace page with colors, images, and text of your choosing. Chapter 12 introduces the tools you'll need to add your own touches to your page.

- **Shore up your security:** MySpace's account settings let you set your profile so it's only viewable to friends. For more about setting this option and for other safety tips, check out Chapters 3, 16, 17 — and watch for 'em throughout the book.

Securing Your MySpace Profile

MySpace allows you to alter your profile settings to limit who can see the information you post to the site. See Chapters 3, 16, and 17 for expanded insight into keeping your MySpace page safe from unwanted contact.

- **Set your profile as private:** The Privacy Settings link on the Change Account Settings page directs you to an option where you can limit full viewing of your profile to users who are on your Friends List. Non-friends can still see your profile name, location, age, profile photo, and MySpace URL.

- **Block photos from other users:** Clicking the Add/Edit Photos link on your MySpace home page directs you to the Upload Photo page. The page includes an option to prevent other MySpace users from seeing your photos. Click the *Only you* button under *Allow your photos to be viewable by:* option to keep your photos to yourself.

- **Limit your blog audience:** After you've composed a fresh entry in your blog, you can determine who can read your entry:

    Diary: Readable only by you.

    Preferred List: Readable by members of your Friends List you select and add to your list.

    Friends: Readable by all members of your Friends List.

    Public: Readable by all MySpace users.

- **Don't accept instant messages:** The Account Settings page offers a link to set instant message privacy. You can choose to allow anyone to send

(continued)

For Dummies: Bestselling Book Series for Beginners

MySpace™ For Dummies®

Cheat Sheet

you IM, limit to your friends only, or block IM altogether. The Privacy Settings link takes you to an option to block your online status, thus never letting other MySpace users know when you're available to receive messages.

✔ **Approve comments:** Your Privacy Settings option also allows you to review comments before they're posted to your profile page. This option is helpful if you want to keep your friends from putting any information on your page that you don't want to share. You can also disable HTML in your profile settings so MySpacers who leave comments can't add photos or video to your comments.

✔ **Block users:** Ignoring unwanted messages usually gets the point across (to most MySpace members) that you don't want to talk. For the persistent few who can't take a hint, you can click the Block User option in the Contact box on the would-be pest's profile page. Adding a user to your Block list keeps your mailbox free from contact with that person.

✔ **Deny, delete, edit, and erase:** Your MySpace page is always under your control. If you ever feel that your profile settings, a comment, a blog entry, or a friend is hurting your privacy, MySpace includes the settings to edit your page. See the chapters in Part II for more info on making changes to your place on MySpace.

Basic HTML for MySpace

There are several things you can do to customize and change how your MySpace profile looks and what appears on the page. Here is some basic *HTML (HyperText Markup Language)* that you can use with your MySpace profile.

Action	HTML to Use
Insert an image into a comment, message, or on your profile page.	`<img src="URL of the image" width="width of image in pixels">`
Insert a link into a comment, message, or on your profile page.	`<a href="URL of web page">Title of link</a>` **Note:** You can add the `target="blank"` option to open up the link in a new window.
Linking an image in a comment, message, or on your profile page.	`<a href="URL of web page"><img src="URL of image" width="width of image in pixels"></a>` **Note:** When you link an image, a border will automatically appear to show that it is linked. If you would like to remove that border you can add the `border="0"` option to your `<img>` tag.
Bolding text	`<b>Enter bolded text here</b>`
Italicizing text	`<i>Enter italicized text here</i>`
Font color	`<font color="Color of Font"></font>`
Font size	`<font size="Size of font from 1-7"></font>`
Special MySpace characters	These MySpace characters can be used in the text that you enter, such as your display name, your headline, and any type of message that you send out. **Heart:** `&hearts` **Trademark:** `&trade` **Copyright:** `&copy` **Registered:** `&reg`

For Dummies: Bestselling Book Series for Beginners

MySpace™
FOR
DUMMIES®

by Ryan Hupfer, Mitch Maxson, Ryan Williams

BICENTENNIAL
1807
WILEY
2007
BICENTENNIAL

Wiley Publishing, Inc.

MySpace™ For Dummies®

Published by
Wiley Publishing, Inc.
111 River Street
Hoboken, NJ 07030-5774

www.wiley.com

WILEY

About the Authors

Ryan Hupfer, a self-proclaimed 'computer nerd', has been consuming, producing, and learning all things Web since his first introduction to dial-up. With a rare mix of being both a social butterfly and a tech geek, he has always strived to find ways to utilize technology in a way that connects people and calls them to action. He is a strong believer in the ability to fulfill and extend the human need to connect with others online and is always looking at ways to leverage emerging technologies to benefit people's lives. By the time he hit his college years, Ryan was deep into the world of computer programming; all while being a bartender at one of Indianapolis' most popular dance clubs. In early 2004 Ryan's odd mix of being both a technology expert and socialite came together when he created his first online social community, www. HupsHoopty.com, which was based on his recent purchase of a brown 1992 GMC full-size custom van. This online community became an unlikely stepping stone and a door for opportunity in Ryan's life and eventually led him to landing his current dream job at Indianapolis-based new media/communications company, MediaSauce (www.mediasauce.com).

In December of 2005, Ryan and Mitch Maxson, both MediaSauce employees, along with Ryan's roommate, a film crew, and two bus drivers, traveled across the United States in a 50-foot tour bus for two weeks in search of their Top 8 MySpace friends — whom they had never met. The tour, called "Hup 'n Dub's Top 8 Tour," was created in an effort to better understand why millions of people were so attracted to the new online social phenomenon. Since the tour, Ryan has been constantly keeping up with all things Web 2.0 and he is extremely inspired and intrigued by the ways that the online world is now flipping the media world upside down. Speaking of media, Ryan was also 'discovered' by a local NBC Indianapolis news station, WTHR (www.wthr.com), when they watched a video podcast that MediaSauce created around the 2006 Final Four, called IndyPods (indypods.mediasauce.com). With his hands in both the traditional and new media world, there's no telling where Ryan will end up next. You can keep up with him on his MySpace page at www.MySpace.com/hupdaddy.

Mitch Maxson spent two years with a small, traditional marketing firm before leaving to co-create his first interactive development firm (Transgres) after graduating from Purdue University. After two years of sustained growth, Transgres joined MediaSauce to pursue a shared vision of broadband-based integrated communications. Today, as a partner and Creative Director, Mitch has helped grow MediaSauce from 8 employees to more than 50 in just two years. As a constant proponent of "what comes next" and the emergence of audience-centric messaging and broadband connectivity, Mitch's focus is on understanding individuals and inspiring new ways for them to interact with their world.

With MediaSauce, Mitch has helped develop a side project known as Roster, which allows fans to connect to their favorite celebrities via video games, and traveled coast-to-coast to explore MySpace Friends in "real life" via The Top 8 Tour. On a more regular basis, Mitch can be found preaching the vision of the integration of communication, entertainment, and media while helping clients better understand their audiences and how to connect with them.

Ryan Williams is a multimedia designer, author, and bassist based in Indianapolis, Indiana. He's shared the stage and studio with everybody and everything from Grammy award-winning hip-hop artists to a full band of bagpipes and drums. He received his master's degree in music technology from the Indiana University School of Music in 2003. He's the author of *Windows XP Digital Music For Dummies* and *Teach Yourself Visually Bass Guitar,* both published by Wiley Publishing, Inc. He has also written several articles and tutorials on music and music technology for several publications and Web sites. He is a frequent panelist on digital music and home studios at music conferences around the nation.

Dedication

I dedicate this, my first book-writing adventure, to my "super rad" parents, Clarence and Alice Hupfer, who have always supported me no matter what crazy thing I was doing.

— Ryan Hupfer

To Pixie, for always supporting me, believing in me, encouraging my ridiculousness, and being the most amazing person I'll ever know. To my family for teaching me how to live, trusting me enough to do it my way, and being there for every question that falls in between. To friends — while technology will continue to impact the ways in which we connect with the world around us, true friends are the ones who come over for dinner or come out to play.

— Mitch Maxson

Authors' Acknowledgments

I would like to thank the Wiley dynamic duo, Steve Hayes and Blair Pottenger, for making their best effort in keeping me on schedule with this book. I would also like to give a hi-five to Mr. Ryan Williams who made Mitch and I look bad because he wrote so dang fast.

Thanks to my partner in crime, the always insightful Mitch Maxson, for making this book such a fun read and for being the greatest writer, ever. Holla!

A HUGE thanks goes to my boss, my mentor and my friend Mr. Bryan Gray, CEO of MediaSauce, for giving me the flexibility to finish this project and for keeping me excited about what I do every single day.

To all of my friends and Ptown homies who first inspired me to find better ways to share our busy lives with each other. All of you mean more to me than you'll ever know.

— Ryan Hupfer

Thanks to Ryan Hupfer for being crazy, but not insane (no matter what they say), and for appreciating my weird brain as much as I do yours. Thanks to everyone at MediaSauce for sharing a vision and enjoying the passionate pursuit therein.

— Mitch Maxson

My contribution to this book would not have been possible without the patience and understanding of Steven Hayes, Blair Pottenger, and the rest of the immensely talented Wiley Publishing staff. Many thanks are also due to my wife Jennifer, who put up with short deadlines and long hours.

— Ryan Williams

Publisher's Acknowledgments

We're proud of this book; please send us your comments through our online registration form located at www.dummies.com/register/.

Some of the people who helped bring this book to market include the following:

Acquisitions, Editorial, and Media Development

Project Editor: Blair J. Pottenger

Senior Acquisitions Editor: Steven Hayes

Senior Copy Editor: Barry Childs-Helton

Technical Editor: Jennifer Hughes

Editorial Manager: Kevin Kirschner

Media Development Manager: Laura VanWinkle

Editorial Assistant: Amanda Foxworth

Sr. Editorial Assistant: Cherie Case

Cartoons: Rich Tennant (www.the5thwave.com)

Composition Services

Project Coordinator: Kristie Rees

Layout and Graphics: Lavonne Cook, Stephanie D. Jumper,Barbara Moore, Barry Offringa, Laura Pence, Rashell Smith, Erin Zeltner

Proofreaders: Laura Albert, Techbooks

Indexer: Techbooks

Anniversary Logo Design: Richard Pacifico

Publishing and Editorial for Technology Dummies

 Richard Swadley, Vice President and Executive Group Publisher

 Andy Cummings, Vice President and Publisher

Mary Bednarek, Executive Acquisitions Director

 Mary C. Corder, Editorial Director

Publishing for Consumer Dummies

 Diane Graves Steele, Vice President and Publisher

 Joyce Pepple, Acquisitions Director

Composition Services

 Gerry Fahey, Vice President of Production Services

 Debbie Stailey, Director of Composition Services

Contents at a Glance

Cartoons at a Glance

By Rich Tennant

page 201

page 163

page 7

page 267

page 55

Fax: 978-546-7747
E-mail: richtennant@the5thwave.com
World Wide Web: www.the5thwave.com

Table of Contents

Introduction

· ·

Greetings, and welcome to *MySpace For Dummies*. The last time we checked, there were over 115 million profiles registered on MySpace. When we started writing this book, there were a mere 70 million. By the time our manuscript gets edited, this book is printed and shipped to your neighborhood bookstore, and you pick it up, that number might be over 150 million profiles. Maybe 200 million? 300 million? In short, this MySpace thing is huge and it's still growing.

Like so many technological tools and services these days, MySpace doesn't come with a user manual or guidebook to help you figure out how the site works. If you're like a lot of people out there in the online world, you enjoy using the Internet to keep in touch with your friends — but you don't have the time, energy, or interest to spend forever figuring out how things work. You just want to have fun and not stress out about the details of using your computer. We understand that feeling — and we're here to help.

Think of us as the friendliest computer nerds you'll ever know. We actually do keep up with all the geeky computer stuff that makes the guys with the pocket protectors and lab coats giddy — but we also know how to filter out the stuff you don't care about and highlight the stuff you need to know. I guess our moms were right — we are quite a catch. And we've packaged it all together in chunks so when you need to know something about MySpace, you can read what you need and move on. Nothing dumb about that, huh?

About This Book

We'll be honest with you — we're shocked that you're reading this introduction. Reading from start to finish isn't what this book, or any *For Dummies* book, is about. In fact, if all you do is pick up the book when you need to know something about MySpace, find your topic in the Table of Contents or index, read the page or two that covers that topic, and put your book back down to gather dust until the next time you need it, we have done our job. Yay us!!!

We don't expect you to become an instant MySpace guru with a half-million friends and the most tricked-out profile page on the site after using this book. We don't expect you'll be able to spout off lectures on the minutiae of MySpace's programming code. We've kept this book simple so you can get the info you need without a computer science degree.

We take a pretty straightforward approach to how we cover MySpace. We know MySpace has a lot of tools you can use — and that you only want to figure out how to use them (and maybe not all of them or all the time). So we've covered what you want to know, including

- Signing up for an account and setting up your profile
- Turning on MySpace's safety and security tools
- Finding friends and keeping in touch with them
- Upgrading your profile with photos, music, and a whole new look
- Showing off your talents on MySpace
- Selling, buying, and marketing on MySpace

Conventions Used in This Book

When we started telling our friends that we were writing a *For Dummies* book on MySpace, a few of them looked at us like we were crazy. The typical question was "How are you going to write a 300-page book on MySpace? It's the easiest thing in the world to use!" But it's like we said — we're card-carrying computer nerds, and most of our friends are kind of geeky as well. So we told them to put their propeller hats back on and go back to their labs.

For the rest of us, we think this book will be ideal when you get stuck trying to get something done on MySpace or you think of something you want to do on MySpace and don't want to waste your time guessing about how to do it. Check out the Table of Contents or the index to find what it is you want to do. Once you've found it, read it, complete your task, and carry on. You won't even be tested on it later.

Along the way, we also share some insight into MySpace that we've gathered during our time logged on to the site. We signed up on the site pretty early on and showed signs of addiction right away. A couple of us, Ryan Hupfer and Mitch Maxson, even commandeered a bus to go around the country and meet our Top 8 friends, getting a taste of how MySpace is changing the culture along the way. We even stopped in the MySpace offices in Santa Monica to meet a few of the people who really make MySpace work. So we've seen everything (so far) when it comes to MySpace, and we share that knowledge with you as we go.

The good folks at Wiley Publishing, the people who actually make the *For Dummies* books, have devised a good system for letting us get our point across when we're explaining how MySpace works.

- ✔ **Bulleted lists.** When you come across a bulleted list like this one, we're usually breaking down a list of MySpace options into smaller chunks for quicker reading. For example, when we cover setting up your profile in Chapter 2, we go over all your options in bullet lists. You don't have to follow the list in order point by point — just jump to what you want to know and follow the guidance you get there.

- ✔ **Numbered step lists.** When you see a list broken down into numbered steps, we're walking you through a specific process toward reaching a set goal. For instance, we offer a numbered how-to list when we tell you how to upload photos to your MySpace page in Chapter 10. Follow the steps and you should get the results you want.

- ✔ **Web addresses.** Here and there throughout the book, we instruct you to type a specific Web site address into your browser. Those references look like this — www.myspace.com. If you're still not sure how things like Web browsers work, you might take a look at *The Internet For Dummies,* 10th Edition by John Levine, Margaret Levine Young, and Carol Baroudi to get some help with the basics of the Internet.

Foolish Assumptions

We're going to be a bit bold and make a few assumptions about you because you picked up *MySpace For Dummies.* We're guessing you've heard about MySpace, want to try it out for yourself, and have access to a computer that lets you get on the Internet and access MySpace. It doesn't matter if the computer is a PC or Mac or something else — MySpace works the same on all flavors of computer.

What we're not sure about is why you want to get on MySpace — yeah, okay, the details are none of our beeswax — but our guess is that you've heard it's a great way to keep up with friends and meet new people with similar interests. Or maybe someone in your family — likely a teenager — is either on MySpace or wants to join MySpace, and you want to know more about it before they sign on. If you're already signed up on MySpace and just want to use more of their tools, we have you covered there as well.

One thing we do assume about all our readers is that you're interested in keeping safe and secure while you're using MySpace. Okay, MySpace has gotten a lot of attention because of some Internet bad guys who have used MySpace to contact other users — especially teenaged users — with illicit and illegal proposals. Unfortunately, those people are a reality in both the real world, and the online world, and to help you stay as safe as possible, we concentrated a lot of information about MySpace safety in Chapter 3. We've also littered safety info throughout the book. We want your MySpace experience to be safe and fun — and we share a lot of pointers to make sure you get that experience.

How This Book Is Organized

We keep promising that this book is set up so you can use only the pieces you need to get the results you want. Well, the first step in this process is dividing all the info into parts that cover the big topics on MySpace. Where you choose to start reading depends on whether you're a complete MySpace newbie (in which case, welcome!), a current member who wants to pump up your page, or a professional looking to use MySpace as a way to get the word about your business or talent out to a lot of people. Here's how we have organized the parts of our book.

Part 1: MySpace Overview and Basics

This is the Part you need to turn to if you're just getting started with MySpace. We cover the basics of what you can do on the MySpace site, how to get signed up with an account, how to set up your profile with the information you want to share with other MySpace users, and how to stay safe and secure when using MySpace.

Part 11: The MySpace Community

The main goal of MySpace is pretty simple: putting their users in contact with each other. This part covers the main tools for making those contacts. We take a look at how to find friends, add friends to your MySpace profile, and stay in touch with those friends via e-mail messages, bulletins, and profile comments. We also cover keeping a Web log — that's what a *blog* is if you're visiting from another planet and haven't heard of 'em — on your MySpace page. This part shares guidance on using MySpace's calendar, event invitations, forums, and creating or joining groups. We also show how you can keep up with your MySpace account on a mobile phone.

Part III: Customizing MySpace

MySpace allows users to decorate profile pages with photos, video, and music tracks posted by the musical artists who have also made a home on MySpace (which makes perfect sense — after all, musicians started it). Truly bold users can even dig into the programming code that runs MySpace to change the colors, layout, and background image they use for their pages. This part walks you through the steps needed to change your MySpace page into something unique.

Part IV: Capturing Your Audience

With millions of users logging on to MySpace every day, the site's become a great way for musicians, filmmakers, comedians, and authors to share their works. Also, with millions of eyes on the site, marketers have turned to MySpace to get the word out about movie releases, television premieres, club events, product availability, and just about every other type of sellable stuff you can think of. This part shows how to use the tools to show off your own talents on MySpace — as well as some ideas on how to get more eyes on your stuff.

Part V: The Part of Tens

In the great tradition of the *For Dummies* series, we close *MySpace For Dummies* with the Part of Tens. There you'll find a few chapters that break down some key points about MySpace into short, easy-to-read sections. We also share some insight that didn't quite fit anywhere else in the book. Flip to this section to read about other Web sites similar to MySpace, a few places you can go for help with your MySpace page, or quick tips on MySpace safety.

Icons Used in This Book

Occasionally you'll encounter a little figure to the left of the text. Those are what we call icons. These figures are sort of like road signs; they point out notes that give you a heads-up when a piece of information is a bit techy or provides a valuable tip. Be on the lookout for these icons:

We've been bumping around on MySpace for a while and have some ideas on how to improve your MySpace experience. The Tip icon points you to these suggestions.

We don't ask you to commit many things to memory, but every once in a while we add in something that's worth keeping in mind while you're using MySpace. Just remember to look for this icon (we haven't come up with an icon for that yet).

Our goal is to steer you clear of the tripwires and pitfalls you might encounter while using MySpace. This icon shows you the detours around the things that might cause problems down the road.

Although we've tried our best to keep all the geeky information out of your way, sometimes we do have to throw in a few bits here and there that explain the technology that makes MySpace work. Don't worry, this icon lets you know when we're about to get nerdy on you. (If you read what's there anyway, we won't tell a soul.)

Where to Go from Here

We're sure you're tired of reading about MySpace and are ready to start exploring the popular Web site. Go ahead and sit down at your computer and log on to www.myspace.com. But be sure to keep this book by your side and flip to the page you need whenever you hit a rough spot.

Part I

MySpace Overview and Basics

The 5th Wave — By Rich Tennant

"You know, I liked you a whole lot more in your About Me survey."

In this part . . .

Before you start your own adventures in MySpace, it might be a good idea to have a look around. Kick MySpace's metaphorical tires and see how it runs. Get an answer to the question "Just what exactly do you *do* on MySpace?" Get the lay of the land from 40,000 feet instead of ground level.

Oh, we could go on and on with the comparisons to what this part is like. Boil away all our jabbering, and what you have is a good look at who's on MySpace, what tools are on MySpace, and how you get signed up and create a profile. We also have a very important chapter on safety. (You might want to grab one of those sticky tabs and put it there right away. We bet you'll be reading it a lot.)

Chapter 1

Diving into the MySpace Pool

· ·

In This Chapter

▶ Understanding why MySpace is so popular

▶ Taking a tour of the features

▶ Deciding whether you should join

· ·

In the brief history of the Internet and the World Wide Web, no Web site has made as sudden and as large an impact as MySpace. In the short couple of years since it first went online, MySpace has grown from a place for bands and musical artists to share their work to a popular online hangout for teenagers and college students to a social and cultural phenomenon that boasts over 100 million profiles and is valued at more than $15 billion.

That growth pushed MySpace into the media spotlight for both good and bad reasons. Technology watchers marveled at how quickly the site grew, and celebrated how it gave people a place where they could share their thoughts, photos, and the things that made them unique individuals. Users connected with old friends and made new ones across the globe. On the dark side, the site gave stalkers and other Internet bad guys one-to-one access to potential victims.

We hope this book clears up all the mysteries of MySpace for you — and shows how you can use the site to share as much (or as little) information as you want with either a worldwide audience or a small circle of friends. In this chapter, we're going to give you a view of MySpace from 30,000 feet. We go over what the site allows users to do, what tools are available to share your story or find others with similar interest, and try to get to the bottom of what makes MySpace so popular with both kids and adults.

Whose Space? MySpace!

At its most basic definition, *MySpace* is a social networking Web site located on the World Wide Web dial at www.myspace.com. A *social networking Web site* is a site that allows users to create individual profiles (shown in Figure 1-1) in hopes of making contact with other site users that share similar interests or goals.

Figure 1-1:
A basic
MySpace
profile page.

Think of social networking sites as big parties that live online. You walk in to a room full of people and see some close friends, some familiar faces, and a lot of complete strangers. You naturally gravitate toward your close friends. Those close friends acquaint you with the familiar faces they know based on

---

The age of user-generated Web content

If you follow technology trends, you may have heard people who spend a lot of time thinking about the future of the Internet using the term *Web 2.0*. That term refers to the recent growth of Web sites that provide a platform for regular users to post content and participate in their own Web experience.

MySpace is the perfect example of a Web 2.0 site. Rather than developing a ton of content on its own, MySpace provides the technology for users to post their own words, photos, videos, music, and other items on their profiles. Some of the Web's most popular sites — including online auctioneer eBay, online encyclopedia

Wikipedia, video-hosting site YouTube, and the many blogs of the "blogosphere" — all fit under the Web 2.0 umbrella.

If user-generated content is part of the definition of Web 2.0, we figure Web 1.0 was back when designers built pages, filled them with content, and you went online just to see what was on the site. Web 1.5 probably came along when you could actually do something with a Web site — such as order a product from a company's Web site. So what's Web 3.0? Those guys who spend all that time thinking about the Internet continue to argue that point.

your mutual friendship. Those new acquaintances then introduce you to the complete strangers they know based on your mutual interests. The same thing happens on MySpace, except there are on the order of 100 million people at the party, so grab your breath spray and lace up your dancing shoes!

The people in your MySpace neighborhood

The MySpace site contains over 100 million profiles. Although that stat is true, it doesn't mean that over 100 million individuals are actually using MySpace. A *profile* is a unique MySpace page that shares information about a user. Along with all the personal MySpace pages, there are profiles for bands, artists, businesses, films, television shows, clubs, cities, and about any other entity you can dream of. Some users even create multiple profiles to address different interests. As you begin to make your way through MySpace, you're going to encounter many different profiles:

- ✔ **Individual users:** The most common profile type is the individual user. These are the people who sign up to share insight into their own lives or personalities on MySpace. Mixed in with the regular folks on MySpace are a number of celebrities (and celebrity wannabes and celebrity impersonators) who use the site to promote their work or just keep in touch with their fans, but in the end, they're really just people like you and me (they just have better hair).

- ✔ **Bands and musicians:** MySpace's musician-friendly tools allow musical artists to share their work on the site and connect with fans, as shown in Figure 1-2. This service is what helped spur the site's fast growth. Every level of act, from the biggest-name bands in the world to the kids making a racket in the garage across the street, can build MySpace pages where they share their music to build a fan base. See Chapter 14 for more information on adding and finding bands on MySpace.

- ✔ **Businesses and marketers:** Any time you collect millions of people together on a single site, marketers will naturally try to find a way to get their messages out to the masses. You can't blame them, it's just their way. MySpace is no exception. Businesses create profiles for their products and product launches in hopes of generating grass roots buzz. See Chapter 13 for more on how marketing works on MySpace.

- ✔ **Films and filmmakers:** Hollywood knows a good thing when they see it. Movie studios have used MySpace to release previews of their films and generate excitement for a feature's opening weekend. You can usually find a MySpace profile for almost any film ranging from big budget blockbusters to art house indies.

  MySpace has also added special features for filmmakers who want to use the site to promote their works. Filmmaker profiles include a special clip player where they can show off their clips to would-be fans. Check out Chapter 15 to find more info on MySpace's filmmaker profiles.

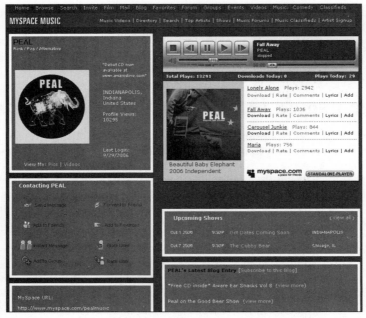

Figure 1-2:
A band
profile
features a
media
player.

✔ **Comedians:** MySpace knows that everybody loves to laugh. Comedians are the most recent artist community to get their own profiles on MySpace. A comedy profile features a player where the comedian can share clips of his or her act, as well as a calendar of appearances, as shown in Figure 1-3. For more on comedian profiles, see Chapter 15.

✔ **Clubs and organizations:** Groups ranging from community booster clubs to school organizations to church groups register MySpace profiles to keep in touch with their current members, as well as to attract new members. MySpace includes tools to build groups where you can collect other members into smaller communities. We cover how to set up and join these groups in Chapter 9.

That list just scratches the surface of the variety of profiles you'll see on MySpace. We've also seen profiles set up for television shows, individual concerts, pets, dance clubs, restaurants, recording studios, cities, music venues, promotional companies, and other Web sites. We've even seen a profile registered for the jukebox at one of our favorite pubs. In short, anytime someone has information they want to share with a big audience, be it individual personality traits or promotion for a product or event, MySpace is becoming the first stop for getting the word out.

Figure 1-3:
Comedians share a laugh and their gigs on MySpace.

The allure of MySpace

MySpace was certainly not the first social networking Web site. You can argue that the idea of social networking on the Internet goes back to when people started putting together mailing lists from their e-mail accounts so they could send mass messages to friends and family — like those tear-jerking stories or adorable pictures of kittens came with instructions that demanded the message be passed on or true love would be within reach. Because MySpace wasn't the first social-networking tool on the Internet, it makes us wonder why it has become the most popular networking site. We have a few theories:

- **Artist-friendly tools:** The biggest thing MySpace offered to users that other social network sites didn't match was the ability for musicians to store and share music tracks on the site with fans. As musicians signed up to take advantage of the service, they publicized their new resource to their fans. These fans, looking to stay connected to their favorite groups or a cool music scene, followed the artists to MySpace and began inviting *their* friends. The site took off from there.

- **Search tools and categories:** MySpace includes the opportunity to include your personal interests and hobbies on your profile. The site also lets you add any schools you've attended, businesses you've worked for, or industries you follow into your page. All these points of contact make it easier for people to filter through to find current friends, old contacts, or other users with shared interests to add to their own friends lists. See Chapter 4 for more info about finding friends on MySpace.

✔ **The dating scene:** The second wave of MySpace users was dominated by young adults, many of whom were single and looking for a way to meet other singles. MySpace offers the opportunity to set up a profile that lets the world know you're on the dating scene and open to contact from interested individuals. (Of course, later waves of users were filled by people who were in relationships and not interested in propositions from strangers.) MySpace also offers means to filter out those contacts. See Chapter 2 for more information on setting up a profile that meets your goals on MySpace.

✔ **Many services collected in one site:** Before MySpace there were sites for social networking, sharing photos, posting music files, showing video, starting a Web diary, sending out event invitations, keeping an appointment calendar, and sending or receiving messages. MySpace collected all those services under one site. MySpace has become a one-stop shop for the things most regular people like to do on the Web.

✔ **Customizable pages:** While you could load tons of information about yourself on other social network sites, you couldn't do much to change the way your personal page looked. You were stuck with the same white/silver/blue look that everyone used. MySpace opened up their pages to modification so people could customize the look, and now those pages are designed with help from editing tools or good old-fashioned *HTML* (short for *HyperText Markup Language,* the language used to design Web pages). A MySpace user can change his or her page from the boring white/silver/blue to including a cool background photo, individualized text fonts, and a customized pointer — all without needing any programming experience — as shown in Figure 1-4. After all, this is your "Space," and if you're going to be having company over, it had best resemble your personality and your style. Skip to Chapter 12 if you want to know more about tricking out your MySpace page.

✔ **Sharing with a huge audience:** Marketers want to get the word out about their products to as many people as they can. Filmmakers and comedians know their success hinges on getting as many eyes and ears on their work as possible. Individuals who have a message they want to share with the masses know it's better to share it once to a lot of people than many times to small groups. With millions of users, MySpace has built the audience for any of these user types. As the MySpace audience grows, so will the number of people who use MySpace to express themselves and build an audience.

✔ **Hanging out with your friends:** Although it's last on our list, the notion of just having a place where you can keep in touch with your friends shouldn't be discounted as a small part of MySpace's popularity. Humans are social animals. In an age where we all find ourselves strapped for time, MySpace provides a forum where we can contact and stay in touch with our friends, or make new friends from any computer hooked to the Internet at any time of day. Being on MySpace is being part of an in-crowd.

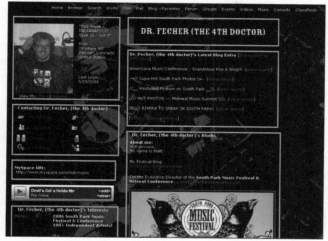

Figure 1-4: MySpace pages can be customized for your own look.

For all the reasons people join MySpace, there are as many reasons that MySpace haters offer for not joining. The popular ones we've heard are they don't have the time to spend on the site or the site is just for kids. We'd argue the latter reason is incorrect, and recent research shows that an increasing number of MySpacers (almost a majority, in fact) are over the age of 25. Admittedly, we haven't found any medical professional who has listed having a MySpace profile as a basic life necessity alongside food, water, and shelter. So if all our reasons for joining up aren't enough to entice you, you should be able to live a full life without MySpace.

The Nuts and Bolts of MySpace

MySpace is a one-stop shop for a lot of services offered on other Web sites. When you begin to peel off the layers of the MySpace site, you quickly discover there's a lot going on at `myspace.com`. After you get signed up at MySpace, you have access to many tools — such as these:

✔ **Web building:** At its foundation, the MySpace service is a basic Web building tool that lets you create your own site and customize it to your liking. Rather than having to start from scratch with HTML or Web building software, you just fill in the blanks at MySpace to create your page. See Chapter 2 for more info about building your MySpace page from the ground up.

✔ **Online photo album:** Along with your profile picture that appears on your MySpace profile page, you can upload other photos that are viewable by other MySpace members (or, if you choose, by your friends only), as shown in Figure 1-5. Similar to a world-wide yearbook, more and more this photo album is the first place someone will go check to see what you look like. Jump to Chapter 10 for more guidance on using the MySpace photo tools.

✔ **Blog:** MySpace provides a built in tool for starting your own Web diary, better known online as a *blog.* Blogs, short for Web logs, are online journals where users record thoughts or report on events. MySpace allows you to make your blog publicly viewable or viewable only to a select audience. You can even mark individual entries as private if you wish. We cover blogging in-depth in Chapter 6.

✔ **Video hosting:** MySpace added a tool for hosting and sharing short video clips. You can find more on how to add and view video in Chapter 12.

✔ **Calendar:** Tired of carrying around your old calendar book? MySpace provides a fully-customizable calendar tool that allows you to enter plans and appointments. You can then choose to share your calendar with friends or keep it private. We cover calendar functions in detail in Chapter 8.

✔ **Address book:** Need a place to store the e-mail addresses and MySpace user names of your closest friends? MySpace's Address Book tool keeps track of that important information. For more information on the Address Book, see Chapter 5.

✔ **Send and receive messages:** Your MySpace account comes with a mailbox similar to an e-mailbox where other MySpace users can send you messages or get replies from you. We cover MySpace messaging in Chapter 5.

Figure 1-5:
Our acquisitions editor shows off photos on his MySpace page.

✔ **Post a bulletin:** You share a bulletin space (shown in Figure 1-6) with all your MySpace friends you add to your profile. The bulletin option is a good way to get a message out to all your friends at once. We cover bulletins in Chapter 5.

✔ **Post an event and invite your friends:** While you can share your personal calendar with your friends, you can share information about a happening with the entire MySpace population by entering it as an event. You can filter the events page by location or time frame to find just the events going on in a certain area during a certain time. After you post an event, you can follow up by inviting your MySpace friends or other contacts that don't use MySpace to the event. We cover the details of the event calendar and invites in Chapter 8.

✔ **Chat with other users:** MySpace provides a forum for posting comments on specific topics to a bulletin board or taking part in live chat in an online chat room. Chapter 9 covers both these features in detail.

✔ **Leave comments:** MySpace offers the chance for your friends to leave comments on your profile, blog entries, or photos. You can do the same for your friends. We like to think of these comments as the online equivalent of yearbook autographs. They're usually brief notes offering kudos or greeting. There's more info about comments in Chapter 5.

✔ **Post a classified ad:** MySpace offers a classified ads forum where you can search for a job, a service, item, or date, as shown in Figure 1-7. You can also offer something for sale if you want. The classifieds pages are divided by geographic region centered around the big cities in the MySpace world. Check out Chapter 9 for more info on the classifieds section.

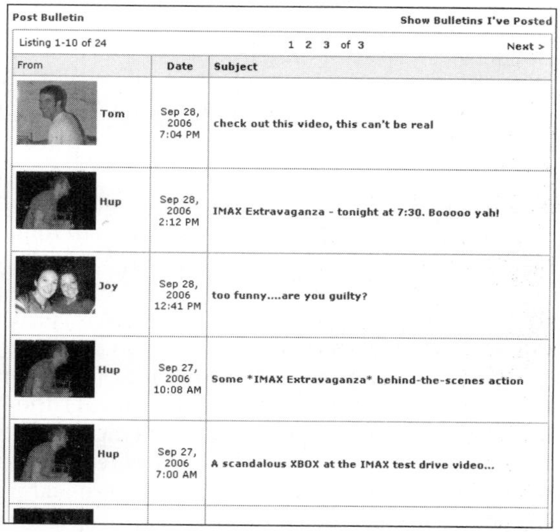

Figure 1-6:
The bulletin board shows messages shared by your friends.

Post Bulletin		Show Bulletins I've Posted
Listing 1-10 of 24	1 2 3 of 3	Next >
From	Date	Subject
Tom	Sep 28, 2006 7:04 PM	check out this video, this can't be real
Hup	Sep 28, 2006 2:12 PM	IMAX Extravaganza - tonight at 7:30. Booooo yah!
Joy	Sep 28, 2006 12:41 PM	too funny....are you guilty?
Hup	Sep 27, 2006 10:08 AM	Some *IMAX Extravaganza* behind-the-scenes action
Hup	Sep 27, 2006 7:00 AM	A scandalous XBOX at the IMAX test drive video...

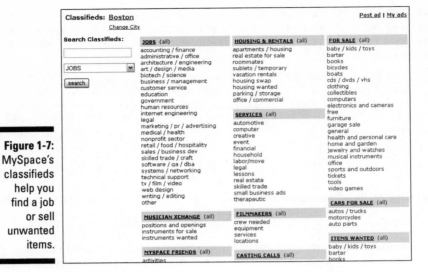

Figure 1-7: MySpace's classifieds help you find a job or sell unwanted items.

The classifieds image contains:

Classifieds: Boston
Change City
Post ad | My ads

Search Classifieds:

JOBS

search

JOBS (all)
accounting / finance
administrative / office
architecture / engineering
art / design / media
biotech / science
business / management
customer service
education
government
human resources
internet engineering
legal
marketing / pr / advertising
medical / health
nonprofit sector
retail / food / hospitality
sales / business dev
skilled trade / craft
software / qa / dba
systems / networking
technical support
tv / film / video
web design
writing / editing
other

MUSICIAN XCHANGE (all)
positions and openings
instruments for sale
instruments wanted

MYSPACE FRIENDS (all)
activities

HOUSING & RENTALS (all)
apartments / housing
real estate for sale
roommates
sublets / temporary
vacation rentals
housing swap
housing wanted
parking / storage
office / commercial

SERVICES (all)
automotive
computer
creative
event
financial
household
labor/move
legal
lessons
real estate
skilled trade
small business ads
therapeutic

FILMMAKERS (all)
crew needed
equipment
services
locations

CASTING CALLS (all)

FOR SALE (all)
baby / kids / toys
barter
books
bicycles
boats
cds / dvds / vhs
clothing
collectibles
computers
electronics and cameras
free
furniture
garage sale
general
health and personal care
home and garden
jewelry and watches
musical instruments
office
sports and outdoors
tickets
tools
video games

CARS FOR SALE (all)
autos / trucks
motorcycles
auto parts

ITEMS WANTED (all)
baby / kids / toys
barter
books

Is MySpace Safe?

MySpace has garnered more than its fair share of public and media attention — partially for it's amazing rise in popularity and use, and partially because some online bad guys have used the site to perpetrate crimes. The most common stories have revolved around adults that use MySpace to contact underage users with propositions of sex. Such stories have been rampant enough that some parents and schools have labeled MySpace as a source of problems and worked to keep young users away from the service.

It would be unfair for us to not address these problems in this book. In fact, throughout the book we offer examples of how the various MySpace tools can potentially leave a profile open to unwanted contact. We also explain how you can set up your profile to prevent unwanted contact. There's a lot of information in Chapter 3 specifically on how to secure your MySpace site from the online bad guys out there. If MySpace security is an immediate concern of yours, we recommend you jump to that chapter.

Our answer to the question "Is MySpace safe?" is a reserved "yes." We think MySpace is safe the same way an automobile is safe if you use your seat belt, drive in good conditions, and follow the rules of the road. If you don't buckle your safety belt, drive on bald tires, and push your speed over the legal limit, you're asking for trouble. The same thing happens on MySpace if you build a profile that potentially attracts unsavory individuals. Remember, think of MySpace as an online party — although most partygoers are just out for a good time with their friends, there are others who show up looking for trouble. Use common sense and commit to being safe. We cover how to tweak your profile to prevent attention from unwanted guests in Chapter 2 and how to stay safe on MySpace in Chapter 3.

As you work your way through this book and gather tips and techniques for keeping a MySpace profile secure, keep a few general comments in mind:

- **MySpace is a reflection of the real world.** In one of our favorite articles about MySpace, the journalist likened the site to a shopping mall. A shopping mall attracts visitors of all ages and all walks of life. Teens gather for social reasons. Adults handling specific errands are mixed in. There are people working in the mall trying to get you to buy things. Also sprinkled in this crowd, however, are a small number of people up to no good, like shoplifting or making illicit contact with teenagers.

  MySpace is a reflection of what's going on in our figurative shopping mall. The main difference between the real world and the MySpace world is that the Internet offers an anonymity that you can't achieve in the real world. Adults can pose as teenagers online to make initial contact.

  Just as a parent wouldn't send a teenager to a shopping mall alone without preparing them to handle any bad situation they encounter, a parent shouldn't let a teenager navigate MySpace without similar advice. MySpace maintains a good set of tips for users and parents of teenaged users on how to address safety concerns. Go to `www1.myspac.ecom/misc/safetyTips.html` for insight on managing your profile or a teenager's profile for maximum security.

- **Think before you post.** If you have a public profile, remember that what you put on your MySpace site is viewable not only by your friends, but also by those MySpace outlaws, your colleagues, classmates, potential employers, and other people you might not want to be sharing certain information with.

  Before you put up that photo of yourself at the beach in your super small bikini or your blog rant about your co-workers, think about who might see it and how they might react. If the outcome might be negative, it's best that you don't add the content to your MySpace page. Always remember, not only can your friends see those pictures, so can your family members, current co-workers, and future employers.

- **Change your profile to change your results.** Almost everything you put on your own MySpace page can be changed or erased. You can limit the people who can view your site to your friends list by setting your profile to private, as shown in Figure 1-8. You can also block certain users from accessing your page. In short, you can completely change your MySpace page at any time if you feel that it's attracting the wrong element. Chapter 3 covers the main techniques for limiting your audience, whereas Chapter 2 explains how to edit your profile.

Keeping an eye on your kids' MySpace pages

Though MySpace offers plenty of tools and advice on keeping kids safe while using MySpace, you can't rely on the site to handle all possible problem users. If your child uses MySpace, we recommend you get your kid's MySpace URL and regularly check the profile. You can even sign on to get your own MySpace ID so you can check the photo album. If your child has a private profile, send a friend request — and *insist* that you be added to the friends list so you can view the page; otherwise (if it comes to a power struggle), no MySpace. Keep an eye on who's leaving comments, what

your kids are putting in their blogs, and what messages they're sending with their pages. You can even check out the pages of some of their "Friends". You might even find your kid has a second profile that you didn't know about. MySpace is a very public forum. Remember the old online rule that e-mail is about as "private" as a postcard? MySpace is even less private. Although we certainly believe your son or daughter has a right to keeping their private thoughts private, MySpace is not an effective venue for storing *any* information one wants to keep private.

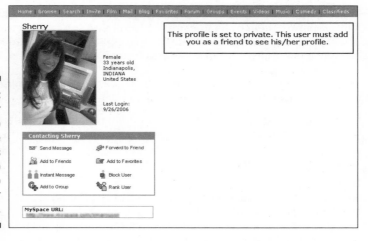

Figure 1-8:
Setting your profile to private limits access to your site to only your friends.

✔ **Ignoring is an option.** Your MySpace Mail is the only way MySpace users who are not your friends can contact you. As with your standard e-mail, the most effective way to resist unwanted contact is to simply ignore it. Deleting unwanted messages without responding usually sends the message that you don't want to talk to the user. If unwanted contact keeps coming from the same source, you can then block the user and report them to MySpace customer service. Chapter 3 has the details on handling those steps.

Chapter 2

Enlisting in the MySpace Army

*T*he first step to getting your own shiny, new page on MySpace is to sign up on the site. If you've ever opened a member account on a Web site such as Yahoo! or registered to use an Internet message board, the process of getting a MySpace account is similar. You give your name, e-mail address, information about what town you live in, and abra cadabra, you're a member.

The big difference between signing up on MySpace and signing up on other sites is that the information you enter when you create your MySpace profile will be immediately shared with anyone who takes a look at your MySpace page. If you're concerned about online privacy or want to keep a low online profile, the information you enter when you sign up on MySpace might be vastly different from someone signing up on MySpace to make contact with new friends.

In this chapter we walk you through the process of signing up to become a MySpace user. We'll show you what information you provide becomes part of your public MySpace profile and what information stays private. We'll also discuss setting up your profile and how to tweak your information to get the results you want out of MySpace.

Becoming MySpace Member #136,485,972

As we're writing this book, MySpace is nearing 115 million registered profiles. By the time the book hits the shelves, our guess is profile #136,485,972 will actually have been claimed by an accountant in the suburbs of Truth Or

Consequences, New Mexico whose favorite movies are *A League of Their Own* and *Close Encounters of the Third Kind,* favorite music includes Elvis Presley and U2, and who joined MySpace for friends and networking. So your number might be higher than that.

No matter how many people signed up before or after you, you'll go through the same enrollment process as the individual users, celebrity users, bands, filmmakers, and everyone else that's staked a claim in the MySpace world.

To begin your own adventures on MySpace, you need to have a few things to get started:

✔ **A computer connected to the Internet.** It doesn't matter if it's a PC or Mac, or if it's in your home or office or someplace else. You need to be connected to the place where MySpace lives — the World Wide Web.

Getting a free e-mailbox

In this modern, wired world, it seems having an e-mail account is about as common as having a nose. It's more rare to find someone without one than it is to find someone with one. Still, the latest stats indicate that only about 15-20% of the total population of the world uses the Internet, so there are still plenty of people getting online for the first time.

If you're in that world majority that's jumping on the Internet for the first time, you're in luck when it comes to setting up an e-mail account. Free e-mail services are plentiful on the Internet. Some of the biggest names in the technology world operate free e-mail services, including Microsoft, Yahoo!, and Google. These services are housed on the Web and are free to use. You don't have to add any special software to your computer to get your messages. You can even access your account from any computer hooked to the Internet anywhere in the world.

When you're ready to grab an e-mail account, check out one of these services:

✔ **Yahoo! Mail:** Sign up for a Yahoo! membership and you automatically get an e-mail account at the popular Web search and services site. Your account will be able to hold 1.0 gigabytes of information (without getting too techy, we'll just say a gigabyte is more space than most average folks need). Your account also includes tools for keeping junk mail out of your inbox. Visit `http://mail.yahoo.com` to sign up.

✔ **Gmail:** If you expect to get a lot of e-mail that you'll need to sort through regularly, Gmail might be the solution for you. Web giant Google operates this service, and they offer over 2.0 gigabytes of space per user (and are adding to the total constantly). The service also provides a unique organization system for your messages. Rather than simply listing messages in order of receipt (the way most e-mail services do), Gmail sorts by topic or sender so you can see similar messages bunched together. The one catch to Gmail is in signing up. You either need to have a mobile phone where you can receive a sign-up code or you need to have an existing Gmail user send you an invitation.

If you've never made your first visit to the Internet and you're already feeling a bit intimidated by the notion of trying out the online world, you might want to put this book down and go find a copy of *The Internet For Dummies*. It's another fine book from Wiley Publishing that covers how to get your PC or Mac ready to go online and how to get connected to the Internet.

✔ **An e-mail address.** MySpace requires you to have an active e-mail address before you can get signed up. The address you provide will be the initial destination for communications MySpace sends you, including notices when you get new friend requests or when someone posts a comment on your page. If you don't have an e-mail account, see the sidebar entitled "Getting a Free e-mailbox," earlier in this chapter, for information on getting an e-mailbox.

✔ **At least 14 years of life under your belt.** MySpace requires you to be at least 14 years old to sign up and use the service. While we admit it's pretty simple to just lie about your age to get an account if you're under 14, we also know that MySpace shuts down thousands of pages per day for users under 14. Our advice is simple — don't sign up until you're old enough. And if you find someone using MySpace who's under 14, report them to the site administrators. You can find more about MySpace safety and security in Chapter 3.

Name, Rank, Serial Number, E-mail Address . . .

Signing up for a MySpace account is a short, painless process requiring very basic contact information. Follow these steps to get your MySpace account started:

1. **Go to** www.myspace.com.

   Type the address in your Web browser's address box and press Enter on your keyboard. You should be sent directly to MySpace's home page.

2. **Click the button that reads SIGN UP! in the Member Login box.**

   You will find the SIGN UP! button on the right side of the screen.

3. **In the JOIN MYSPACE HERE! box, enter the requested information in the text boxes.**

   MySpace requires certain information to start an account, as shown in Figure 2-1. Your initial sign up screen asks for the following:

   • **E-mail address:** Enter the address you will use to receive all messages from MySpace. The e-mail address you enter can't already be in use by another MySpace account.

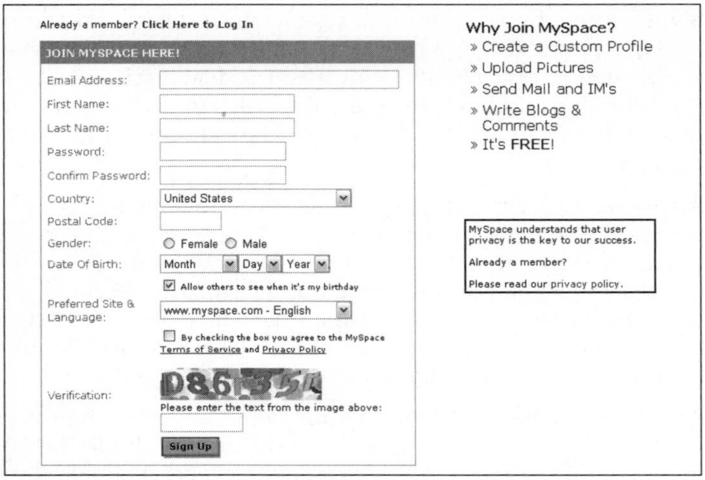

Already a member? **Click Here to Log In**

JOIN MYSPACE HERE!

Email Address:

First Name:

Last Name:

Password:

Confirm Password:

Country: United States

Postal Code:

Gender: ○ Female ○ Male

Date Of Birth: Month Day Year

☑ Allow others to see when it's my birthday

Preferred Site & www.myspace.com - English
Language:

☐ By checking the box you agree to the MySpace
Terms of Service and Privacy Policy

Verification: **D86T354**

Please enter the text from the image above:

Sign Up

Why Join MySpace?
» Create a Custom Profile
» Upload Pictures
» Send Mail and IM's
» Write Blogs &
  Comments
» It's FREE!

MySpace understands that user
privacy is the key to our success.

Already a member?

Please read our privacy policy.

Figure 2-1:
The sign up
page is your
first stop in
setting up a
MySpace
account.

- **First Name:** This will be the default Display Name for your account. The Display Name is the name other users see when they visit your profile page. You can change your Display Name at any time, so don't worry about your real first name causing any privacy issues. For more on changing your display name, see the section "Name," later in this chapter.

- **Last Name:** Similar to your first name, this doesn't have to be your actual name.

- **Password:** This is the password you'll use to keep other people from accessing your MySpace account. MySpace requires you to use at least one non-letter character in you password.

The best passwords are words or codes that aren't easily guessed by others. One good way to create a password that's not simple to figure out is to use a word or words that are easy for you to remember, but replace certain letters with numbers. In this plan, OpenSesame could easily become 0p3nSe5ame and keep anyone trying to guess your password confused. (Of course, now that we've already put that sample password in front of every reader of this book, it wouldn't be a good one to use. But you knew that.)

- **Confirm Password:** Re-type the password you just typed into the previous box to confirm there were no typos in the initial entry.

- **Country:** This drop-down menu lets you select the nation from which you'll be accessing MySpace most of the time. It's like your choices with the names — if you prefer to stay anonymous, you can select a country other than the place of your residence.

What's wrong with lying about my age on MySpace?

When we covered signing up for a MySpace profile, we mentioned it's okay to enter a false date for your birthday. That point is actually only partially true.

People lie about their ages for a lot of reasons. People over 30 might claim they're still in their 20s so they come off as college-aged hipsters. We have one friend in her 50s who claims she's 39 on MySpace because her business is dominated by younger folks. In cases such as these two, telling little white lies about your age on MySpace is okay. You're still a liar, but if you're okay with it, so are we.

There are a couple of specific cases when lying about your age on MySpace is not a good thing. If you're under 14 years old and sign up as being old enough to use MySpace, you're in violation of MySpace's terms of agreement and your profile will be subject to deletion. Perhaps more noteworthy, if you're an adult over 18 and you claim you're under 18 in order to make closer contact with users under 18, you're not only in violation of MySpace's terms of agreement, you might also be subject to arrest and prosecution depending on the nature of your communication.

If you discover any other users who are violating MySpace's terms of agreement by lying about their age, contact MySpace's customer service to report those users. (You can find more information on how to file such a report in Chapter 3.) If you discover one or two folks telling a little white lie about their age just to fight the effects of Father Time, do them a favor and keep their little lie a secret (it might come in handy as blackmail later on down the road).

Do note, however, that whatever country you select will appear in your profile. Choosing a country other than your own might result in visits from users looking for other users residing in your country of choice, so choose wisely.

- **Postal Code:** Type in the postal code associated with your home address. In the United States, the postal code is more commonly known as the ZIP code. Again, if you want to remain somewhat anonymous on MySpace, the sign up page will accept "00001" as a postal code even though the number is not associated with a real place.

- **Gender:** You have a choice of two, male or female. Do us all a favor and don't be a creep. Click Female if you're a female and Male if you're a male. If you're uncertain, please figure it out prior to creating a profile.

- **Date Of Birth:** Enter the month, day, and year of your birth. As with most of the other fields, MySpace can't verify your birth date so you're free to enter a false date if you want to keep your actual date of birth private. For some reason, you can't be older than 100 years old when signing in. We're not sure what MySpace has against centarians, but thus far there hasn't been a big enough groundswell to warrant changing it.

If you want to share your birthday with your friends once you've added a few to your profile page, keep the box marked "Allow others to see when it's my birthday" checked. If you want to keep your birthday a secret, be sure to uncheck that box.

- **Preferred Site & Language:** This drop-down menu lets you decide which MySpace site you want to call home. As MySpace has grown, it's added sites for the UK, Australia, Germany, France, and Ireland. This box defaults to whichever site you initially started the sign up process from.

- **Agree to terms and conditions:** To complete your sign up, check this box that verifies you've read MySpace's Terms of Service and Privacy Policy. You can click the links below the box to read either.

  If you're like us, you've probably signed up for many Web sites and loaded many pieces of software on a computer that required you to verify the terms of service before finalizing the process. And (also if you're us) you probably just clicked the button or box assuring that you've read the terms without actually ever looking at a word.

In the case of MySpace, we highly recommend you actually read the Terms of Service and Privacy Policy before setting up a profile. Both documents are clearly worded without a lot of legal mumbo jumbo that usually makes these documents read like a foreign language. They also define what you can and can't do on MySpace, as well as what MySpace does with the info they collect from you. If you see any part of the Terms or Service or Privacy Policy that makes you uncomfortable, we recommend you stop your sign up and don't join MySpace. For a quick rundown of the highlights of both, see the sidebar titled "MySpace rules that make MySpace rule," later in this chapter.

- **Verification:** This is your last stop on the sign up screen. Simply type what you see in the Verification box into the text box beneath it. This step verifies that bots, or automated programs designed to sign up multiple profiles, cannot do their job on MySpace.

The verification code always reminds us of those colorblindness tests you have to take at the optometrist's office. In fact, if you actually are colorblind, you might have trouble with this piece and will need a friend to help you out.

The verification code is case-sensitive, so make sure all the capital letters are capitalized and the lower-case letters are lower-case.

4. **Click the Sign Up button.**

   MySpace then takes you to a screen where you can upload photos. We go into detail on how to upload photos to your MySpace profile in Chapter 12. Click the Skip for now link. You then travel to a page where you can invite friends to join. Click the Skip for now link on that page as well to travel to your MySpace home page, as shown in Figure 2-2.

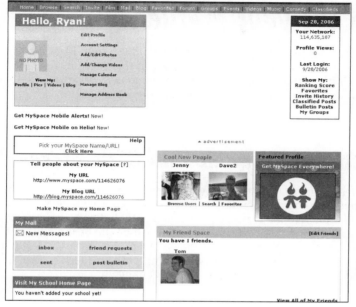

Figure 2-2:
Your new MySpace home page provides a jumping off point to customizing your profile.

MySpace rules that make MySpace rule

As with any community, MySpace needs a good set of rules to make sure everyone plays nice. Without rules, there is chaos. Considering that MySpace is a community with over 100 million user profiles ranging from 14 year olds to adults to bands, filmmakers, and comedians, you begin to understand why they need a clearly stated set of rules to make sure everything operates smoothly.

Verifying that you've read MySpace's Terms of Service is part of the sign up process. Before you get started on MySpace, we highly recommend you actually read through the Terms of Service to make sure you understand what you can and cannot do with your MySpace profile. Among the things prohibited by MySpace are:

✔ Content posted to your profile that you own or hold copyright on.

✔ Commercial use of a MySpace profiles, including collecting users' names or e-mail addresses for the purposes of sending unsolicited business messages.

✔ Content deemed offensive, racist, harassing, or exploitative is prohibited.

✔ Content showing nudity or linking to an adult-themed Web site is prohibited.

✔ Content listing individuals' telephone numbers, e-mail addresses, or street addresses.

✔ Content deemed false or libelous.

✔ Impersonating another person

Protecting members from people sending unwanted business solicitation and junk mail is serious to MySpace. In fact, their Terms of Service even outline a means by which they can fine users $50 per incident when those users are in violation of the site's anti-junk-mail rules.

Showing Off Your Profile

Perhaps even more important than the actual sign up is the process of setting your profile preferences, which we cover in this section. Your *profile* refers to all the information about yourself that you make viewable on MySpace. You can change or completely erase most of the information in you profile at any time.

Setting your name and Web address

The best place to start turning your barren new MySpace page into a place that best fits your personality is by setting your MySpace Name and URL. Your MySpace Name is the name permanently linked to your profile, though it doesn't have to match your Display Name (see the next section). You can change your display name any time you want, but not your MySpace Name. The First Name you entered in the sign up process (see the previous section) is your default MySpace Name until you change it.

A *URL,* short for *Uniform Resource Locator,* is a fancy name for the Web address of your MySpace page. All pages are assigned a temporary URL that includes MySpace's URL followed by your profile number. In our example, our default URL is `http://www.myspace.com/114626076`. Your MySpace Name replaces your profile number in your URL and it becomes permanent as well. Follow these steps to change your name and URL:

1. **Click the Click Here link in the Pick your MySpace Name/URL! box on your home page.**

   The box is located in the upper left part of your page.

2. **Type your MySpace Name/URL in the boxes under "Pick your MySpace Name/URL."**

   You will have to type the Name/URL twice to confirm you did not make any typos.

3. **Click Submit.**

   A confirmation screen will pop up confirming the Name/URL you selected and reminding you that you cannot change it. Click OK if you're satisfied with your selection. Click Cancel if you want to make any changes.

   Clicking OK will actually take you to another confirmation screen to make sure you're completely satisfied with your name, as shown in Figure 2-3. Yes, these MySpace people are quite serious about this "you can never change it" business.

Who is Tom and why does he think he's my friend?

The first time you see your new MySpace profile, you notice that you already have a friend you probably didn't know you ever had. His name is Tom and he has a big job. He's everybody's first MySpace friend.

When you join MySpace, you walk into a room that's already filled with over 100 million other users. Would you want to walk into a room packed like that in real life without a buddy by your side? In the MySpace world, think of Tom as that buddy. Always smiling, giving you a perpetual thumbs up, Tom is the kind of guy that looks like he'll stick by you in the wild world of MySpace. Of course, you're new to MySpace and are probably wondering "Who is this Tom guy, anyway?"

Tom is actually Tom Anderson, one of the co-founders of the site and the current President of MySpace. Legend has it that Tom was in a band when he began thinking of ways to spin the budding world of online social networking in a direction that could help musicians. MySpace's musician-friendly roots sprang from that idea, and the site took off.

Nowadays, Tom is the spokesperson for MySpace and is also probably one of the most recognizable people in today's pop culture. Whenever an unfounded rumor about MySpace begins to spread, Tom sends out a message to squelch it. When MySpace's technology starts going haywire, Tom shows up to calm fears. He's your good buddy who wants to make sure everything works okay for you while you're making your way through MySpace. Tom Anderson's MySpace profile (shown in the figure below) at www.myspace.com/tom provides a good source of updated info about the site.

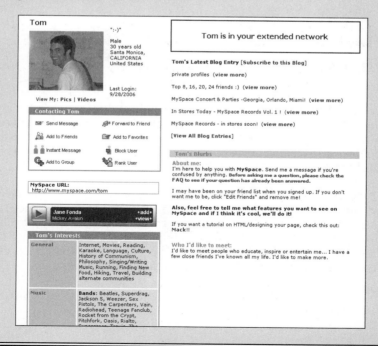

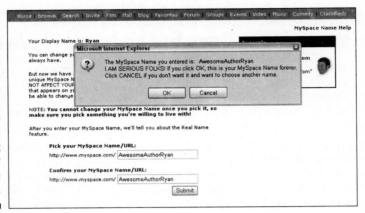

Figure 2-3:
MySpace
means
business
when they
say you
can't
change your
MySpace
Name/URL.

Your next stop is a confirmation screen noting your MySpace Name/URL. At this point you have the option to re-enter your real first and last name if you want them associated with your profile. Though your real first and last names are never displayed on your profile page unless you use them in your profile name, entering them will bring up your profile if another MySpace users does a search on your real name. If you'd prefer to not associate your real name with your profile, you can simply skip this step by clicking the Skip link.

Answering the question "Who does this person think they are?"

Everyone has a different goal in mind when they sign up for MySpace. If you're interested in expanding your social network and meeting new people, you probably want to include a lot of information about yourself to better link up with like-minded users. If you're primarily interested in keeping in contact with a small circle of friends you already know, it's not as important to include a lot of personal info.

MySpace makes it very easy to add, erase, or change your profile information whenever you want. Simply go to your home page and click the Edit Profile link in the Hello box on the left side of your screen, as shown in Figure 2-4. The click takes you to the Profile Edit page. The Profile Edit page is divided into eight separate screens you can select to edit different parts of your profile. We discuss these eight screens in the sections below.

Figure 2-4:
The Hello
box
provides
links to edit
your profile,
change
account
settings, or
view your
public
MySpace
page.

Interests & Personality

The Interests & Personality section, shown in Figure 2-5, allows you to enter
information about your personal interests as well as the reasons why you're
using MySpace. All the information you enter on this page appears in your
main MySpace page.

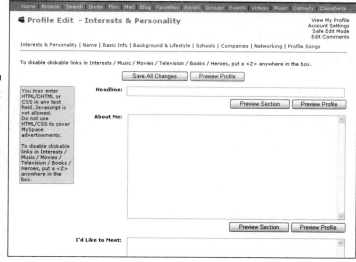

Figure 2-5:
The Profile
Edit page
includes
links to all
the pages
where you
can make
changes to
your profile
settings.

The categories in the Interests & Personality section include:

- ✔ **Headline:** The Headline is a brief sentence meant to sum up you or your profile. Think of it as the hook that pulls viewers deeper into your profile. Our recommendation is to keep your headline brief and general. Let the rest of your profile do the talking about your personality.

- ✔ **About Me:** Your About Me space allows you to tell the world anything you want about yourself. We've seen MySpace profiles use this space to add more detail to the basic profile information — say, a laundry list of likes and dislikes — or as a place to put a favorite quote from a philosopher, or as a mini-diary to update what's going on in their immediate lives. What you put in the About Me box is limited only by your own creativity.

- ✔ **I'd Like To Meet:** This box lets you define specifically who you want contacting you on MySpace. This space is a great opportunity to really define your reasons for being on MySpace. If you want to expand your professional network, list your specific occupation. If you're looking to meet people who share a specific hobby or interest in a certain geographical area, you can put in a specific request, such as "New Yorkers addicted to the TV show *Lost*." The more specific you are, the more likely you are to be contacted by the type of people you want to meet on MySpace.

- ✔ **Interests:** This box is a great place to list your hobbies, academic pursuits, sports you play, or other pastimes that define your life.

- ✔ **Music:** What is the soundtrack of your life? Let other MySpacers know what tunes get you through the day. Feel free to list band names, album titles, song titles, or genres of music you like or don't like.

- ✔ **Movies:** Do you have a favorite movie you can quote line for line? List it in this box so other fans of the film know you're on MySpace.

- ✔ **Television:** When you get finished with a hard day at school or the office, do you like to kick back and watch reruns of *The Simpsons* (the way we do)? Share your favorite shows in this space and let the world know what your viewing habits are.

- ✔ **Books:** Other than *MySpace For Dummies,* have you read any good books lately? Let your friends know what they should be reading by listing your favorites here.

- ✔ **Heroes:** Who do you look up to as a personal hero? A politician? A professional athlete? Your parents? Let the MySpace universe know what you aspire to be by sharing the names of the people who inspire you.

All the items you entered in these fields are automatically displayed as clickable links on your MySpace profile page. Clicking the entries on a profile page takes you to a MySpace search page associated with the words you clicked. For example, if you list *MySpace For Dummies* as one of your favorite books, the words "MySpace For Dummies" will generate a link in your profile. When you or someone else clicks that link, your browser goes to a MySpace search page that shows other user profiles that include mentions of *MySpace For Dummies* along with advertising links. If you want to turn these links off in your profile, type <Z> anywhere in the text box of the particular category in which you want to disable links and the links will be instantly turned off.

When you've entered all the information you wish to share, click the Save All Changes button at the bottom of the page to place your interests on your profile page. If you want to see what the page will look like before you save it, click the Preview Profile button found throughout the page. You can also click the Preview Selection button under any of the text boxes to get a look at that specific section.

Unfortunately, telling people a little about yourself can also pull in attention from unwanted would-be friends or general annoyances. Using certain buzz words like "sexy" and "single" can attract attention from users looking for dates or adult chat. Listing political party affiliations or even certain sports teams can pull in people looking for an argument. Always consider all the reactions you might get from what you add to your profile before you post it. Remember, if you have a public profile, what you put on MySpace can be seen by family members, colleagues, and complete strangers. Make sure you're sharing the information you're comfortable with all these people knowing.

The good thing is all parts of your profile can be changed at any time. Simply return to the Edit Profile link on your home page and you can change what you choose to share. Don't be afraid to tinker with the information on your MySpace page as often as you want to make sure you hear from the people you want to hear from and keep the jerks out.

Name

Click the Name link at the top of the Profile Edit page to make two major changes to your profile.

✓ **Display Name.** This is the name that appears at the top of your MySpace page. It is also the name that other users see when they encounter your profile link when you appear in other users' friend spaces, when you send messages, or when you post bulletins. Display names range from the simple to the silly. Most users prefer to keep it to the name or nickname they're typically known by.

We've noticed a lot of younger users mixing up capital and small letters with other type elements for their display name. After all, they figure, why be `Ashley` when you can be `aSh7Ey!!!?` We personally don't recommend that approach if you're over 18 because, well, it's pretty silly and comes across as kid stuff . . . which is fine . . . for the kids.

> ✔ **First Name/Last Name.** Back when you established your permanent and unique MySpace Name/URL you had the option to include your real first and last name so you could be found in MySpace searches. This option allows you to add in your first and last name if you skipped the step when setting up your URL or to change or erase your names if you prefer.

Basic Info

Click the Basic Info link to fill in specifics about your occupation, ethnicity, body type, height, and the reason you use MySpace. On your first visit to this page, you'll notice that MySpace included your gender, birth date, country, and postal code information you entered when you signed up. They even turned your postal code into the actual city and state or region the code is associated with. Feel free to change or erase these automatically filled fields if you wish.

How you fill out the "I am here for" field can be an important decision that determines what type of user contacts you. If you choose only the Friends and Networking box, you're less likely to get people cruising MySpace for some adult action than if you also check Dating or Serious Relationships. Our completely unscientific research has indicated that users that do not check Dating and Serious Relationship are less likely to get unwanted propositions than those who choose to check those boxes.

Background & Lifestyle

This set of choices allows you to share your marital status, sexual orientation, hometown, religion, education level, and income with other MySpacers. You can also include if you smoke, drink, or want to have children someday. You can fill in each of the fields with the answers they recommend, choose to leave the field blank, or select No Answer.

How you choose to fill in the Marital Status field can help determine the type of user that contacts you on MySpace. Once again, our completely unscientific research based on chatting with hundreds of MySpace users has revealed that users that select the Swinger or Single options are more likely to get unwanted propositions than those who select Married or In a Relationship. In fact, we know single people who have switched their status to Married or In a Relationship to curtail unwanted advances.

Schools

Adding the names of the schools you attended to your profile is an easy way to find and make contact with other MySpace users that attended the same schools as you. Clicking the Schools link at the top of the Profile Edit page takes you to a search screen where you can find a high school, college or university, or trade school you attended, as shown in Figure 2-6.

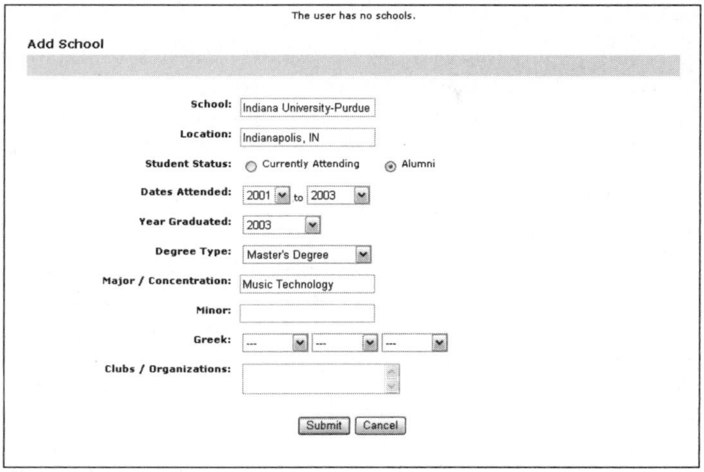

The user has no schools.

Add School

School:	Indiana University-Purdue
Location:	Indianapolis, IN
Student Status:	○ Currently Attending ◉ Alumni
Dates Attended:	2001 ▾ to 2003 ▾
Year Graduated:	2003 ▾
Degree Type:	Master's Degree ▾
Major / Concentration:	Music Technology
Minor:	
Greek:	--- ▾ --- ▾ --- ▾
Clubs / Organizations:	

[Submit] [Cancel]

Figure 2-6:
List the school you're attending or institutions you've graduated from on the Add School page.

To add a school to your profile:

1. **Enter the name of the school you want to search for along with the country and state or province in which it's located and click Search.**

   MySpace automatically generates a list of all the schools in the system that match the name of your school.

2. **Click the link on the name of the school you attended.**

   If you cannot find the name of your school on the list, scroll to the bottom of the page and select the city where your school was located from the scrolling menu next to the word City and click Select again.

   If your school does not appear after the second search, click the Submit Your School link at the bottom of the page to send information about your alma mater to MySpace for consideration to add to the list of schools.

3. **Enter the information in the text boxes and click Submit to add to your profile.**

   MySpace gives you room to enter the school name, location, status (current student or alumni), dates attended, year graduated, degree type, major/concentration, minor, and if you were affiliated with any Greek letter organizations or other clubs. The more info you enter, the more likely your fellow students or alumni can track you down on MySpace.

Companies

You can add the companies you work for currently or worked for in the past to your profile. Click the Companies link at the top of the Profile Edit page. You can enter the company's name, city, state/region, and country, as well as your title, the division you worked in, and the dates you were employed into your profile.

Networking

MySpace provides an online venue for networking with people either in your profession or a field you're interested in. Click the Networking profile at the top of the Profile Edit page to add networking information to your profile. MySpace provides drop-down menus where you can select the field, sub-field, and role that you want to network in. You can also add a description of what specific field, business, or position you're looking for.

The selection in the field category is pretty limited. As we were finishing this chapter, there were only 14 fields to choose from. All the fields were in either the arts, media, or technology worlds. Until MySpace expands on these offerings, you're out of luck if you're a doctor, lawyer, or teacher looking to network with others in your field.

Profile Songs

MySpace is the most music-friendly of all the social networking sites. Bands can load their music on their sites for fans to listen or download. Users can even include single songs on their profiles. If you hear a song on MySpace you'd like to add to your profile, simply click the Add link associated with the song. Also, no need to worry about breaking any music copyright laws that I'm sure you've heard about on the news — adding songs to your profile is about as legitimate as it gets. You can find more information on finding friends in Chapter 4 and information about setting up band profiles and uploading your own songs in Chapter 15.

Profile Videos

Although music is probably the most popular form of media on MySpace, video is definitely second and getting closer by the day, well that is if MySpace has anything to do with it. With just a click of your mouse you can add one or your videos or any other video that a fellow MySpacer has uploaded onto your My Video Space on your profile. Sound cool? Check out Chapter 11 to find out more information on all things MySpace video.

After you feel comfortable with all of the information that you've entered into your profile, click the View Profile link in the upper right-hand corner of your Profile Edit page to take a look at what everyone will see when they stop by. Your profile page, as shown in Figure 2-7, will now be filled out with all of the information that you entered. It was *totally* worth the time, right?

Figure 2-7:
The profile
page with
profile
information
added.

Making Account Changes

Change is inevitable in life. Okay, some people seem to make MySpace their
life — and we suppose change is inevitable on a MySpace account as well.
Fortunately, MySpace makes it easy to get under the hood of your account
and make changes that effect how it operates for you, as well as for the users
that encounter your page.

You make changes to how your MySpace page operates on the Change
Account Settings page. You can reach this page off your MySpace home page.
Click the Account Settings link in the Hello box on the left side of the screen
and you're whisked to the My Account Settings box (shown in Figure 2-8)
where you can tinker with your page.

There are a number of settings you can change from this page.

- ✔ **E-mail Address:** You can alter the e-mail account associated with your
  page. Simply enter the name of the account you want to use and click
  Change at the bottom of the box.

- ✔ **Change Password:** Click the Change Password link to access the Change
  Password screen. You'll be required to enter your current password and
  new password, as well as a verification code presented in the same
  format as the one you entered when you initially signed up.

My Account Settings	
Email Address:	[redacted]@myspace.com
Change Password:	- Change Password:-
Notifications:	☐ Do not send me notification emails -help-
Newsletters:	☐ Do not send me MySpace newsletters
Privacy Settings:	- Change Settings-
IM Privacy Settings:	- Change Settings-
Mobile Settings: New!	- Change Settings-
Groups Settings:	- Change Settings-
Calendar Settings:	- Change Settings-
Blocked Users:	- View List-
Profile Views:	- Reset Count-
Profile Settings:	- Change Settings-
Music Settings: New!	- Change Settings-
Away Message:	- View / Edit Away Message-
Preferred Site & Language:	www.myspace.com - English
Time Zone Settings:	(GMT -08:00 hours) Pacific Time (US & Canada)
	-Change-

Figure 2-8:
The Account Settings page.

✔ **Notifications:** Click the box to turn off notification e-mails from MySpace.

✔ **Newsletters:** Click the box to stop delivery of MySpace newsletters to your e-mailbox.

✔ **Privacy Settings:** In order to protect MySpace users who wish to keep their profiles limited to friends only, MySpace has added a number of privacy controls designed to limit who can see or comment on your site. Click the Change Settings link to reach controls that allow you to

- Require other users to provide your e-mail address or last name before they can add you to their accounts as a friend

- Approve any comment added by another user before it's posted

- Hide your online status

- Block your birthday from friends

- Block picture forwarding from your account

- Allow only friends to leave comments on your blog entries

- Block friend requests from bands

- Only allow friends to send group invites

- Only allow friends to view your full profile

Skip up to Chapter 3 to find more information about safety strategies and the available privacy settings on MySpace.

✔ **IM Privacy Settings:** Controls who is allowed to send you instant messages.

✔ **Mobile Settings:** In a nod to the wireless world, MySpace will now send text messages to your mobile phone when you get a new friend request, message, event invite, or a comment on your profile, blog, or an image. Check out Chapter 7 for more on how MySpace works with your wireless device.

✔ **Groups Settings:** Controls notices on new posts in your MySpace groups. See Chapter 9 for more information about joining MySpace Groups.

✔ **Calendar Settings:** Click the Change Settings link to alter the default view of your calendar, set sharing filters, set the day the week begins on, change time intervals, set working hours, and establish reminder settings. For a more detailed discussion of the calendar, jump to Chapter 8.

✔ **Blocked Users:** Displays the users you've blocked from your account. Take a look at Chapter 3 for more info on blocking users.

✔ **Profile Views:** Clicking the Reset Count link sets your counter displaying the number of times your profile has been viewed back to zero.

✔ **Profile Settings:** This control allows you to display the MySpace Groups you belong to as well as to disable the use of HTML in profile, image, and blog comments. The HTML controls are handy if you want to keep other users from dropping audio, video, or image files onto your MySpace page. You can get more info on dealing with comments in Chapter 5.

✔ **Music Settings:** Adding music to your MySpace page is a nice touch. Unfortunately not everyone is a fan of a song suddenly blaring at them as they bop around the Web. This control allows you to keep songs on both your profile and other users' profiles from automatically starting when you pay their pages a visit.

✔ **Away Message:** This control allows you to set a message that will automatically be sent to other users that send you messages while you're away from MySpace for an extended period.

✔ **Preferred Site & Language:** The drop-down menu allows you to change the preferred site you selected when you initially signed up for MySpace.

✔ **Time Zone Settings:** You can change the time zone used to display the time of your messages and comments. New members on the US site are automatically set to the home time zone of the MySpace offices, Pacific Time.

Once you've marched your way through this list of decisions and options, you're officially a part of the MySpace universe. As you might expect, this initial creation is only the beginning of the fun.

Chapter 3

Staying Safe on MySpace

*L*et's be honest — we share this world with a lot of dangerous individuals who still eat, work, drive cars, go to the mall, and use computers just like you and me. Though it would be great if we didn't have to worry about sinister strangers, the truth is that by paying attention and being educated and aware, it's much easier to stay safe.

Many people are afraid of things they don't understand — so if you're reading this book for yourself (or if you're hoping to learn enough to catch up to your kids), you deserve a pat on the back for taking the initiative. After all, we're careful to teach our kids not to take candy from strangers and how to cross the street; keeping them safe in today's constantly connected online environment is every bit as important. For millions of people, MySpace has moved from being just another technology to an integral part of their day-to-day lifestyle.

In this chapter, you'll learn many tips that will help keep you safe in MySpace. More important than any technical specifics, however, are the big ideas — use common sense and remember what MySpace *is* and what it *is not*. As with any social gathering spot, there will be people who won't be in your best interest to befriend — keep an eye out and be careful. You wouldn't hand out your phone number, address, or daily schedule to everyone you meet on the street (or even at the library), so don't do it here.

Enjoy all that MySpace has to offer. Hang out with friends. Make some new ones. Just be safe while you're doing it!

Having a Private Profile on MySpace

As the name MySpace states, this is *your* space. This means you can, within reason, essentially add anything you want to your profile page. You've got a great deal of freedom when you're creating your profile, which is one of the main reasons why MySpace has become so popular. But with freedom comes responsibility, and at some point the line needs to be drawn when you're deciding what type of information (particularly personal information) you openly publish for the masses.

Determining who can see what — that's actually a big deal when you understand that there are potentially *millions* of people who can read your profile. MySpace has realized this, and for this reason there is an option to have a private profile. A *private profile* allows you to limit who can view your profile information; you can narrow it down to only the individuals listed in your friends list. Then anybody you haven't added as a friend has no way to view your info — it's just that simple.

When you make your page private, any non-friends who come to your page will only be able to see your profile picture, basic information (age, location, and so on), and your Contact Box. Also, in the place of your other personal info, a message appears: This profile is set to private. This user must add you as a friend to see his/her profile. Figure 3-1 shows what this looks like.

Figure 3-1:
A Private
Profile
restricts any
non-friend
from seeing
most of your
personal
MySpace
information.

So, why would you want a private profile — and what happens if you decide to go private? Here's a list of points that help answer these questions; it also tells you what you need to know about private profiles in general:

✔ **A profile is publicly viewable by default:** When you first register on MySpace, a majority of your profile can potentially be viewed by anyone with Internet access, not just registered MySpacers. While adding your information to your profile page, keep in mind that what you post can be viewed by friends, family, co-workers and anyone else who might stumble upon your MySpace page while surfing the Web.

✔ **A private profile offers automatic protection for young MySpacers:** One of the things that MySpace takes very seriously is protecting younger users. To begin with, no one under the age of 14 is technically allowed to register on MySpace, but there is no real way to enforce this rule. But, by default, any MySpace who is older than 14 and younger than 18 will be given a private profile.

✔ **Granting full profile access to just your friends is smart:** Although MySpace gives you the ability to meet all kinds of new people from around the world, you might decide that you only want to interact with people whom you already know and are friends with outside of the MySpace realm. By creating a private profile, you can allow only those you're already friends with to see the information that you add to your space. If you become friends with someone new and want to let them see your full profile, simply add them to your MySpace friend list.

✔ **Flexibility of profile settings gives you control:** Nothing that you change in your settings, such as making your profile private, is permanent. If for some reason you'd like to open yourself back up to anyone and everyone on the Internet, you're just a few clicks away. And if you try it and don't like being open to everyone on the Internet, you always have the ability to change back.

If you decide that you want to make your MySpace profile private, follow these steps:

1. **After you've logged in, click the Account Settings link in the list that's directly to the right of your profile picture.**

   You wind up at the Change Account Settings window, as shown in Figure 3-2. This is where you can manage many different parts of how your MySpace page works.

2. **Click the Change Settings link for the Privacy Settings option.**

   This will open the Privacy Settings window, which has several controls that allow you to change the various privacy settings.

3. **In the Privacy Settings window, scroll down to the Privacy Settings box.**

4. **In the Privacy Settings box, choose the radio button for My Friends Only in the Who Can View My Full Profile section (shown in Figure 3-3).**

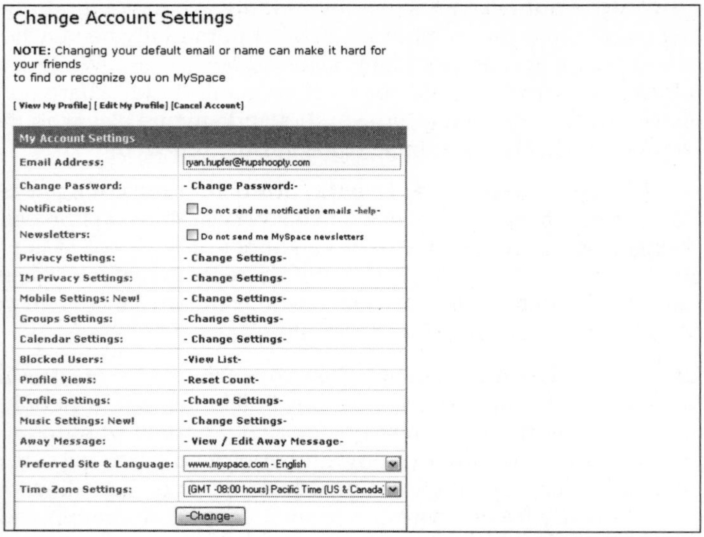

Figure 3-2:
The Change
Account
Settings
window is
the place to
go for all
settings that
deal with
safety and
privacy.

By default, MySpace will have your profile viewable to the public. This means that anyone, not just other MySpacers, can view most of your profile information at any given time. To set your profile to private mode, change the selection from Public to the My Friends Only option.

5. Click the Change Settings button.

Figure 3-3:
Making your
profile
private
by only
allowing
your friends
access to
your full
profile.

The Who Can View My Full Profile section

After you select the My Friends Only option, there's only one thing left to do — save your new privacy settings. This is done by (you guessed it) clicking the Change Settings button at the bottom of the Privacy Settings box. After you click the Save Settings button, a message appears above the Privacy Settings box, letting you know that your privacy settings have been updated. (I bet you feel safer already.)

With your profile set to private, all non-MySpacers will be unable to view your profile at all, and you will have to add any registered MySpacer to your friends list before they can view your full MySpace profile.

Although you may feel a little more safe now that your profile is set to private, remember that some of the fun and power of MySpace is allowing people from anywhere and everywhere to view what you have to offer. Having a private profile makes a curious visitor jump through some hoops to check out your information, which might make some impatient people give up. If you're using your MySpace profile to promote and expose your professional self (or your organization) for marketing purposes, then you might want to think twice before making the switch to a private profile.

Additional Privacy Settings

As you read in the previous section, there is a big difference between having a public and private profile on MySpace. Whether or not you decide to make your own profile private is up to you, but before you make the decision, you should know that there are a few other ways that MySpace allows you to control your account's privacy settings. By knowing what each of these options are, you can make sure you feel safe and comfortable in the sometimes-overwhelming world of MySpace.

Each of the privacy options discussed in the following sections are found in your Account Settings window, which can be accessed by clicking the Account Settings link located directly to the right of your profile picture on your home page.

The Privacy Settings window

The Privacy Settings window is opened by clicking the Change Settings link for the Privacy Settings option. When you arrive at the Privacy Settings window, you see a list of check boxes(as in Figure 3-4); these turn certain MySpace privacy options on and off.

Figure 3-4:
The Privacy
Settings
window has
several
privacy
options that
can be
turned on
or off.

Here's a breakdown of what actually happens when you put a check next to each of these cute little boxes:

- ✔ **Require email or last name to add me as a friend:** This adds an additional layer of security as far as friending is concerned. Whoever wants to send you a Friend Request will be prompted to fill in either your last name or your email address — which basically means you won't be receiving Friend Requests from complete strangers. This option is unchecked by default.

- ✔ **Approve Comments before Posting:** In the MySpace world, the content displayed on your page isn't always posted by you. A very popular example of this is the Profile Comment, used regularly to communicate with fellow MySpacers.

  Even though someone must be your official friend before posting a Profile Comment on your page, that doesn't mean you're always going to like what that person ends up posting. This option adds another layer of privacy and security by allowing you to approve comments before they show up on your profile page. This option is unchecked by default.

- ✔ **Hide Online Now:** If you don't want others to know when you're logged in and when you're not, check this box and the Online Now image won't show up next time you log in. This option is unchecked by default.

- ✔ **Show My Birthday to my Friends:** When you first register on MySpace, you asked for your date of birth. If you check this box, your friends will be alerted when your birthday is getting close. As a user, you may find this a very handy way to keep up with your friends' birthdays, which aren't always easy to remember. This option is unchecked by default.

- ✔ **No Pic Forwarding:** When checked, this option restricts other users on MySpace from using the Email to a Friend links under each of your pictures to forward your pictures to other individuals. This option is unchecked by default.

✔ **Friend Only Blog Comments:** Your MySpace Blog is a great place to write about your personal interests as well as whatever is on your mind at any given time. If you aren't looking for what potential strangers think about your Blogging masterpieces, then you can check this option and make them unable to leave online comments. If you're looking for any feedback you can get about your blog, then leave this option unchecked (as it is by default).

✔ **Block Friend Request From Bands:** MySpace was essentially grown from a foundation of bands who grew to love what the site had to offer them and their music. While this is what helped MySpace achieve its incredible growth, it also means there are a ton of bands on the site who are looking for any potential fans they can find. If you feel like you're being overwhelmed by their friend requests, check this option — and all requests from users with a band profile will be blocked. Power to the people. This option is unchecked by default.

✔ **Friend Only Group Invites:** MySpace groups out there are being created every single day — a horde of them — all looking for potential members. By default, the moderators of these groups can invite any other MySpace user to join their groups; all they have to know to do that is your email address. If you want only your friends to be able to use this option to invite you to groups, then check this option. This option is unchecked by default.

As you just read, the Privacy Settings window allows you to really tighten down your MySpace account options. You may or may not have noticed that each one of these options is left unchecked by default. That means MySpace doesn't put very many automatic restrictions on your account. If you want more control than you already have, you have to be proactive about it and change it yourself.

Instant Messaging Privacy Settings

The one and only way to connect you directly with another MySpace user in real-time chat is through the MySpace Web site, using *Instant Messaging (IM)*. (There is also a MySpaceIM application, discussed in Chapter 7.) This type of instantaneous interaction makes it easier to carry on a conversation with other users you want to know better. But even though you may like using IM to chat with your friends, you might not necessarily like getting random IM requests from complete strangers — and that happens. It's your choice to control how (or whether) others can IM you. No matter what you choose, you select your particular setting by going to the IM Privacy Settings window (shown in Figure 3-5) via the Account Settings menu.

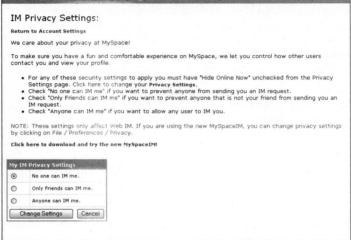

Figure 3-5:
There are
three
available
privacy
options in
the IM
Privacy
Settings
window.

There are three available IM Privacy Settings, but you can only choose one of the following options:

✔ **No one can IM me:** If selected, no one at any time can ever intitiate an IM session with you through the MySpace Web site. You still have the option of initiating the IM session with someone if you wish to do so, but thisis still the highest level of IM security.

✔ **Only Friends can IM me:** If this option is selected, only your MySpace friends can open up an IM conversation with you. Selecting this is the most common setting, and it's the MySpace default for a new user.

✔ **Anyone can IM me:** If selected, you're opening up the chance for anyone who is registered on MySpace to IM you at any time. Feeling a little adventurous? Then this is probably the option for you.

Blocking the unwanted of MySpace

You know that creepy guy who keeps trying to talk to you, even after you've made it blaringly clear that you have absolutely no interest in his job, his car, his hobbies, his medical condition, or anything that he might have to say? Well, not only does he have a profile on MySpace, but so do all of his similarly creepy friends. And so does the guy who leaves fliers on your car in the parking lot.

The point is, just as in real life, there are also people on MySpace who will stop at nothing to annoy and irritate you. Thankfully, this is one of those instances where the online world may well provide better solutions than real life. Though there is no way to reach through your monitor to slap, punch, or scream at someone (no matter how much they might deserve it), there are ways to keep them at bay — blocking them.

Blocking a user means that person will no longer be able to contact you at all through MySpace. That means he or she won't be able to comment your page — or send you any message that you actually receive. If you block users who are in your friends list, they're removed. If they send out a bulletin, it won't show up in your My Bulletin Space. Blocked means blocked out — they'll be cut off completely from communicating with you via MySpace. And don't worry — other users don't know when you block them; they have no idea what blocked lists they are on. All they might notice (if they get a clue) is that you aren't answering. So by all means block away!

If you block someone, that person can still view your profile unless you have it set to private (see the section "Having a Private Profile on MySpace," earlier in this chapter). If the blocked person creates a different account on MySpace, he or she can use the new account to contact you — and if that happens, just block that user's new account as well.

So why would you want to block a fellow MySpacer? Here are a few reasons that might potentially land someone in your Blocked Users list:

- ✔ **Annoying:** Lets face it, some people are just annoying. There are lots of reasons why they are annoying — and if someone gets on your nerves just one too many times, blocking them might be a valid option.

- ✔ **Did they really just say/show that?:** People say and do some "interesting" things on MySpace, and one day someone might cross the line from funny to just downright disgusting. If you aren't amused with that once-entertaining user anymore, and wouldn't mind it if you never heard a thing from that direction again, then get your block on. You won't hurt their feelings, I promise.

- ✔ **Blind date gone bad:** You go on a date with a potential significant other and now you have someone messaging you 50 times a day to tell you how awesome you are. Creep potential aside, a person can only take so many compliments in one day . . . block!

- ✔ **Attack of the MySpace spammer:** Every now and then you might get a few messages from users telling you to check out their webcams — or a band from across the nation telling you how awesome their new CD is and why you should buy it. These types of MySpace spammers would look great hanging out together in your Blocked Users list.

Adding a user to your Blocked Users list

Feel like you've come to the point where you need to make room for someone on your almighty Blocked Users list? Follow these steps to make sure you don't have to deal with that not-so-special someone on MySpace ever again:

1. **Go to the MySpace profile of the person you would like to block.**

   The only place to block a user is directly from their profile.

   You can block a user even if they have their profile set to private.

2. **Locate the Block User link in the user's Contact Box.**

   After you find the profile of the user you'd like to block, locate their Block User link. It's located in the user's Contact Box on their profile page, as shown in Figure 3-6.

The Block User link

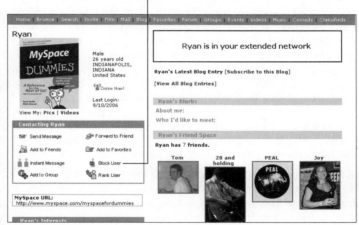

Figure 3-6:
The Block User link is located in the Contact Box on any user's profile page.

3. **Click the Block User link.**

4. **Confirm that you want to block the user.**

   MySpace usually likes to make sure that you want to do certain things before it does them; blocking another user is a typical example. After you click the Block User link, MySpace will ask you, `Are you sure you want to block this user?` If you do, click OK.

5. **Confirm the blocked user . . . again.**

   Even after you click OK for the prompt in the previous step, you will be taken to one more confirmation page, as shown in Figure 3-7. MySpace will ask you once more, `Are you sure?` If you still want to go through with it, click the OK button and the user will be officially blocked. Refreshing and oh-so-powerful at the same time, huh?

Figure 3-7:
After you click the Block User link, MySpace prompts you to make sure you really want to block the user.

Managing and unblocking your blocked users

Once you've finished blocking someone (see the previous section), they will show up in your Blocked Users list. Just like the other settings covered in the previous sections, the Blocked Users list is found in the Account Settings window. Your Blocked Users list is where you can see the users you've blocked, and it's also where you can unblock them if you ever feel the need to do so. Follow these steps to check out your Blocked Users list:

1. **Once logged in, click the Account Settings link in the list directly to the right of your profile picture.**

   This will take you to back to the Change Account Settings window.

2. **Click the View List link next to the Blocked Users option in the My Account Settings box.**

   When you click the View List link you will be taken to the Blocked Users window, as shown in Figure 3-8.

3. **All blocked users are listed. To unblock a user, click the Unblock User link.**

   All the user profiles you've blocked appear in the Blocked Users window. Feeling nice (or has somebody decided to behave)? You can unblock a user by clicking the Unblock User link to the right of the user's profile picture; they're instantly able to contact you again. Almost too easy, isn't it?

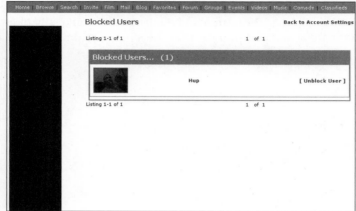

Figure 3-8:
The Blocked
Users
window is
where you
can view
and manage
which user
profiles
you've
blocked.

Alerting MySpace for Safety's Sake

Odds are, if you're getting messages from MySpace users that you think are inappropriate, unsafe, or questionable as far as content goes, then other users are thinking the same thing. Whether it's a message that you think is spam or a profile that has crossed the line between appropriate and inappropriate content, you should feel confident that if you let MySpace know what's going on, they'll do something about it. MySpace is very dedicated to making your experience as safe and secure as possible, and they have many different ways for you to report things that make you feel uncomfortable or uneasy— and don't worry, you'll be able to stay anonymous.

Here's a list of a few ways MySpace makes your MySpace experience as safe and enjoyable as possible:

✓ **Flagging spam/abuse:** Received one message too many from that MySpace spammer? Let MySpace know that you're sick of it by flagging the message as Spam/Abuse. You can do this by clicking the Flag spam/abuse link that is included on every received message. The link is located to the right of the date on each received message, as shown in Figure 3-9. After you click the link, the message will be deleted from your Inbox; it will be sent to MySpace for review.

✓ **Reporting inappropriate content and abuse:** The great thing about MySpace is anyone with a profile can post basically anything on the profile page. Sometimes, the bad thing about MySpace is the same thing — people can post basically anything, and that "anything" might be something that you feel is inappropriate. There are a couple of ways to let MySpace know about a MySpacer whose content or actions give you a not-so-great feeling.

- If you would like to report a MySpace profile, click the Report Inappropriate Content link in the footer of every MySpace profile page, as show in Figure 3-10. You will be taken to a report form where you can let MySpace know what's up.

Figure 3-9:
The Flag spam/abuse link is included on every received message.

The Flag spam/abuse link

MySpace page footer links

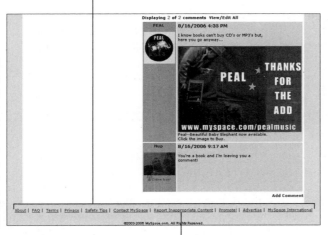

Figure 3-10:
The Report Inappropriate Content link can be found in the footer links of every MySpace profile page.

The Report Inappropriate Content link

- If you have general questions or comments, or would like to report other MySpace abuse, click the Contact MySpace link that's included in the footer links at the bottom of every MySpace page. This link takes you the more detailed Contact Request form shown in Figure 3-11, where you can select Reporting Abuse as your subject and one of many other subtopics (such as Spammers and Underage Users).

✔ **Privacy questions and concerns:** If direct email is more your style and you have something that you would like to send MySpace regarding safety, privacy, abuse, or anything else, they've set up an email address just for you. Send your email to `privacy@myspace.com` to let them know what you're thinking.

✔ **Safety Tips:** Before contacting MySpace, you should always check out the resources they've posted online for users. There are some great Frequently Asked Questions (FAQ) posted; you can access them by clicking the FAQ link located in the footer links at the bottom of every MySpace page (refer to Figure 3-10). From general information to safety tips for parents, this is a great resource that you should check out when you have questions.

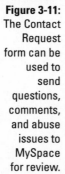

Figure 3-11:
The Contact Request form can be used to send questions, comments, and abuse issues to MySpace for review.

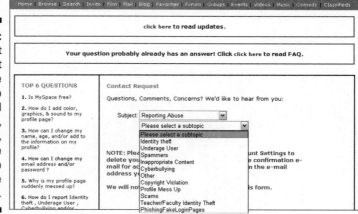

MySpace can be an intimidating place. Just like the first time you set foot in a new school, college campus, workplace, or party, there are lessons to be learned about how to act and protect yourself. Not everyone you'll meet along the way deserves suspicion, but it's often much better to be safe rather than sorry. Be patient. Be smart. Be safe.

Part II
The MySpace Community

In this part . . .

Take a virtual walk around our MySpace neighborhood with us. There's our buddy, Mike the DJ — who tools around town on his vintage scooter. And over there's Ben. He just got married last weekend. (We read about it in his blog.) It looks like Kristen has a new picture up; she just posted a bulletin telling us she opened her own realty office. Of course there's Tom. Everybody knows Tom.

Those are just a few of the friends we've linked up with on MySpace. We've had invites come in from a lot of others, too — and have spent time searching the site for our real-life neighbors, co-workers, old classmates, and people with the same interests as ours. We've also used the site to send them messages and keep up with what they're doing. This part shows you how to do the same.

Chapter 4

Friending the MySpace Way

. . . .

In This Chapter

▶ Getting familiar with the Friend Request

▶ Finding new and old friends on MySpace

▶ Managing your friends with the Address Book

▶ Knowing how to determine who's a friend and who isn't

▶ Setting up your Top Friends within MySpace

. . . .

*B*uilding connections and making friends has been a central part of the human condition since we first lumbered out of the cave and figured out that banging two rocks together was only fun when it would attract a crowd and get some attention. Whether you're deathly shy or an uncompromising social butterfly, making and maintaining friendships is one of the most valuable experiences of our lives. We make friends at school, work, and pretty much anywhere we have the opportunity to share common ground with other individuals. Today, MySpace is that common ground for millions of people, and friending on MySpace is an easy alternative to striking up a conversation with that girl who happens to be choosing your favorite movie at the rental shop. It also makes it easier to stay in touch with many more people with whom you may have lost touch otherwise.

So, whether you secretly desire the celebrity status of having millions of MySpace friends or just want to communicate more efficiently with your closest handful of "real-world" friends, friending on MySpace may be the solution.

Getting Your Friending On

A friend in everyday life is normally defined as someone whom you know, like, and trust. You can make a new friend anywhere you go, and depending on what type of person you are, you may have just a few friends or a lot of friends. Regardless of the number of friends you have, someone else can only become your friend if it's mutual; nobody gets to be your friend unless you want them to be. This same rule also holds true in MySpace and the result — known as *friending* — is the underlying foundation of MySpace.

As you make the leap into the MySpace world, friending will be one of the main things that you will be exposed to the most. There are many ways to interact with the millions of members who are on MySpace, and the ways that you can interact with them differs greatly depending on whether you are friends. Friending can be a great way to connect with people and groups whom you already know, and maybe some that you don't But before you jump on the friending bandwagon, you should know some more details on how to add, find, accept, and reject all the potential friends who are out in the wide world of MySpace. MySpace, here we come — get ready to get your friending on!

The Almighty Friend Request

To understand MySpace, you must first understand the single most fundamental thing that makes it what it is — the Friend Request. The Friend Request is probably one of the simplest and most utilized aspects of MySpace, and it is used as a way to create a mutual friendship within the MySpace world. It takes two to tango, and if you don't want to be someone's friend (or vice versa) it's not going to happen. If the Friend Request is officially accepted, then the two parties involved are considered friends and the world is a better place.

Whether or not you are friends with someone on MySpace can make a big difference in how you can interact and communicate with that person. In the following sections, we will take a detailed look at what it really means to be a MySpace friend — as well as the ins and outs of friending.

Breaking Down the Friend Request

Congratulations! You've found some people whom you consider, for one reason or another, worthy of friending. Or, maybe you haven't found them . . . but you know they're out there. This section will give you a better understanding of how to search the millions of MySpacers so you can find that needle in a haystack, send out a Friend Request, and what happens when you receive one.

Finding some friends

So many potential friends, so little time. As you make the big move into the MySpace world, your first goal may be to find yourself some potential friends. There are millions of users who are active in the MySpace community and are just waiting to be friended, so let's go find them.

There are a few potential ways that you could find a prospective friend on MySpace:

- ✔ **Locate a user with a direct MySpace URL**
- ✔ **Browse for a user**
- ✔ **Search for a user**

Locating a user with a direct MySpace URL

Using a direct MySpace URL to locate an individual is becoming easier to do. More and more bands, people, companies, and other MySpace users are broadcasting their MySpace URLs though fliers, e-mails, stickers, billboards, TV commercials, and any other method of advertising and promotion. If one of these URLs catch your eye and you can remember it, plug it into your browser and you will be taken directly to that MySpacer's profile page.

Browsing MySpace for a user

Browsing for a user on MySpace is another method you can use to find a friend. With more than 100 millions users, there is bound to be a few people out there that you can relate too — it's just a matter of finding them. Browsing for users is MySpace's way for you to sift, sort, and filter through the masses, making it easy to find the types of MySpacers that you're looking for.

To browse MySpace for users, follow these steps:

1. **Click the Browse link at the top of your MySpace home page.**

   The Browse link is the second link from the far left side, located just to the right of the Home link. This will open up the Browse Users window.

2. **Choose a Basic or Advanced browse.**

   When the Browse Users window opens, there are two options when Browsing, Basic and Advanced.

   - **Basic:** The Basic option limits the number of browse options that MySpace lets you use to narrow your results. These options are limited to sex, age, relationship status (such as single and married), reasons for using MySpace (such as dating and friends) and whether or not to return haven't posted a profile photo.

   - **Advanced:** The Advanced option allows you to better pinpoint your search results by offering you many more search options. From body type to education level, this option is definitely for the users who know exactly who they're looking for.

   You can switch between the two by clicking the tabs on the upper-right corner of the Browse Users window, as shown in Figure 4-1.

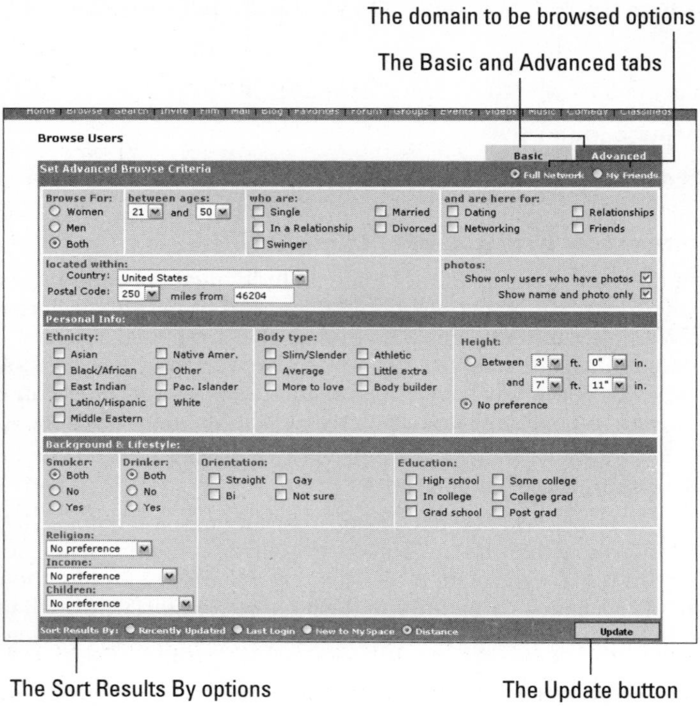

The domain to be browsed options

The Basic and Advanced tabs

Figure 4-1:
There are
two options
when
browsing
users,
Basic and
Advanced.

The Sort Results By options   The Update button

3. Select your browse criteria.

After you select Basic or Advanced, you then need to select all your browse criteria. There are many different criteria that you can filter your results by, such as gender, age, interests, and many, many more.

You can also choose to browse the Full Network or just My Friends (refer to Figure 4-1). This option comes in handy as your friends list begins to grow more and more.

- **Full Network:** The full network allows you to browse each one of the millions of users who use MySpace, even if they aren't in your friends list.

- **My Friends:** This option searches only your friends list for results. The more friends that you have, the more useful this option becomes when you are browsing through MySpace.

4. Select a sort method.

The Browse Users window also allows you to sort your results. The Sort Results By options are Recently Updated, Last Login, New to MySpace, and Distance (refer to Figure 4-1). By default, the results are be sorted by Distance.

5. **Click the Update button to view your browse results.**

   After you click the Update button (refer to Figure 4-1), your browse results will be shown beneath the Set Browse Criteria box. A maximum of 3,000 users will be returned.

   After your browse results are shown, you can click any other users' names to view their profile pages. When you're on a user's profile page, you're ready to send the Friend Request on over. To find out how to send a Friend Request, see the section "Sending a Friend Request," later in this chapter.

Searching MySpace for a user

Searching for a user on MySpace is yet another way for you to find a friend. Where as browsing for a user is a very broad way to filter through the users upon users of MySpace, *searching* allows you to locate who you're looking for in more of a precise and specific way. You can search for users by a specific display name, e-mail address, and school to name a few. Usually searching is used to find a very specific person or group of people based on fairly strict search criteria.

You can search for a user on MySpace by following these steps:

1. **Click the Search link at the top of your MySpace Home page.**

   The Search link is located just to the right of the Browse link. This will open up the MySpace Search window.

2. **Choose your method of search.**

   As shown in Figure 4-2, there are four methods for searching MySpace:

   - **MySpace Search:** This is the most broad method of MySpace searching. You can search for any keyword within 7 areas that MySpace lists in an easy-to-use dropdown menu; MySpace, Blogs, General Interest, Music Interest, Movies Interest, Book Interest, and the Web.

   - **Find Someone You Know:** This method allows you to find someone you're specifically searching for. This could be a friend, family member, or someone else whom you already know. You can search by Name, Display Name, or E-mail Address.

   - **Find Your Classmates:** This method searches MySpace by a School Name, Country, and State/Province. This is a quick and easy way to find users who you know from your high school or college years.

     Searching is the only way for you to search for your long, lost classmates. Browsing will allow you to find MySpacers who have attended high school or college, but it will not let you browse a specific high school or college.

- **Affiliations for Networking:** This method allows you to dig up other users who may have the same affiliations as you do. It's human nature to find others who are into the same things you are, and this method makes it a little bit easier for everyone. Whether you're into film, nightlife, or television, someone with the same interests are just a click away. Almost too easy, isn't it?

3. **Click the Search or Find button and search to your heart's content.**

   After you narrow down who you're looking for, click the applicable search button to see your results. Depending on your method of search, you may even be able to drill down even deeper into your results.

   For instance, if you search for your alma mater, you will eventually be able to filter your search results even more by graduation year, male/female, age, and more. MySpace lets you really pinpoint the people who you're trying to find — which is good, considering there are millions and millions of MySpacers out there.

After you find your needle in the haystack, simply click that person's profile link or profile picture — and you go directly to that user's profile. Whether you send the user a Friend Request is completely up to you, but if you want to go through with it, check out the section "Sending a Friend Request," later in this chapter.

To send or to receive, that is the question

After you become a member of the MySpace community, individuals, bands, companies, groups, comedians, and filmmakers are just a few of the types of MySpacers that you might run into while going about your business. Whether you find them or they find you, sooner or later you will be making some friends. When it comes to friending, there are a two ways that you can offi-cially become someone's friend:

- ✔ **You send a fellow MySpacer a Friend Request.** There they are, staring at you through the screen. It might be someone whom you searched for as a graduate of your high school class. It might be an old friend whom you lost touch with. Perhaps it's a friend of a friend who seems to always have something funny to say, or someone you've never met who just so happens to share your love for pickled beets. Who knows, it might even be someone you saw on television or read about in the newspaper. Whatever the specifics, you've found someone you admire enough to link yourself to via the social network of MySpace

- ✔ **A fellow MySpacer sends you a Friend Request.** Every piece of informa-tion you make available on MySpace is a possible reason why people will be drawn to your profile. Someone out there is interested in the fact that you're both into bowling and fine wine. They may find you because you know someone they know, or because you went to the same school they did. They may be new to your area and are hoping to find others who share common interests. Whatever the reason, you're a likeable person and people want to get to know you better. It is up to you to decide if the requester is someone worthy of being your friend.

Sending a Friend Request

Sending a Friend Request is the most important step in the overall friending process on MySpace. MySpace, as the tagline says, is "a place for friends," so what are you waiting on? Lets stop talking and go find some friends! Although there are many different ways to search out and find users on MySpace, there is only one place where you can initiate the sending of a Friend Request. That one place is the Add to Friends link in any user's Contact Box, as shown in Figure 4-3.

Even though the Add to Friends link is the only place that MySpace provides for sending another MySpacer a Friend Request, you can use the web address of the link in other places as you please. You can usually copy this link by right-clicking on the Add to Friends link and selecting the Copy Shortcut option. For instance, you can send another user a message with your Add to Friends link address so they could add you directly from that message, instead of them having to click the link in your Contact Box. The actual link will look something like this: `http://collect.myspace.com/index.cfm?fuseaction=invite.addfriend_verify&friendID=99804220`.

The Add to Friends link

Figure 4-3:
The Add to
Friends link
in any user's
Contact Box
is the only
MySpace-
provided
way to
initiate a
Friend
Request.

The steps to sending a Friend Request are as follows:

1. Locate the user's Contact Box on his or her profile page.

Normally, the user's Contact Box will be located directly under the user's profile photo on the profile page.

2. Click the Add to Friends link in the Contact Box (refer to Figure 4-3).

The Add to Friends link is located on the left hand side of the Contact Box, second link from the top. After you click the link, the Confirm Add Friend screen appears, as seen in Figure 4-4. This is MySpace's way of asking you, "Are you sure you want to send a Friend Request to this user?"

3. Click the Add to Friends button on the Confirm Add Friend screen to send the Friend Request.

When you've clicked the Add to Friends button, the Friend Request will be sent. A message will then come up letting you know that a request has been sent to the user.

Wondering whether or not your sent Friend Request ever went through? Having second thoughts about that last Friend Request that you sent off? By clicking the Pending Requests link in your Mail Center menu, you will be taken to the Pending Friend Requests window where you can see the status of every Friend Request that is still pending. From this window you can click the Send Message button to send a reminder to the pending friend to ask what the hold up is. Or, if you want to cancel the pending Friend Request, simply click the Cancel Request button.

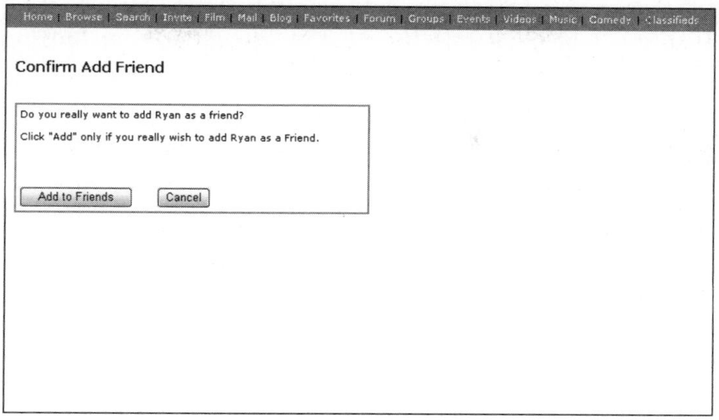

Home | Browse | Search | Invite | Film | Mail | Blog | Favorites | Forum | Groups | Events | Videos | Music | Comedy | Classifieds

Figure 4-4:
The Confirm
Add Friend
confirmation
screen
double-
checks that
you want to
send the
Friend
Request.

Confirm Add Friend

Do you really want to add Ryan as a friend?

Click "Add" only if you really wish to add Ryan as a Friend.

Add to Friends   Cancel

Accepting a Friend Request

Just as you will be searching and finding users to become friends with, other MySpacers will be doing the same. This means that you might be the user that shows up in someone's search, which could also mean that you might be getting a Friend Request sent your way. It always takes two to tango, and you might be surprised on who ends up requesting to be your friend.

Accepting a Friend Request is a quick and easy process, but before you can start adding friends you first need to know that you have Friend Requests waiting for your approval. As with many of the other alerts within MySpace, the fact that you have pending Friend Requests waiting is communicated loud and clear after you log in. As shown in Figure 4-5, a New Friend Requests! alert is shown in you're My Mail section whenever you have Friend Requests that you haven't viewed.

Figure 4-5:
A New
Friend
Requests!
alert is front
and center if
you have
pending
Friend
Requests
you haven't
viewed.

The New Friend Requests! alert

My Mail

✉ **New Friend Requests!**

inbox	friend requests
sent	post bulletin

TIP

If you receive a Friend Request while you're in the middle of MySpacing, a red "NEW!" alert will be located to the right of Friend Requests link in your Mail Center menu, as show in Figure 4-6.

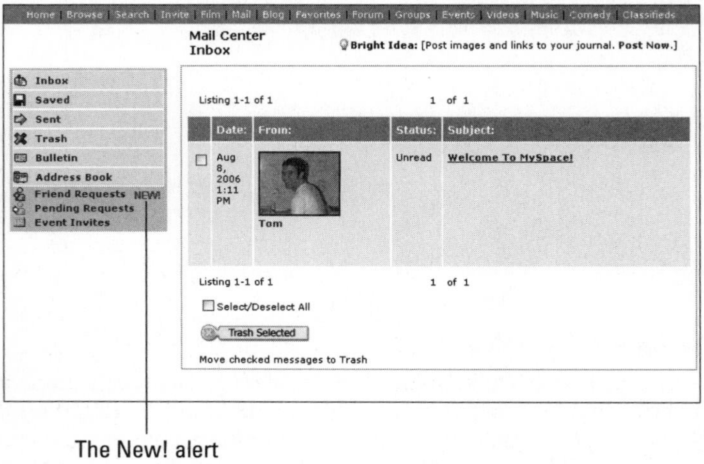

Figure 4-6:
A red NEW! alert will also let you know that you have unviewed Friend Requests.

The New! alert

To begin accepting those friends that are anxiously awaiting your approval, follow these steps:

1. **Click the New Friend Requests! alert or the Friend Requests link in your MySpace Mail Center menu.**

   This will take you directly to the Friend Request Manager window, which is where the fate of these pending friendships are in your hands.

2. **In the Friends Request Manager window, you have 3 choices — choose one and go with it.**

   Your three choices, as seen in Figure 4-7, are as follows:

   • **Accept:** You can make the user's day and accept them as your friend by clicking the Accept button. After you click the Accept button, the user will be removed from the Friend Request Manager window and appear in your friends list.

   • **Deny:** Don't think that the pending friend deserves to be in your short list of who's who in MySpace friends? Click the Deny button and the user will be removed from the Friend Request Manager window without being added to your friends list.

Examples of received Friend Requests

Think of MySpace as a giant cocktail party. You show up, and at first you spend some time looking around and finding the people who you already know. That guy from work. The girl you sat next to in 8th grade biology. Your bowling team members. Eventually, you start talking to those folks, who then introduce you to the other people they know. The more people arrive at the party, the bigger your circle of friends grows.

The same goes with MySpace. You never know whom you'll meet. You may have made a big impression on someone you met only once in passing. You may have thought (or hoped) you'd never see or hear from certain people again. You just never know who is out there looking for (or coincidentally finding) you.

1. My R.A. from my freshman year of college

I hadn't heard from Jim, my resident assistant in the dorms my freshman year, for over 6 years until his face popped up in my Friend Requests window. Of course I accepted — and in the process, I learned that he now lives in Savannah, Georgia, and he is married and has a daughter. Oh yeah, he's also a helicopter pilot for the Navy! I would have never talked to him again if it hadn't been for MySpace.

2. My cousin from Maryland

I normally only catch up with my family from Baltimore once a year during our traditional summer vacation. That's all changed thanks to MySpace. One day I received a Friend Request from my cousin, who lives in Maryland, and we now are updated on things all year long. Don't worry, we still go on vacation — grandma still needs the updates as I have yet to get her up and running on MySpace.

3. Darth Vader on the Top 8 Tour

While I was on the road during my Top 8 Tour, I ran into a very interesting character when driving through Phoenix., Arizona. When we got off of the bus there was a man dressed head to toe in a Darth Vader outfit. He was out cruising the country as Darth Vader and we happened to run into him. Awesome, huh? Well, after we hung out for a while (and after I tried on his Darth Vader helmet) we had to part ways. I never thought I would hear from him again until I checked my MySpace account — and there he was in all his Darth Vader glory, just hanging out in my Friends Request window. He had signed up and sent us a request as soon as he made it to an Internet connection. Once again, MySpace was the connector.

- **Send Message:** This is MySpace's way of letting you find out a little more info on this so-called pending friend. Not real sure you want to add that particular user? Just send off a message — maybe the response will make you feel a little better about approving or denying them.

Figure 4-7:
You have
three
options
when you
receive a
Friend
Request —
Approve,
Deny, or
Send
Message.

In a hurry? You can Approve/Deny multiple users at once by checking the boxes next to the user's profiles pictures or by checking the Select/Deselect All box and clicking the Approve All/Deny All button at the bottom of the Friend Request Manager window. *Warning:* Be careful, though, when using this feature — there is no confirmation screen so make sure that your decision is final.

What Being a Friend Really Means

You've started sending and accepting the truckload of Friend Requests that you've received. Now all you need to know is what it actually means when you hit the Accept button and become friends. We'll go through what you and your new found MySpacers can do now that you're officially friends.

As you can see in the following list, becoming friends with another user allows you both to interact and communicate much more openly and freely. By friending another user, you're telling yourself that you trust them enough to not abuse the benefits of being MySpace friends. Here is a quick break-down of things that you or any of your newfound friends can do now that you're officially MySpace friends:

✔ **Profile comments:** Profile comments (discussed in further detail in Chapter 5), are one of the most commonly used communication methods on MySpace. When a friend leaves a comment on your profile page, it is out there for the entire world to see, so make sure that you keep up with what people are saying.

✔ **Photo comments:** As you create your MySpace profile, you will most likely fill it up with photos of you, your friends, and other things that let people know a little bit more about you. Even if another registered user isn't your friend they can still view your photos, but they must be your friend to leave a comment about them. Want to learn more about photo comments? Check out Chapter 9.

✔ **Video comments:** As with photos, any registered user can view any video that you post on MySpace, but they must be your friend to comment them. Comments are a great way to get feedback from your friends on all the things you post, so if you want more opinions, then you might want to add some more friends. More details on MySpace videos can be found in Chapter 10.

✔ **Instant Messaging:** By default, only friends can Instant Message you through MySpace — and most users keep it this way. To find out more about Instant Messaging, turn to Chapter 5.

✔ **Bulletin views:** Bulletins, which are discussed further in Chapter 5, are messages that are sent to the Bulletin Space of every one of your friends. This means that the more friends you have, the better the chance that someone reacts to the Bulletin that you just sent out. Bulletins are a great way to keep up with all your friends, but you won't be seeing anything in your Bulletin Space unless it has been sent by someone who has earned a spot on your friends list.

✔ **Viewing of Private profiles:** For privacy reasons, MySpace allows you to make your profile private, which means that only your friends can view the majority of what you've added to your MySpace page. If you run into someone who has a private profile and you'd like to interact with that person, then you'd better send a Friend Request and cross your fingers in hopes that your new prospective friend will friend you back. If that doesn't happen, you'll never get to see the full profile. More privacy and safety information can be found in Chapter 3.

Managing the Masses

Once you've started making and adding friends, you'll need to be able to manage them. Whether it's keeping up with your Friend Requests, dealing with unwanted friends, or making sure your growing friends list is in check, this section has got you covered.

Using the Address Book

Before you know it, you'll have more friends than you know what to do with. Some will be people you see every day at work, and others you may never see face-to-face. With all these different people, personalities, and preferences, it can be easy to confuse Angela from Miami with Mia from Los Angeles.

A quick and easy way to keep track of your ever-growing friends list is to use the Address Book. It works much the address book of your favorite e-mail program; MySpace allows you to add contacts names and information so it can group them into more manageable pieces. You can take all the guesswork out of how you met the contact by jotting down a few things in the Contact Notes section. This comes in especially handy when you begin to meet "friends of friends" or people even farther removed from your current everyday circle of co-workers and former classmates.

Adding a Contact

You can add someone to your Address Book by following these steps:

1. **Click the Inbox link in your My Mail section.**

   This will take you to the Mail Center window.

2. **Click the Address Book link in the Mail Center menu.**

   The Address Book link, as seen in Figure 4-8, is located just below the Bulletin link in your Mail Center menu.

The Address Book link

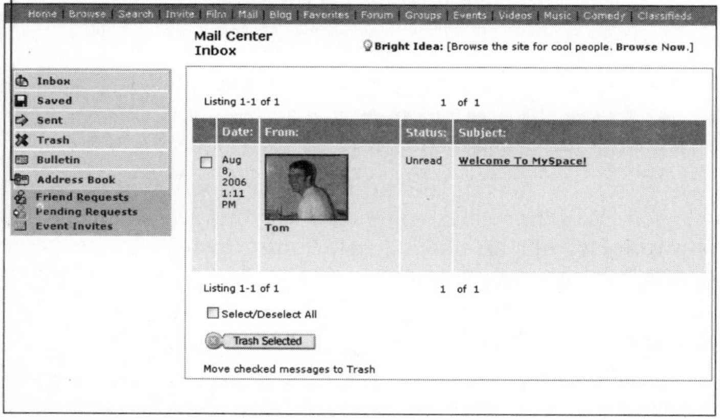

Figure 4-8:
The Address Book link is located directly under the Bulletin link in your Mail Center menu.

3. **After clicking the Address Book link, you're taken to the main Address Book window, as shown in Figure 4-9.**

Figure 4-9:
The
Address
Book
window.

4. **Click the Add A Contact link located at the left side of the screen.**

   This will take you to a form where you can input all of your contact's information.

5. **Fill out all known contact information.**

   You can get as detailed as you want as far as your contact's information is concerned. The only information that is required is the contact's e-mail address, but the more information that you can add the better. You can store multiple e-mail addresses, phone numbers, messenger screennames, and notes for each contact that you enter into the Address Book.

6. **Click the Save & Add Another button.**

   This will save your contact and clear out the form so you can enter in another contact if you want.

   The quickest way to add a contact is to use the Quick Add Contact feature at the bottom of the Address Book window. This method is much faster, but it doesn't allow you to enter additional contact information that you may want to store. But if you're in a hurry, this is definitely the way to go.

   After you add your contacts to the Address Book, you can sort them, search them, view their profiles, and message them all from one location.

Creating a Contact List

You can also create lists so you can keep your contacts managed in a way that makes sense. For instance, you can create a list for your co-workers or for your family. This will make it easier to keep track of who's who in your Address Book. Setting up a list is quick and easy — just follow these steps to get your first list up and running:

1. **Click the Lists link in the main Address Book menu.**

   The Lists link is located directly below the Add A Contact link. This will take you to the Contact Lists window.

2. **Enter a name for your new list in the New List field.**

   Use a name for your new list that will allow you to easily identify it and know who is in the list.

3. **Click the Add button.**

   Click the Add button next to the New List field and your new list will be created. You will then be taken to a form, shown in Figure 4-10, that allows you to add and remove contacts to and from the list that you just created.

Figure 4-10: After a list is created, you can then add and remove contacts.

4. **When you've finished adding and removing contacts to your list, click the Save List button.**

   After you have your list set up the way you want it, click the Save List button and your list will be modified and saved.

   You can create as many lists as you'd like — as your friends list grows more and more, the Contact List can help you make sense of it all.

To Friend or not to Friend?

As you begin your friending spree, you will receive friend requests from some users who you know right off the bat and some that may be a little more, how do I say this, unfamiliar. Being able to decide whether or not the user is friend-worthy is very important, as you don't want to let just anybody into your online circle of friends.

Keep these points in mind as you wander through the seemingly never-ending world of MySpace and you should be just fine:

- ✔ **Unusual or misspelled display names:** Make sure to take a good look at the display name of the user that is trying to friend you. If they are a spammer or someone that you might not want to associate with, this could be one of your first clues.

- ✔ **No profile picture:** If a user doesn't have a profile picture on the account, then it's likely you're looking at a spam account. Anyone who would legitimately want to become your friend would at least take the time to add one picture to his or her profile.

- ✔ **Profile research:** If you still aren't sure about the Friend Request you receive, simply click the link to their profile and do a little research on the user. Pay attention to the comments that other people have left on the page, check for links or images that take you to a third-party Web site, and take a look at their picture gallery to see if they look legitimate. Within a couple of minutes you should be able to tell if they are potential friend material.

- ✔ **Send a message:** If all else fails and you think it's worth the time, click the Send Message button on the Friend Request and ask the person directly why he or she chose to send you a Friend Request. If the answer sounds good to you, you can accept; if not, you can deny. It's your world, they're just trying to become part of it.

The Top Friends Phenomenon

The Top Friends section in MySpace is the new social thermometer in the Internet world. Deciding how many Top Friends you want to have, who makes it to your list, and the implications of each are all details that you cannot overlook.

If MySpace is the world's school cafeteria, your "Top Friends" are those whom you've specifically chosen to sit at your table for lunch. Just as in junior high, the decision as to whom to include in this very public group will be noticed, and much joy and drama can come as a result of who is and who is *not* included in this list. Each time a person visits your profile page, they will be greeted by not only by the information you publish about yourself, but also by the smiling faces (or other, less welcoming photos) of your "Top Friends."

Choose your Top Friends wisely — they will be "vouching" for you each time someone visits your MySpace page.

Getting your Top Friends in order

Your Top Friends are front and center when someone stops by your profile page, so knowing how to manage them is a must if you're going to become part of the social MySpace landscape. To some, it's a big deal to be in someone's Top Friends, and as crazy as it seems, that means it's not to be taken lightly. But not to worry, to get up to speed on all this Top Friends business all you need to do is read this section.

Your My Friend Space

The first thing that you need to understand when talking about Top Friends is your My Friend Space. Your My Friend Space, as shown in Figure 4-11, is found on the right hand side of your MySpace home page. This area doesn't show all of your friends, but it is where you can view, edit, and interact with those who are lucky enough to make it into your sacred Top Friends list. Who is included in your Top Friends, why they are there, and when they will move on and off the list will change more than you will like to admit. Keeping your Top Friends updated is something that will become habit after a while, but first you need to learn how to manage it.

The My Friend Space

Figure 4-11:
Your My Friend Space is where you can view, edit, and manage your Top Friends.

Managing your Top Friends

Getting your Top Friends in order is a piece of cake because MySpace makes it easy to manage. To get your Top Friends up and running, all you need to do is follow these steps:

1. **Click the Change my Top Friends link in your My Friend Space.**

   When you click the Change my Top Friends link, which is in the lower-left corner of your My Friend Space, you will be taken to the Edit Your Top Friends! window, as shown in Figure 4-12.

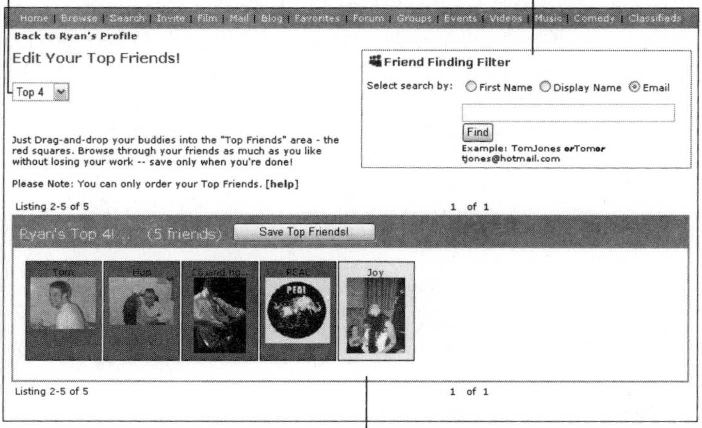

The number of Top Friends to display   The Friend Finding Filter

Figure 4-12: The Edit Your Top Friends! window allows you to change your Top Friends quickly and easily.

The Top Friends management area

2. **Using the drop-down menus, select the number of Top Friends you'd like displayed (refer to Figure 4-12).**

   MySpace gives you the option of displaying 4, 8, 12, 16, 20 or 24 Top Friends. How many friends you have — and how many of those you'd like displayed as Top Friends — will help you determine how many you choose. Note that if you have five Top Friends and you want them all displayed on your page, you'll need to select a number higher than the number of Top Friends you have (in this case, 8). Also, the lower the number of Top Friends, the more important the people you choose for the spots will feel. Depending on how many you select, the same number of red spaces for friends will be added below in your list of friends.

3. **Find the friends you'd like displayed as your Top Friends.**

Now comes the tough part — deciding who you'd like to be in your Top Friends list. Don't be too hard on yourself, the choices that you make here are by no means permanent and they can be changed quickly.

4. **Drag the selected friends into the red Top Friend spots.**

Your friends will be displayed in front of you so you can easily drag friends in and out of the red Top Friend spots as needed. Depending on how many friends you've collected, this could be several pages long and it might be fairly difficult to find the friends who you're looking for. You can freely drag any of your friends into any of your Top Friend spaces, which means that you not only need to decide who's in your Top Friends, but you also need to decide who goes where. Who will get the coveted first spot on the upper left corner? That's for you to decide.

Having trouble finding that certain someone in your long list of friends? As long as you know the person's e-mail address, the easiest way to find a friend who's in your list is by using the Friend Finding Filter in the upper-right corner of the Edit Your Top Friends window (refer to Figure 4-12). After entering in your friends e-mail, click Find and if something matches, the needle in the haystack will appear at the bottom of the red Top Friend spaces. If that's who you were looking for, click and drag your new Top Friend into the red space that it deserves . . . for now.

5. **Save your new Top Friends.**

This is the moment we've all been waiting for. It's now time to make this thing official by clicking the almighty Save Top Friends! button. After you save your new Top Friends, your My Friends Space on your home page and your Top Friends on your public profile will display your changes.

It will be only a matter of time before people begin to notice that they've been added, removed, or moved to a new spot in your Top Friends list. You might be surprised with some of the reactions you get — your Top Friend spots are a big deal, whether you want to admit it or not.

Deleting a Friend

Believe it or not, you may find yourself in a situation where you need to delete a friend from your Friends list — de-friend if you will. This could be due to many different reasons, but regardless of why you want to delete a friend, if you know that it's time, then you definitely need to know how. Good riddance. Follow these steps to delete the unwanted friend from your Friends list forever:

1. **Click the Edit Friends link in your My Friend Space.**

   Click the Edit Friends link in the upper-right corner of your My Friend Space on your home page. This will take you to the Edit Friends window, as shown in Figure 4-13, where all your current friends will be displayed.

2. **Find the friend you'd like to delete.**

   Here comes the hard part, finding the friend you'd like to delete from your Friends list. Unfortunately, MySpace doesn't make this too easy on you, so if deleting this friend isn't urgent, you may want to just forget about it.

   But if you're dead set on deleting the friend, you need to first find that person by flipping through your friends that are listed in the Edit Friends window. The friends aren't listed in any particular order, so finding the one friend might take a little while depending on how many friends you have.

Figure 4-13:
The Edit Your Top Friends window allows you to change your Top Friends quickly and easily.

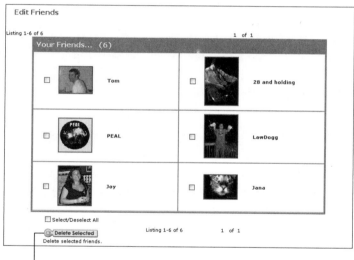

The Delete Selected button

3. **Check the box next to your friend and click the Delete Selected button (refer to Figure 4-13).**

   This will completely delete the friend from your Friends list forever (or at least until you decide to add them back). Also, there isn't any delete-confirmation alert, so there's no room for second thoughts; be 100% sure that you want to delete them.

If you'd like to delete all your friends with one click of a button, you can check the Select/Deselect All box and click the Delete Selected button. Or, if you want to delete multiple friends at once, check the Select/ Deselect All box, go back and uncheck the friends you want to keep, and the click the Delete Selected button. Use this option *only* if you want to delete an entire page (or multiple friends) at one time.

Chapter 5

Staying in Touch via MySpace

In This Chapter

▶ Getting to know your MySpace Mail Center

▶ Keeping track of your MySpace contacts

▶ Exploring the methods of MySpace communication

*F*inding friends on MySpace is only half the battle — the second half is working out the best way to communicate with them. MySpace is centered around communication, and your method of communication may vary depending on who you're sending a message to, what that message is, and how you want it answered. Whether you're messaging a long-time friend or trying to get the word out about your next big get-together, MySpace provides you with a wealth of tools to get the job done. This chapter examines the tools you'll have at your disposal to get the information it takes to find the perfect mix and get the results you want.

Getting to Know the Tools

MySpace has created a wide array of tools that allow you to contact individuals in many different ways. The more familiar you can become with the tools, the better. These tools include

- ✔ **MySpace Mail Center:** The one-stop shop for all things communication. The look of the Inbox will remind you of your Web e-mail or Outlook Inbox, with the additions of a few new features. *Messaging* is the term used for the e-mail functionality within MySpace.

- ✔ **Comments:** A quick and efficient way to keep in contact with your social circle, comments allow your MySpace friends to leave you a quick note on your page for all to see. These are the virtual equivalent of stopping by your friend's house and leaving a note on his front door.

- ✔ **Bulletins:** This is MySpace's version of mass communication — the one way to hit all your MySpace friends with one message. Bulletins are a great way to get the word out quickly to a lot of people.

✔ **Instant Message (IM):** Don't want to wait for a message response? IMing on MySpace is for you. IM is a real-time chat session between any two MySpace friends at any time.

This type of IM, which is accessed using the Contact Box on an individual's profile, is not to be confused with MySpaceIM. MySpaceIM is a downloaded application installed on your PC outside the MySpace Web site. MySpaceIM is discussed in more detail in Chapter 7.

In the sections that follow, we take a more in-depth look at each of these communication tools.

For information on blogging with MySpace, check out Chapter 6.

Message Management with the MySpace Mail Center

When you simply want to send someone a one-to-one message through MySpace, messaging is the way to go. When looking at all the various ways to communicate through MySpace, messaging will most likely seem the most familiar. It's similar to normal, everyday e-mail operations on a Web-based e-mail service such as Hotmail or on e-mail clients such as Outlook.

Messaging, as opposed to Instant Messaging (discussed in the "Instant Access with Instant Messaging" section later in this chapter), isn't a simultaneous, real-time chat with another user. It's best to think of messaging as your MySpace e-mail — one message sent to one user's MySpace Inbox for reading the next time that user logs in.

Messaging is available between users even if the users aren't technically "friends," meaning that you can send a message to any and every MySpace user you choose (though that doesn't mean they'll respond). A *friend* — in MySpace-speak — is a mutually accepted addition to two user's friends lists on MySpace. A MySpacer sends a friend request to another; if the request is accepted, they're officially friends (for more information on friends, see Chapter 4). This makes messaging a great way to meet new people, ask questions, and learn more about other users before actually accepting them as official friends. You can also use the messaging feature as a way to communicate with users who are requesting to be your friend — especially if you aren't familiar with who they are. Often messaging is the first communication you have with a person on MySpace.

Your Mail Center (shown in Figure 5-1) is your one-stop shop for nearly all things MySpace. Whether you're sending, receiving, or deleting messages, this is a place to get used to. It's also the place you'll find yourself excitedly checking in hopes of finding the latest correspondence.

Figure 5-1:
The
MySpace
Mail Center
utilizes
many
common
e-mail
actions,
along with a
few new
ones.

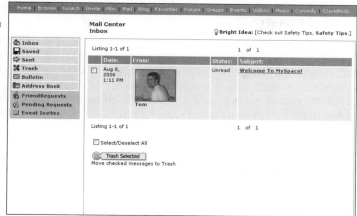

You can access your inbox in the Mail Center by following these steps:

1. **Log in to your MySpace account.**

2. **Scroll down your home page to the My Mail section, located on the left side of the screen (shown in Figure 5-2).**

Figure 5-2:
The My Mail
section is
where you
find the link
to your
inbox.

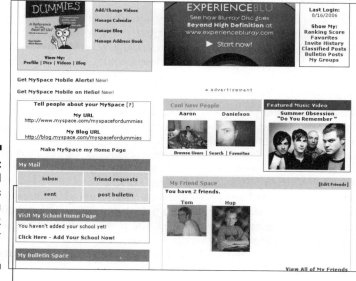

The My Mail section

In the My Mail section, you see links for Inbox, Friend Requests, Sent, and Post Bulletin.

3. **Click the Inbox link in the Mail Center section, and you're there.**

The Mail Center may remind you of other e-mail clients you've seen, but with a few additions — such as a Bulletin link (discussed later in this chapter in the section "Creating and sending a Bulletin"), an Address Book link (discussed in Chapter 4), friending links, and a link that takes a user directly to your Confirm Add Friend confirmation page (also discussed in Chapter 4).

The following list walks you through the Mail Center's parts and pieces that deal directly with Messaging:

- ✔ **Inbox:** Links to your received messages, sorted with newest messages at the top — Mail Center does not allow for any other type of sorting. The messages are tagged with the date and time received, profile link and picture of the sender, message status (read/unread/replied), and message subject. The check box in the left column is used when moving messages to the Trash folder.

- ✔ **Saved:** If you want to make sure that you don't delete a message from that special someone, the Saved folder is where you want to put it. To save a message, simply open it up and click the Save button following the end of the message. Doing so moves that message from your Inbox to the Saved folder.

- ✔ **Sent:** This is where you cannot only see what messages you've sent, but you can also see whether it's been read yet. The same status options used in the Inbox are used for sent messages (read/unread/replied). If you want to hold on to a sent message, be sure to save it (see the previous bullet on how to do that); all sent messages in the Sent folder are automatically deleted after 14 days.

- ✔ **Trash:** Whenever you delete a message, you aren't really getting rid of it forever — at least not yet. What you're really doing is sending your deleted message to the Trash folder. This helps with those "Whoops, I didn't mean to delete that!" moments. All messages are held in the Trash folder for 30 days before they are automatically deleted. Even though you can still view all messages in the Trash folder, there isn't a way to bring the message back to your Inbox. This is why MySpace double-checks with a confirmation screen before sending messages to the Trash. If you want to make sure that the message is never seen again and you don't want to wait 30 days before the automatic deletion, click the Empty Trash link when you're in the Trash folder and the Trash will be emptied right then and there.

As stated previously, the other links (Bulletin, Address Book, and so on) found in the Mail Center do not deal directly with Messaging, but don't worry — we cover them in Chapter 4.

Creating and sending a message

When surfing around MySpace, you're never far from creating and sending your next message. The first step is to find the user that you want to contact. When you find a user, the most common way to send a Message is by using the Send Message link on another user's profile. This is especially important when introducing yourself to someone new.

After you land on a profile that you think looks message-worthy, follow these steps to contact the individual:

1. **Locate the MySpace user you want to contact. You can find users in a couple of different ways:**

   - **A known contact:** You can type in the specific MySpace link for a known contact (www.myspace.com/*xxx*) or, if the known contact is in your Address Book, you can contact the person from there as well. For more on the Address Book, see Chapter 4.

   - **Browse:** Browsing is a great way to find other users by using certain designated criteria. Click the Browse link at the top of your MySpace homepage. It's located between the Home and Search links. This will bring up several browsing options such as gender, age, and location so you can narrow your results. When the results are displayed, click any of the profile pictures to be taken directly to that user's profile page.

   - **Search:** Searching is a keyword based method of finding other MySpace users that gives more of a snapshot view of a user's info when searched. Click the Search button at the top of your MySpace homepage, which is directly to the right of the Browse button. This takes you to the main search page, where you're able to search users by keywords, display name, real name, e-mail address, school/university, or networking affiliations. After you've entered your search criteria and are given results, click the profile picture (or click the View Profile link) of any user to be taken to the profile page.

2. **When you've found the user you want to contact, locate the Contact Box on the user's profile page.**

   The Contact Box is usually located directly following the profile picture on each MySpace page. The Contact Box, as shown in Figure 5-3, has several options available. The link to send a Message is always in the upper-left corner of the Contact Box.

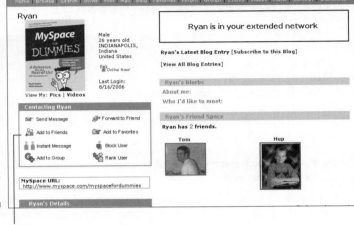

Figure 5-3:
Most
communica-
tion begins
by clicking
an option
in the
MySpace
Contact
Box.

The Contact box

3. **Click the Send Message link in the Contact Box.**

This will take you to the Send a Message window in the Mail Center, which will automatically be in the correct mode so a new message can be composed, as shown in Figure 5-4. The To information is already set based on the user whom you're contacting. You'll notice that composing a MySpace message is similar to composing an everyday e-mail.

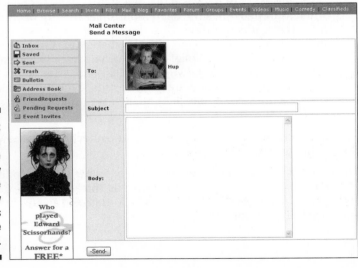

Figure 5-4:
The Send a
Message
window
is where
new
messages
are
composed.

One thing many people like about MySpace is that it gives all users the flexibility to customize almost anything on their profile pages. Customizing, which is covered in Chapter 12, is a great way to give your profile page some personality, but it can also make it look completely different from the standard MySpace profile; the Send Message link (as well as the entire Contact Box) could look and read differently. Instead of `Send Message`, it could say `Give me a shout` or `Message Me`. Although the look of the Contact Box can change, the position of the different links won't. The Send Message link will always be in the upper-left corner.

4. Fill in the Subject and Body fields for the Message in the Send a Message window.

When composing your message, you do not need to include a Subject, but to send, you must enter some content into the body of the message. Messages can include HTML, which means that links, images, and so on can be used in the body.

5. Click the Send button at the bottom of the Send a Message window.

After you've typed in everything that you want, press the Send button and off it goes. After your message is sent, a confirmation message box (see Figure 5-5) appears to let you know the message was sent successfully. Pat yourself on the back: You've now officially sent your message.

Figure 5-5:
A confirmation appears once your message has been sent.

After sending your message, you can check its status by heading to your Sent folder in your Mail Center. Depending on what action the recipient has taken, the status can be Read, Replied, or Unread. This takes the guesswork out of figuring out whether your message has been opened. It also enables you to know if someone is too busy, or just plain uninterested, in communicating with you.

Replying to a received message

As mentioned earlier, any user on MySpace can send a message to any other user any time they feel like it; sometimes you won't be initiating the contact, but you'll be replying to it. As your list of friends grows, so will the number of messages you'll be responding to. Follow these steps to reply to a received message:

1. **Click the New Messages! Alert.**

   Before you can reply to a message, you need to somehow know that you've received one. MySpace enables you to know that a message is waiting in your Mail Center Inbox through alerts displayed on your homepage after login. The New Messages! alert, as shown in Figure 5-6, will be clearly displayed in the My Mail section when a new message is waiting for you. By clicking the New Messages! alert, you'll be taken directly to the Inbox window of the Mail Center.

The New Messages! alert

My Mail

✉ New Messages!

| inbox | friend requests |
| sent | post bulletin |

2. **Click the Subject link to open the Message.**

   The most recently received messages will be listed at the top of your Inbox. Any new message will have a status of Unread in the Status column. Click the Subject link to open up the message for reading.

3. **Click the Reply button.**

   By clicking the Reply button at the bottom of the message, the Read Mail window in the Mail Center will open so a reply message can be composed. As shown in Figure 5-7, the subject line will add an RE: and the original message will be quoted in the body of the reply message as reference for the recipient. This is similar to how e-mail treats replies.

4. **Compose a reply message.**

   Fill out a reply message in the Body section of the Reply Message window above the original message text.

5. **Click the Send button.**

Click the Send button at the bottom of the Reply Message to send your reply. After the reply is sent, a confirmation message box enables you to know that it was a successful reply.

Figure 5-7:
The reply message automatically adds an RE: into the message's Subject line and the original message will be quoted in the Body.

Forwarding, saving, and deleting received messages

Of course, replying isn't the only option you have after receiving a message. There are times when the message you've received doesn't require immediate action. In fact, there are times when a message doesn't deserve your attention at all. As shown in Figure 5-8, you can also Forward, Save, or Delete any message that may find it's way to your Inbox.

Here is a breakdown of how to do each:

✔ **Forward a Message:** If you would rather pass along the received message to someone other than the message sender, forwarding is for you. Click the Forward button and you're taken to the Forward Message window of the Mail Center. This window looks similar to the Send a Message and Reply Message windows, except for one main difference — the To: dropdown box. The To: dropdown box, as shown in Figure 5-9, is filled with the names of each of your MySpace friends so you can choose whom you want to forward the message to. Pick a friend, compose your message, and click the Send button to forward it off.

Figure 5-8:
You can
Reply,
Forward,
Save, or
Delete any
received
message.

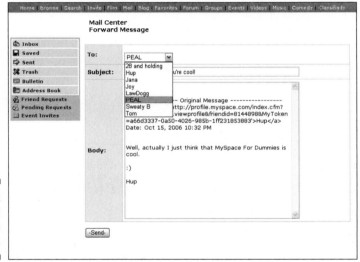

Figure 5-9:
Forwarding
a message
to a friend.

You can only forward messages to individuals in your friends list, which is sometimes handy but also limiting.

✔ **Saving a Message:** Worried that you might lose a message that you've received? If you click the Save button at the bottom of the Reply Message window of the Mail Center, you won't need to worry anymore. This sends the message to the Saved folder for safekeeping. When the message is sitting in the Saved folder, you're still able to reply, forward, or delete it just as you could when you first received it.

✓ **Deleting a Message:** If you feel like deleting the received message from your Inbox, click the Delete button at the bottom of the Reply Message window of the Mail Center. After the Delete button is clicked, the message will be permanently moved to the Trash folder. When sent to the Trash folder, there is no way to get it out. MySpace will automatically empty messages in your Trash folder that have been there for 30 days, but if you want them completely deleted, immediately click the Empty Trash link at the bottom of the main Mail Center links (see Figure 5-10).

Not all messages are what you want to receive. Whether it's some spam that's trying to sell you things you don't need or something unquestionably inappropriate, MySpace has ways to deal with unwanted messages. Flip to Chapter 3 for more information on ways to deal with the messages that you aren't too fond of.

The Empty Trash link

Figure 5-10: To completely delete your Trash folder, click the Empty Trash link.

Communicating with Comments

When looking at all the different ways to communicate with your fellow MySpace friends, Profile Comments are the most popular *and* the most public way to stay in touch. A Profile Comment can be left to say happy birthday, to post an upcoming event reminder, or to rehash last night's concert. No matter the reason, Profile Comments are a fun and effective way to keep up with everyone else's world. Leaving a voice-mail is like *so* five years ago.

One of the most powerful things about MySpace is the ability to dig deeper and find out more information about any particular user. When browsing a user's profile page, the Profile Comments section can give a great snapshot of what the user's friends are like, what they have been up to lately, and who they hang out with regularly. Another thing to remember is that you must be friends with someone to leave them a Profile Comment; users cannot comment randomly without first being added to your friends list. This reduces the amount of "Comment Spam," and allows only those users you've given the green light a chance to add something public to your profile page for all to see.

If you comment me, I'll comment you

As you begin to comment your friends and they begin to comment you, there are a few things that you should keep in mind. Comments are a big part in the success of MySpace and it opens the door to a fairly public and open method of communication between millions of people. The following are a few items related to Profile Comments that you should be aware of while MySpacing:

- ✔ **Anyone can view Profile Comments:** Just because you must be some-one's MySpace friend to post a Profile Comment doesn't mean you have to be a friend to *read* it. When posted, a Profile Comment is ready for the entire Internet to see, so make sure that whatever has been posted is something that you don't mind others, such as co-workers, bosses, family, friends, and anyone else with an Internet connection and a curi-ous mind reading.

- ✔ **Proper Profile Comment etiquette:** MySpace is all about give and take, meaning that if someone has taken the time to comment you, you should take the time to comment them back. Use generic Profile Comments sparingly and try to personalize what you say as much as possible. This also works the other way as well; if you want someone to Comment your page, take the initiative to leave them a Profile Comment first.

- ✔ **HTML is okay, just don't overdo it:** As long as you allow it in your settings, users can incorporate HTML code when posting a Profile Comment on your page. HTML code can be used effectively when post-ing pictures, videos, and links. But be careful of overdoing it — if you want the view something that's a little more lengthy, add a link for them to check it out instead of posting a lengthy Profile Comment.

You can disable HTML in your Profile Comments by clicking the Account Settings link on your Home Page and then clicking the Change Settings link in the Profile Settings section. If you do not want users to post HTML, check the box next to Disable HTML Profile Comments and click the Change Settings button. More information regarding profile manage-ment and control is covered in Chapter 3.

10 popular reasons for leaving a Profile Comment

There are many different reasons for leaving a comment on another MySpacer's profile page. Here are 10 of the more popular reasons for reaching out and commenting someone.

1. Looks like I have a new friend.

Did that special someone finally add you to that coveted friends list? Show them your appreciation by giving them an obligatory "Thanks for the Add" comment.

2. Your show last night ROCKED!

What better way to let your favorite band know that their show was incredible than by leaving them a comment? It will let them, and everyone else who browses their page, know how much of a fan you really are.

3. Do you still exist?

If you haven't seen one of your friends, co-workers, or family members in a while, leave them a comment to see if they are still somewhere on planet Earth. A simple "Hello, is anyone home?" comment would work nicely.

4. Dude, you're awesome.

If you happen to like what you see on someone else's page, comments are a great way to let them know. Whether it's a sweet profile design, a hilarious video or a new, goofy profile pic, tell them your thoughts through a quick comment.

5. Looks like we had a good time last night.

The only thing better than having a good time is letting others know how much of a good time that you actually had. Whether it's posting a few pics, videos, or just recapping the night in a few sentences, leaving something to show everyone how much fun you had is always a great reason to leave a comment.

6. I don't feel like working right now.

Say you're at your job, staring at your computer screen and not really motivated to work at the moment. What better way to spend your time than posting a few comments to catch up with your friends?

7. Give and you shall receive.

It's always fun getting a new comment and most will not give a comment unless they've received one. It's a give and take comment world out there, so go post a few comments and wait for the responses to be posted back on your page. To increase your chances of getting a reply, ask a question or add some personalization to the comment.

8. I love what you've done with the place.

Most MySpacers like to keep their profiles fresh and new; many people update the look of their profile pages on a regular basis. If you like, dislike, or have noticed updates to your friends' profiles, let them know with a comment. Everyone loves feedback (especially positive!), so feel free to let the comments fly.

9. I know a lot of people will see this.

If you're looking for ways to get noticed on MySpace, a comment on a popular user's profile page might do the trick. Be careful with this though, an irrelevant comment could get you some bad feedback or it could be deleted from the user's profile page all together.

10. Look at what I found!

Find a hilarious pic, an interesting video, or a crazy blog on the Internet? Let everyone else know about it by leaving a comment with links to the newfound goodies so they can check it out as well. Other users who browse the user's page can see it too if it catches their attention.

✔ **Managing your Profile Comments:** If you want to approve all comments before they are displayed on your Profile page, click the Change Account Settings link on your Home Page and click the Change Settings link next to the Privacy Settings section. Check the box next to Approve Comments before Posting and click the Change Settings button.

✔ **I am like *so* popular:** The amount of Profile Comments on a user's page is directly related to the public perception of how popular the user is with his/her friends list. When someone takes the time to leave a legitimate Profile Comment on another user's page, it shows that they are interested in what that user is up to. The more Profile Comments, the "busier" the profile is, which shows the amount of interest in that particular user. By persuading other users to add Profile Comments to your page, you're creating a profile that shows how much people care about you and what you're doing. For a band looking to get booked for shows, this could mean the difference between looking like you have a great following and looking like you don't have fans.

Posting a Profile Comment

Posting a Profile Comment is one of the easiest and most effective ways to communicate with the members of your friends list. Creating and posting a Profile Comment can be done by following these steps:

1. **On your Friend's profile page, scroll down to the Friends Comments section.**

   The Friends Comments section is usually listed directly following the Friends Space on your friend's profile page, as seen in Figure 5-11.

Figure 5-11: You can find your Friends Comments section under your Friend's Space.

The Friends Comments section

2. **Click the Add Comment link at the top of the Friends Comments section.**

   This takes you to the Post a Comment entry form.

3. **Fill out the Body of the Comment entry form and click the Submit button.**

   Enter the Profile Comment you want to leave for your friend. Include any HTML code that you'd like to include as well. If the user doesn't allow HTML in the Profile Comments, that too is displayed on this form so you're aware of the setting.

4. **Confirm the Profile Comment and post the comment or edit it.**

   A Confirm Comment screen appears and gives you a preview of how your Profile Comment will appear once posted. If the preview looks the way you want it to, click the Post Comment button to post. If you need to make changes, click the Back button on your browser to edit.

Deleting a Profile Comment

In case you have second thoughts about that Profile Comment that you just posted about you-know-who doing you-know-what, fear not, Profile Comments are as easy to delete as they are to post. Follow these steps to delete a Profile Comment that you've posted:

1. **On your Friend's profile page, scroll down to the Friends Comments section.**

   You just posted the Profile Comment here, so you should be able to find this pretty easily.

2. **Click the View All link at the top of the Friends Comments section.**

   This link will take you to a page with all your friend's comments listed, as shown in Figure 5-12.

3. **Find the Profile Comment you want to delete.**

4. **Click the Delete My Comment link at the bottom of the Profile Comment you posted.**

   The Delete My Comment link will only show up at the bottom of the Profile Comments that you've posted. When you click the link, a confirmation message will ask whether you're sure that you want to delete the Profile Comment. If you're sure, click OK and the Profile Comment will officially be deleted.

The View All link

Figure 5-12:
The View All
link is just to
the left of
the Add
Comment
link.

Messaging the Masses with Bulletins

MySpace was built in a way that allows any one person the ability to send
messages to other users in a quick and easy way. Whether you want to send a
personal message to a friend or broadcast a message to anyone who will
listen about your upcoming garage sale, MySpace has a way to do it. The
number of people who you can contact is limited only by the size of your
friends list. This variety is a big part of what makes MySpace a useful way to
quickly get the word out to the masses about anything and everything.

A Bulletin is MySpace's way of giving the millions of users a way to broadcast
a message to every one of their friends via Bulletin Space. The more friends
you have, the more likely the Bulletin will get noticed and (hopefully) viewed.
There are many reasons why you may want to send out a Bulletin, such as:

- **Don't Forget:** Bulletins are an easy, non-intrusive way to give friendly
  reminders to all your friends. If you're having a big party, getting married
  or having your 10-year class reunion, sending out a bulletin can help
  remind people what's happening.

- **My Thoughts:** Although it might not be the most relevant information,
  sometimes you just want to let your friends know what you're thinking
  during random moments of your life. Just remember, the thoughts that
  you type into a Bulletin are going to also be available to every single one
  of your friends. Filling out surveys and sending them in a Bulletin is also
  a popular way to tell others a little about yourself in a fun and interesting way.

✔ **Your Thoughts:** It's always good to know what other people think about things and a Bulletin is a quick way to get feedback and opinions on different subjects. Sometimes the truth hurts, so be careful what you ask for.

✔ **Updates:** Just posted some new pictures or post a new blog? Maybe you just updated your profile layout? Send out a Bulletin to let your friends know what's up. It's always a good to keep your friends in the loop.

✔ **Awareness:** Let your friends know about the music tour that you're leaving for, the purchase options for that cool new T-shirt that's now for sale on your Web site, or that you're looking for a new house. No matter what you want them to be aware of, you can let them know by sending a Bulletin.

✔ **Getting viral:** By forwarding on a Bulletin that you think worth seeing, you've increased the audience for that particular message. Instead of just being sent to the original sender's friends list, you have now sent it to your own friends list as well. A forwarded Bulletin can become viral and reach hundreds, thousands, and potentially even millions of users quickly.

Locating the My Bulletin Space

If you're wanting to take a look at the Bulletins that you or your friends have recently sent out, sign into your account and browse on over to the bottom-left corner of your MySpace home page. There you should see a box with the heading My Bulletin Space, as shown in Figure 5-13.

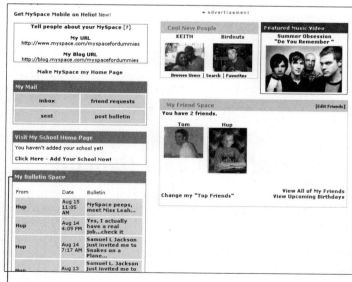

Figure 5-13: The My Bulletin Space is where the most recently posted Bulletins can be viewed.

The My Bulletin Space box

If one of the Bulletins looks interesting enough to deserve your undivided attention, click the subject under the Bulletin heading to open it up. After it's opened, you can read, interact with, or just plain ignore the Bulletin. The Bulletin is pretty straightforward and has only two options once opened, as shown in Figure 5-14:

✔ **Reply to Poster:** Press this button if you want to send a message, comment on, or give feedback to the original sender of the message. If you aren't familiar with the sender, simply click the sender's profile picture to view that person's profile. The reply you send will be sent to the Inbox of the user as a MySpace Message.

✔ **Delete from Friends:** If you have had one too many Bulletins sent to you from a particular user, click this button to delete that person from your friends list permanently. With two simple clicks, the user vanishes from your friends list.

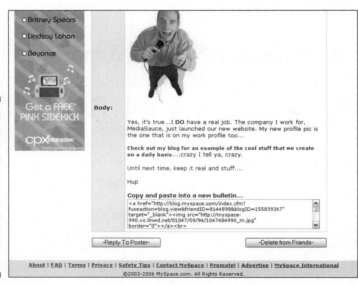

Figure 5-14: You get two button options when you receive a Bulletin: Reply to Poster and Delete from Friends.

Creating and sending a Bulletin

So now it's time to send out that oh-so-important message to your friends that you've decided to run for president. Okay, maybe it's not *that* important, but you still want to get a message out to your fellow MySpacers. Whether your friends are ready or not, you're going to create and send a Bulletin to the masses.

When creating a Bulletin, you basically have a blank template to work with, as seen in Figure 5-15. Before you start typing away to your heart's content, it's always good to think about why you're sending out the Bulletin and what message you really want to get across. Considering that Bulletins are the only way to message several people at one time, many people abuse this feature by sending them out all the time for no particular reason. If you send out a large number of Bulletins, you risk a chance of not getting your friends' attention when you really need to — not to mention that your friends could become annoyed and delete you off of their friends list permanently — consider it the "Boy Who Cried Wolf" of the new millennium.

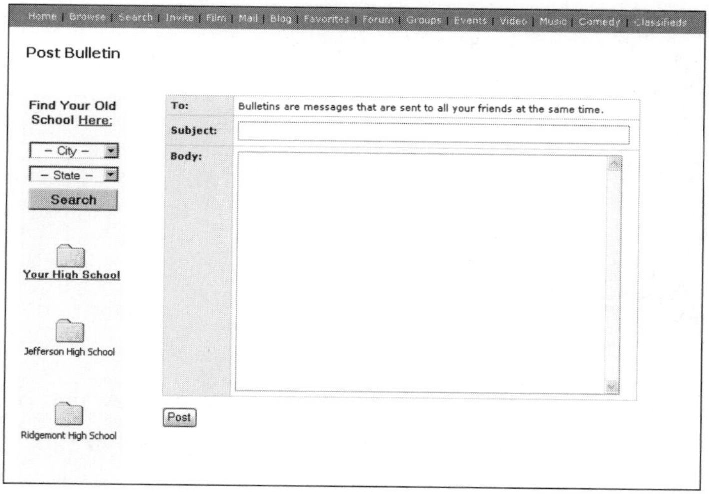

Figure 5-15:
A Bulletin is a great way to send out a message to your entire friends list.

To create and send a Bulletin, follow these steps:

1. **Click the Post Bulletin link on your Home Page.**

   The Post Bulletin link is in the bottom-right corner of the My Mail section on your MySpace Home Page, as shown in Figure 5-16.

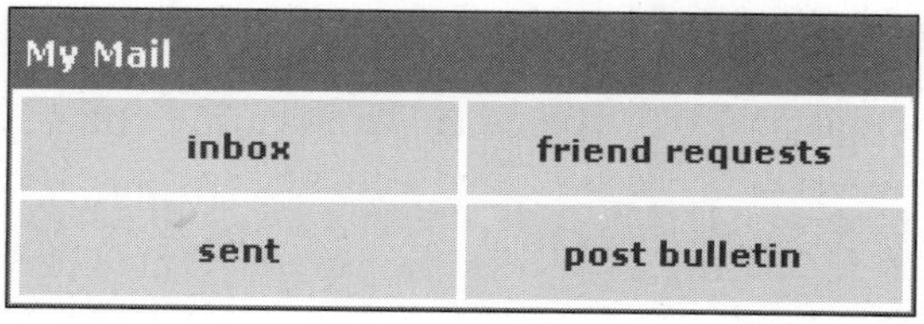

Figure 5-16:
The link to post a Bulletin is located in your My Mail section.

2. **Fill out the Subject and Body of your Bulletin message.**

MySpace requires that both a Subject and Body is entered before a Bulletin is sent. If you aren't sure if your message looks the way that you want, don't worry. There is a confirmation page that enables you to preview your message before you send. Figure 5-17 shows the Bulletin text before posting to the preview/confirmation screen.

Figure 5-17:
Fill out the
Subject
and Body
before you
proceed.

3. **Click the Post button when you're ready to preview and confirm.**

4. **Check your Bulletin layout and click Post Bulletin or Edit.**

The preview/confirmation screen, as shown in Figure 5-18, enables you to see your Bulletin layout in the same way that your friends will view it when opened. Use this final check to look for any misspellings or design fixes that need to be taken care of. If you notice some changes that need to be made, press the Edit button to go back to the text version of your Bulletin and make the changes. If the Bulleting looks good and you're ready to release your message into the wild of MySpace, click Post Bulletin and watch it go!

You can add some more interactive elements into your Bulletins by inserting some simple HTML code. Bulletins are flexible and will allow you to add most HTML tags for images, videos, and links. By adding the HTML code into your message, you make it that much easier for your friends to interact with it. The easier and more engaging that you can make your Bulletin, the better.

If you aren't too familiar with HTML code, an easy way to figure out how to add these elements is by finding an interesting Bulletin that gets sent to you, hitting the Reply to Poster button, and looking at the HTML code and text that makes up the Bulletin's message. When you reply to the Bulletin, the HTML code for the Bulletin will be included in the reply message. All you need to do is copy and paste the message into a new Bulletin, make any needed changes, and test out your new HTML. Use the preview/confirmation screen to test out your code before you send.

Figure 5-18:
The preview/ confirmation screen is your last chance to check your Bulletin before sending to your friends.

Whoops! Deleting a Bulletin

If for some reason you think that you might not want people to see the Bulletin that you just posted, there is an easy way to delete it from MySpace quickly. Follow these steps to get rid of it:

1. **Go to the My Mail Space on your home page and click the Inbox link.**

   This will take you to your Mail Center.

2. **Click the Bulletin link on the left side of the screen.**

   The Bulletin link is directly under the Trash link. This link takes you to your Bulletin Board window.

3. **Click the Show Bulletins I've Posted link on the top-right side of the window.**

   When you click the Show Bulletins I've Posted Link (as shown in Figure 5-19), you'll be taken to a list of the Bulletins you've posted yourself. Remember, any Bulletins you post will expire in 10 days and will not be available for viewing.

The Show Bulletins I've Posted link

Figure 5-19:
The Show
Bulletins
I've Posted
link in the
Bulletin
Board
window.

4. **Check the box to the left of the Bulletin that you want to delete, and then click the Delete Selected button located below the list of Bulletins.**

By checking the box to the left of the Bulletin and clicking the Delete Selected button (as shown in Figure 5-20), you deleted the Bulletin from MySpace completely, and it will be removed from all your Friends' My Bulletin Space as well. Also, there is no confirmation prompt when you delete one of your Bulletins, so make sure that you definitely want it removed before you delete it.

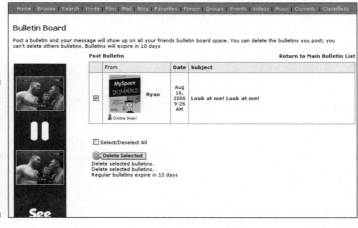

Figure 5-20:
Be sure to
check the
box before
clicking the
Delete
Selected
button.

Be heard

So, you've decided to create a bulletin. It's a big moment. All the eyes will be on you, but I suppose that's the whole point. So, how do you get the attention of your audience? It helps if you have a reputation for sending out pertinent information, but even if this is your first message, you're going to have plenty of folks eager to hear what you have to say. The first step is perhaps the most important — filling out the subject line. Above all, it is best to be clear and direct about whatever it is you're planning on talking about. Sure, you have an obscure movie quote or a funny bit of wordplay that would be perfect, but save it for the main text — it has been proven that the more direct the subject line, the more likely your message will be opened. If you are extending a special offer or prize, you might want to include that, as well. Allow the recipient the ability to quickly decide if the topic is something interesting to them. Although you can't provide a message (or a bulletin) that's perfect for everyone, you *can* find one right for the right individuals. When they've decided the message is worthwhile, it's up to them to decide whether the offer you've extended is worth the cost (even if the price is just time or energy)!

Instant Access with Instant Messaging

It may seem hard to believe, but increasingly, even messaging or an e-mail takes too long to get the information or connection that you need. Sometimes, you need to know right now, this instant, pronto. Instant messaging, or IMing, is your answer. It's much like the rise in popularity of text messaging on mobile phones; Instant messaging on your computer gives you all the immediacy of a phone call without any of that pesky effort of having to actually *speak* to someone.

The first thing you need to know is that you can only IM with your friends on MySpace, so IMing with complete strangers is out of the question. When you find that oh-so-special friend who deserves the grace of your IM invitation, follow these steps to get your conversation started:

1. **Find the Contact Box on the profile page of the user you'd like to IM.**

   The Contact Box is normally directly under the user's profile picture. Although each Contact Box can look different, the Instant Message link will always be located in the left row, third from the top, as shown in Figure 5-21.

2. **Click the Instant Message link.**

   When you click the Instant Message link, a new chat window pops up. A Connecting animation flashes while MySpace attempts to connect you to your friend.

Figure 5-21:
Locate the
Instant
Message
link in the
user's
Contact
Box.

3. **Wait for the chat window to load, and then chat away to your heart's content.**

   When you connect up with your friend, you see a full chat window (as shown in Figure 5-22), and you can start chatting with your friend in real time. A discussion thread is created to help you keep track of the conversation.

Figure 5-22:
After you're
connected,
you see the
full chat
window.

Tying It All Together

After looking at all the different ways to communicate with other users on MySpace, we want to point out that these tools are even more powerful when used together than they are individually. When you're truly trying to get a message out to your friends, be aware of each type of communication, how they're used, and whom they can reach. Always remember your audience; consider how you might reach them best with your intended message. As you move forward with your MySpace adventures, keep the following tips in mind to communicate effectively with your MySpace audience:

✔ **Keep it personal:** People hate being bothered or spammed, regardless of whether they're your MySpace friends. When sending any type of message through MySpace, try to make it as personalized as possible. The reactions you get from a more personalized approach will be worth the extra time it takes to do it.

✔ **Mix and match:** Look at ways to mix all the different communication methods together. Looking to attract attention to something on your MySpace page? Send out a Bulletin that announces it — and send out a few select messages to your friends, letting them know about it. Encourage comments and feedback by asking for focused opinions.

✔ **Make it easy to interact:** When sending out a Bulletin, Message, or posting a Profile Comment, add links, shortcuts, and anything else that makes it easier for the viewer to interact. If you want a friend to post a Profile Comment on your page, send out a Bulletin with a link that takes your friends directly to where they can post one quickly. Take out as many steps as possible.

✔ **Don't reinvent the wheel:** As you learn more about MySpace, you'll pick up on ways other users code their messages to create effective ways to communicate. If you come across a Bulletin that you think rocks, simply hit the Reply to Poster button to view the code used to create it. Take that code and apply it to what you're doing. In a community like MySpace, there is no need to start from scratch.

Figuring out how to effectively communicate with your fellow MySpacers will become easier and easier as time goes on, but it will always be something that you must stay on top of. Just as with everything else in life, the more you give, the more you receive. Knowing what message to send to whom — and at what time — is one if the most important things you'll need to master as you move forward. Also, if you ever get stuck or have questions about something, remember that MySpace is a community — ask the other users questions. You'll be surprised how willing other users will be to help you out.

Chapter 6

Blogging on MySpace

Y ou've probably heard the word "blog" before, even if you've never written or read one. Everyone from your local newscaster to those wordy folks who put together dictionaries have acknowledged the existence of these online writings. Politicians and pundits rant about the "blogosphere," wondering what these words mean for upcoming campaigns and opinion polls. Musicians and fans count on blogs for grassroots promotion of their songs. It seems everybody has a blog these days.

So what is a blog? The short answer is that it's short for "weblog," but that really doesn't say much. The full story is that a *blog* is a collection of writings about whatever you want to write about. Think of a blog as an online notebook or journal where you can write down what you're thinking and feeling about any subject you want. You're the only writer and editor involved.

This chapter takes a look at creating your blog and what you can do to change its visual appearance on-screen. When you're done, you'll have a place all your own to let the world know how you feel.

What Should I Blog?

The short answer to this question is simple — whatever you want! That's probably not all that helpful, though, and it certainly makes for a short chapter. The whole thing is up to you, but it's good to keep some things in mind as you set out on your blogging career.

Knowing your audience

It's always a good idea to keep in mind who you're talking to while you write your blog. That way, you'll have an idea of what will interest your readers and how you're going to talk to them. Even if it's just a quick update of your daily activities, you'll want to phrase it to be read by your friends or family. You'll also want to keep in mind what information you want to be public — does your grandmother (assuming she knows how to use MySpace) really need to know about that road trip to Las Vegas?

You don't have to have a MySpace account to be able to read the blogs of MySpacers — keep this in mind as you begin blogging through MySpace.

Writing about what you know

You're going to be more likely to contribute to a long and productive blog if the subject matter interests you. If you really want to discuss existential literature online, feel free to add to that canon of knowledge. There's no shame in using your blog to keep your friends and family up to date on your life, either. Base your blog on your interests, and don't feel pressure to write about something you don't know.

If you'd like a jump start, MySpace lists several categories you can file your blog under. To see the categories MySpace has made available to you, follow these steps:

1. **Click the Blog link located under your profile picture on your MySpace page, as shown in Figure 6-1.**

2. **Click the Post New Blog link to access the Post a new Blog Entry window.**

Figure 6-1:
The Blog link is located on your MySpace profile page.

The Blog link

3. Click the Category drop-down menu, as shown in Figure 6-2, to see the list of some of the categories you could blog about.

Pick a category, or you can decide not to categorize your blog entry by selecting None. You can also use the categories to get ideas for other topics you could write about. Ultimately, it's up to you.

Figure 6-2: Viewing the Category options MySpace has made available to you.

If you know a lot of information about something, that knowledge is something you can share through your blog. For example, you can help people know more about car maintenance if you want to share your expertise as a mechanic. Blogging about something you're good at will help people and keep them coming back to read your work.

You can also look at other MySpacer profiles and see what subjects people are blogging about. It's not a good idea to just say "Me, too!" and copy the writing style and subject of somebody else's blog, but looking at what's out there can give you an idea of what's available and what holes need to be filled.

Creating and Posting Your Blog

When you have a pretty good idea of what you want to blog about, it's time to make your first post. Click the Blog link under your profile picture, and then click the Post New Blog link to get things underway. It's quite easy to get going.

It's all subjective

At the top of the Post a New Blog Entry window are fields to choose the date and time you're posting (set by default for you by MySpace), along with a subject line and the Category drop-down menu. The Subject field is the title of the blog post you're writing, and you can select an applicable category for your post if you'd like. Again, you don't have to enter anything in the Subject field, but this information will give the reader some advance notice as to what they're going to read.

MySpace defaults to Pacific Standard Time, or PST. Take that into account when you're not posting on the west coast, and change the time to your correct zone when you make a blog post.

Your subject line is the teaser for your entire blog post, and it should both summarize what's going to be talked about inside your writings. Something like "Crappy Day" or "Hi" probably won't get a huge amount of attention, but something with a little flair or craziness might do the trick. This is especially true if you're trying to market something through MySpace, like a small home business, but it applies to all forms of writing. You need to entice the reader and make them want to read your blog. Don't just write "New Shirt," but try something more like "Her Majesty Is RESPLENDANT In Her New Garments."

Your body of work

The large text field is where you actually write your blog entry. If you're an experienced writer, you already know what to do — go on and write your entry. If you haven't written much before, don't be afraid. There are plenty of other people taking their first steps into blogging right along with you. Just imagine yourself talking to someone about what your blog subject is and then type out what you would say. Blogs aren't formal papers — you can throw all the anxiety about that bungled book report in 4th grade out the window. Make it informal and conversational. You'll reach a lot of readers with that style.

You can also include links to Web pages, photos, songs, videos, and other items in your blog. To add links to items within you blog follow these steps:

1. **In the Post a New Blog Entry window, the Advanced Editor toolbar should appear by default and is located above the Body section of your blog, as shown in Figure 6-3.**

   If you do not see the Advanced Editor toolbar, click the Go to Advanced Editor link in the Body section, as shown in Figure 6-4.

Figure 6-3:
The
Advanced
Editor
toolbar will
help you
insert links
to Web
pages,
photos, and
more into
your blog.

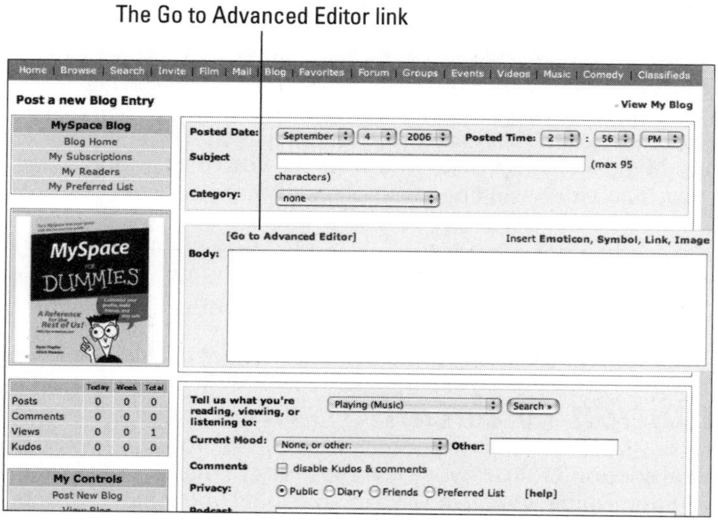

The Advanced Editor toolbar

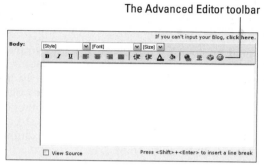

The Go to Advanced Editor link

Figure 6-4:
The Go to
Advanced
Editor link.

2. **To insert an item into you blog, select the appropriate button from the Advanced Editor toolbar. Your options include**

- **Insert Link:** The button featuring the globe and a chain link below it

- **Add Image:** The button featuring an image of a picture

- **Insert Symbol:** The button featuring a key from a keyboard

- **Insert Emoticon:** The button featuring . . . well, an emoticon

3. **When you've clicked a button to insert an item, fill out the information in the window that pops up and click OK (if you're inserting a link or image), or make a selection from the options that appear (if you're inserting a symbol or smiley).**

4. **The link or image will be inserted automatically into your blog entry.**

Some browsers might not handle the Advanced Editor correctly. In that case, you'll use the Simple Editor (refer to Figure 6-4). You'll still be able to enter the link, but you'll have to enter it manually. For example, when you click the Link button, it'll ask for the URL and the text. You'll then have to cut and paste the result it gives you into the body of your blog. For example, a link to the main page of MySpace would look like this:

```
<a href="http://myspace.com">MySpace!</a>
```

To insert an image, the link would look like this:

```
<img src="http://sampleimage.com/sampleimage.jpg">
```

You can also embed any videos that you or somebody else has put on MySpace. Just go to the Video section under your (or somebody else's) profile, and MySpace will provide the code for you to copy and paste into your blog text. The video will appear in place of that text when the blog is posted.

It might eventually be faster for you to type these links by hand instead of using the buttons. In any case, you can use the automatic or the manual entry to insert links, pictures, symbols, and emoticons into your blog.

Attention to detail

The final section of the Post a New Blog Entry window, as shown in Figure 6-5, lets you determine who gets to read your blog and what you want them to know about yourself. The first drop-down menu lets you insert a link to what music you've been listening to, what you've been reading, what DVDs or videos you've been watching, and what video games you've been playing. You don't have to include all (or any) of this, but MySpace gives you an optional list of CDs, books, DVDs, and games to choose from. Click the Search button to look for your current pastime and let the world know how much that new album impressed you.

You can also let the reader know your overall mood by selecting one from the drop-down menu or writing in your own. The drop-down menu will attach an emoticon to your mood as a visual clue. Again, you don't have to include this if you don't want to.

Figure 6-5:
The final
details of
your blog
post.

By default, readers can leave comments or kudos (a kind of virtual high-five) on your blog entries. If you don't want to let them do this, click the Comments check box to disable that ability.

The Privacy radio buttons below the Comments check box determine who gets to read your blog. Your options are

- ✔ **Public:** This is the default setting, and it means your writings are free and open to whomever stumbles on your profile.

- ✔ **Diary:** This setting means that only you can read the entry. Everybody else is blocked from accessing it.

- ✔ **Friends:** Only those on your Friends List can view your blogs. This keeps your information confidential. For more about your Friends List, see Chapter 4.

- ✔ **Preferred List:** Only those on your Preferred List can view the entries. To set up your Preferred list, click the My Preferred List link on the left side of your blog entry page and search out your friends. This way, you can select exactly who reads your blog.

Each blog entry can have its own privacy setting. For example, you can make one entry a diary, and the rest can be public. This helps you control exactly what you tell the world and what the truth actually is.

There's also an option for Podcast Enclosure at the end of the section, but you won't use that unless you actually have a podcast. Feel free to ignore it. If you do have a podcast, though, you can put the link to your podcast file there. For more information on podcasting, check out *Podcasting For Dummies* by Tee Morris and Evo Terra (Wiley Publishing, Inc.).

When you're finished with your blog entry, click the Preview & Post button at the bottom of the page. MySpace will show you what your blog entry currently looks like. You can then choose to post that blog, edit it, or cancel out and dump the blog entry entirely, as seen in Figure 6-6.

Figure 6-6: MySpace allows you to review your blog entry before posting, editing, or canceling it.

Customizing Your Blog

What your blog looks like is an important part of presenting your writings to the public. You not only want to concentrate on what you're writing, but how the reader is going to see it. While the overall look of your blog will have the same characteristics of your overall profile (for more on customizing your MySpace page, see Chapter 12), there are still some color and text changes you can alter to make your blog stand out.

Making general page settings

Click the Blog link at the top of your MySpace account to get to the blogging view, as shown in Figure 6-7. You have several options available to you in this screen.

Look at the section labeled My Controls, located at the bottom-left side of the screen. There are links to post a new blog, view your previous writings, customize your blog, and access the blog safe mode. Click the Customize Blog link to access the Customize My Blog window, as shown in Figure 6-8.

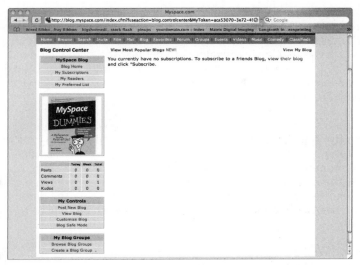

Figure 6-7:
The Blog
Control
Center.

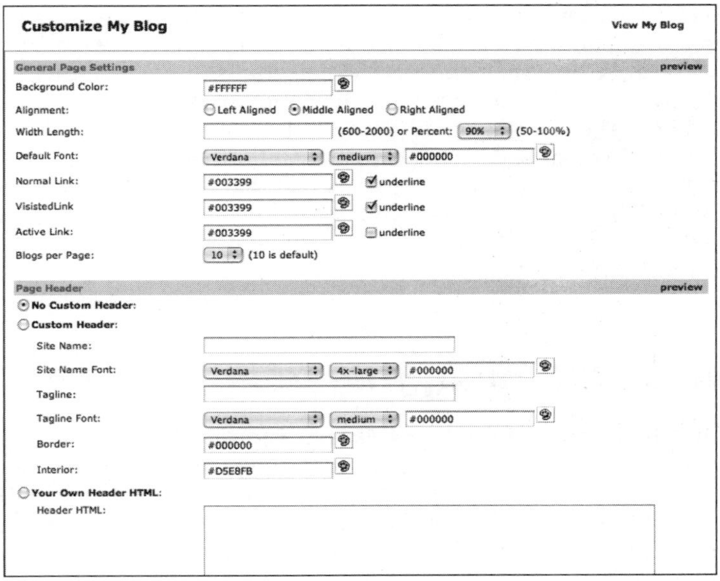

Figure 6-8:
Customizing
your blog.

This view should look familiar to you if you've customized your main
MySpace page (for more on customizing your MySpace page, see Chapter 12),
but lets take a look at the controls anyway. The first section of the window is
the General Page Settings. These settings include the background color of the
page, the font, and where your blog will appear in the readers' Web browsers.
By default, the blog will appear in the middle of the browser with the Verdana
font, but you can feel free to change it to whatever you want.

Technically, the letters and numbers appearing in the color choice fields describe the color in hexadecimal terms, so the browser can choose the right color to display. Luckily, you don't have to keep track of your conversion tables and hexadecimal equivalents to get just the right shade of lavender for your blog. Just click the palette button located to the right of the fields to see the available color choices. Click your color choice, and MySpace will set up the code for you.

The palettes give you basic color choices, but you can try adding and varying shades by changing the letters and numbers in the code. Try choosing a basic color and varying it manually. Without getting too technical, you can use the numbers 0 through 9 and the letters A through F (from low to high) to change the colors. The first two parts of the code following the number sign represent the amount of red, the second two represent the amount of green, and the last two represent the amount of blue. Mix and match to your heart's content.

Using the Width Length window, you can set the width of the blog within the MySpace page, either in exact pixels or by the percentage of the page. Feel free to experiment and see which setting you like best. You can always change it back later. Any links you put in your blog will stand out from the normal text, and the Normal Link, Visited Link, and Active Link controls lets you determine how they appear. You can choose a color (either through code or using the palette button next to the control) and whether the link will be underlined. The Normal link is just what it implies, whereas the Visited Link is what the Normal Link changes to after it has been clicked. The Active Link changes the color of the link being used at that exact moment in time. Finally, the Blogs Per Page control lets you determine how many entries are displayed on each page of the page. The default number is 10, but it can range from 1 to 15.

Heads up: Modifying your page header

The header gives your reader a heads up (appropriate, isn't it?) as to what they should expect from your blog. In the Page Header section (shown in Figure 6-9), you can give your blog a title and a little explanatory text, along with some custom color choices. Consider the header your calling card to your potential reader. It should give them a brief but catchy introduction to your writings.

By default, the Custom Header is turned off so the reader will see nothing if you don't want him or her to. To turn on the header, click the Custom Header radio button and fill in your options.

Figure 6-9:
Modifying
your header.

The Site Name field sets up the main page title, whereas the Tagline field creates the descriptive text for the right side of the header. You can also change the colors of the background, the font, and the border by clicking the palette button and choosing a color. The choices shown in Figure 6-9 create the header shown in Figure 6-10.

Figure 6-10:
Just one
of many
possible
custom
headers.

If you're familiar with HTML, you can add your own header information in the last field of this section. This could include putting pictures or banners in the header for an extra touch.

Inserting incorrect HTML can cause problems displaying the page. Unless you're sure what you're doing, you might want to leave this section alone.

Customizing . . . on the side

Whereas the header introduces the blog itself, the Side Module gives the reader some background on you, the writer. You can include as much of the information as you want, or you can leave it all out. It's your choice.

The top of the Side Module section, as shown in Figure 6-11, lets you choose which side of the page to put the Side Module on and what colors you want to use for the border, text, and body. You can make it look the same as the rest of the blog, or you can give it its own identity.

Side Module		preview
Side Module Position:	Left	
Font Color:	#000000	
Alignment:	○ Left Aligned ◉ Middle Aligned ○ Right Aligned	
Border:	#000000	
Interior:	#FFFF00	
Show Gender:	◉ YES ○ NO	
Show Status:	◉ YES ○ NO	
Show Age:	◉ YES ○ NO	
Show Sign:	◉ NO ○ NO	
Show City:	◉ NO ○ NO	
Show State:	◉ NO ○ NO	
Show Country:	◉ NO ○ NO	
Show Signup Date:	◉ NO ○ NO	
ShowSubscription	◉ NO ○ NO	
Show Blog Groups:	◉ NO ○ NO	

Blog Post Settings		preview
Blog Background Color:	#B1D0F0	
Spacer Color:	#FFFFFF	
Date Background Color:	#B1D0F0	
Date Format:	Wednesday, March 10, 2004	
Date Alignment:	◉ Left Aligned ○ Middle Aligned ○ Right Aligned	
Subject Font:	Arial medium #000000	
Subject Bold:	✓	
Time Format:	6:08 AM – 12 hour Clock	

Figure 6-11: Customizing your side module.

The radio buttons in the second part of the Side Module section allow you to choose what parts of your profile you let the reader see. For example, if you want the reader to see your gender but not your astrological sign, select Yes for the Gender button and No for the Sign button. Make your choices, and you're ready to go.

The main event: Blog Post Settings

The Blog Post Settings section, as shown in Figure 6-12, controls the meat and potatoes of your blog: the actual writing. This section controls how the writing appears to the users — and your writing is where they'll be spending most of their time with your blog. Therefore, it's probably a good idea to make it easy on their eyes. Red text on a black background may seem like a good idea at first, but you'll notice some eye strain as you go on. Don't hurt the reader you're trying to inform or entertain. Dark text on a lighter background is probably the best way to go.

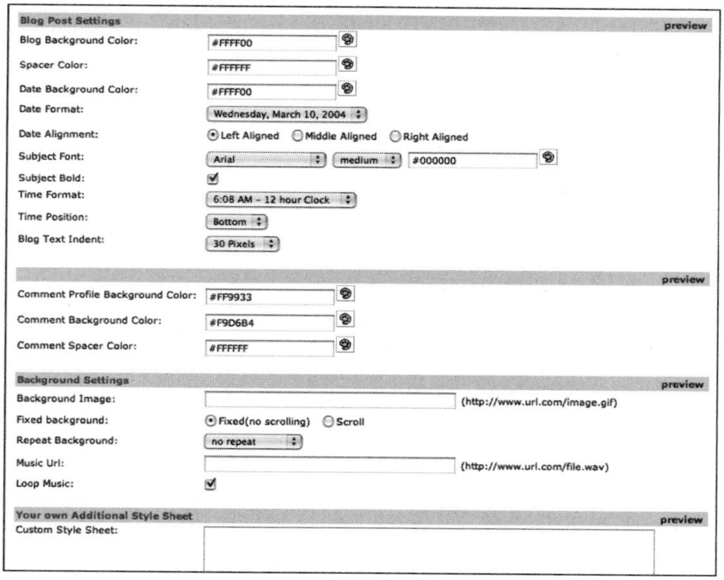

Figure 6-12:
Setting the
look for your
blog posts.

The commands in this section are similar to the rest of the controls in the Customize My Blog window, so the controls should look familiar. Choose the colors and font you want to use for the main section of the blog. Each blog post will also get a specific time and date stamp, and you can choose where on the page you want those to appear. This section also includes color settings for the comments others leave on your blog.

Changing the background

The next section of the Customize My Blog window is Background Settings (refer to Figure 6-12). This section gives you the option to put a picture or song behind your blog. To use a picture, make sure you have the picture you want to use already loaded on a Web server. This can include any picture you've uploaded to your MySpace account (look at Chapter 10 for more information). When your picture is uploaded, put the address for that picture in the Background Image field. From there, you can adjust the picture to either stay in place (fixed) or move as the reader scrolls through your writings. If it's a smaller image, you can choose to have it repeat (like tiles) vertically, horizontally, or in all directions.

Use the background picture choices wisely. Don't let an especially eye-catching image distract the reader from actually taking in what you write.

If there's a song you'd like to have the reader listen to while they peruse your work, just put the URL of the song in the Music URL field and it'll play. If you want to keep the music going after the song ends, check the Loop Music button to repeat the song until the reader closes the page. Because this function requires a URL, you'll have to use a song that's already been uploaded to the Internet. Unfortunately, there's no button you can click that will automatically load a song into this field. You'll have to get the exact address from the person hosting the song on the Internet, or you'll have to host it yourself. MySpace doesn't provide the URLs for the songs they host in band jukeboxes, so more than likely you'll be looking at different Web sites for addresses to use in this field.

Music files can be large, so it might be a good idea to use a shorter section of the song and let it loop around. That way, the reader gets the page loaded more quickly.

Don't let the background music distract the reader. Use it to enhance the mood of your writing, not take away from it.

Using a Custom Style Sheet

At the bottom of the Customize My Blog window is the Your Own Additional Style Sheet section. This space allows you to add your own style information. To do this, you'll have to format it as a *Custom Style Sheet.* That mouthful is also known as a *Cascading Style Sheet,* or *CSS* for short, and it's how the look of many Web pages you see are defined. Think of it as a list of instructions that your browser gets ahead of the actual Web page that tells it how to display that page.

There are plenty of resources for you to look up that will show you how to build your own CSS. Although it will allow you to highly customize the look of your MySpace page, CSS can be a little complicated. You don't have to put anything in the field if you don't want to, and in fact it's better to avoid it until you know what you're doing. There are also services you can use that will build the CSS for you. Look at Chapter 12 for more information on custom profile editors and what they can do for you.

It's sometimes hard to predict how different Internet browsers (such as Internet Explorer or Firefox) will interpret CSS information. Try testing your blog on different browsers to see how it works before deciding on a final layout.

Safe Blogging

The Blog Safe Mode option is found in the My Controls box on the left side of your blog page. Selecting the Blog Safe Mode option (shown in Figure 6-13) allows you to look at your blog without any additional HTML or commands. This means you can go in and fix any problems in your blog that might cause it to display incorrectly. Use this view if you're having problems seeing your blog and you need to remove problem code. Otherwise, you can leave this view alone.

Figure 6-13:
The Blog
Safe Mode
option in the
My Controls
box.

The Blog Safe
Mode link

More than likely, you won't have to use this view too often. Unlike your comments section, where others can leave HTML-based comments that might screw up your profile, you're the only one in control here. Still, it's a valuable tool to have in case something does go wrong. There's nothing wrong with having a backup plan when it comes to putting something on the Internet.

Your Subscription

MySpace gives you a way to keep up to date with certain blogs. When you find one you want to keep tabs on, just click the Subscribe link on the main blog page of that profile, as shown in Figure 6-14. Confirm that subscription, and you'll automatically receive a notice in the My Mail section of your profile when a new blog entry is posted. Just follow that notice to see that new entry.

Figure 6-14:
Subscribing
to a blog.

> **Last Updated:**
> Oct 11, 2006
> Send Message
> Instant Message
> Email to a Friend
> Subscribe
> Invite to My Blog

You can also use subscriptions to let people know what you're reading and who's reading your writings. Click the My Subscriptions link in the MySpace Blog box (shown in Figure 6-15) to see who you're subscribed to. Clicking the My Readers link lets you know who has subscribed to your blog. You won't see all your readers — just the ones who have subscribed.

Figure 6-15:
The
MySpace
Blog box
allows you
to see your
subscrip-
tions and
readers.

> **MySpace Blog**
> Blog Home
> My Subscriptions
> My Readers
> My Preferred List

More generic statistics are displayed below the subscription section, as shown in Figure 6-16. You'll be able to see how many times your blog page has been loaded by week and in total, along with how many comments have been left and who gave you kudos.

View your Blog statistics

Figure 6-16:
Your blog
statistics.

Spreading the Word

When you have a blog, it's time to let your potential readers know — assuming you want other people to read them. There are several ways you can do this, and most of them are provided by MySpace for simplicity's sake. You can make people aware of your blog in the following ways:

- ✔ **Bulletins:** Use the Bulletins feature detailed in Chapter 5 to let all your friends know you're keeping a blog. It's a quick and easy way to get the word out, and by using the Bulletin feature, you know that your readers already have access to the Internet and can read what you write. Invite them to subscribe in your bulletin so they can always stay in touch.

- ✔ **Comments and Messages:** If you have someone specific you want to tell about your blog, drop them a message or leave a comment on their profile page. They'll get the message.

- ✔ **E-mail:** Tell the folks for whom you have e-mail addresses about your blog — drop them a quick note. You don't have to have a MySpace account to read blogs, so this is a good opportunity to let those outside the site know about your blog.

- ✔ **Other Web sites:** If you participate in forums or discussions on other Web sites, put a link to your blog in your signature or profile. This link can be found under the Tell People About Your MySpace section of your main profile page, as shown in Figure 6-17.

Figure 6-17:
Spreading
the word of
your blog.

Tell people about your MySpace [?]

My URL
http://www.myspace.com/myspacefordummies

My Blog URL
http://blog.myspace.com/myspacefordummies

✔ **Blog Groups:** Create a blog group by clicking the Create a Blog Group link in the bottom left corner of your blog page, as shown in Figure 6-18. You'll be asked to name your group, describe it in a few words, and select a category that defines what your group is all about. That group will be entered in the main directory of blogs on MySpace, allowing readers interested in your particular subjects to search you out and read what you've written. You can also browse blog groups in this section and make connections with other like-minded individuals.

Figure 6-18:
Creating a
blog group.

Comments, Please?

Every blog entry includes an Add Comment button at the bottom of the page. People will click that link when they want to leave you a small message. You can also leave one or two kudos here. Just type in your comment and click Post, and your comment will be added to the blog (if that function has been enabled by the owner of the blog — see the section "Attention to detail," earlier in this chapter).

Both the blog writer and readers can post comments; you can have an ongoing discussion with your readers using this feature. This is a great way to talk about your blog and the subjects you write about. These entries will appear in sequential order, making it seem like you're having an online conversation. Blogging doesn't have to be only one-way!

Leaving comments on other blogs is a good way to encourage conversation on your own writings. Be more active in discussing blogs, and you'll have others do the same for you.

Set up a consistent schedule for posting your blogs. People are more likely to come back again and again if you put up fresh entries on a regular basis.

Chapter 7

Keeping Up with MySpace

*T*here's so much to keep up with on MySpace that it's nice to have some help in tracking it all. After all, don't you want to know every time somebody tries to send you a message, a bulletin, or a picture that neither of you can believe somebody would actually want to share with the public?

MySpace can track these events for you, even if you're not logged in to the site. There are e-mail reminders, visual clues, and even text messages to your cell phone. If you can't stand to be out of contact with MySpace for too long, consider getting some fresh air — and read on with this chapter.

Alert! Alert! Alert!

MySpace automatically notifies you when you receive a new message, event invitation, comment (either on your profile or your blog), or friend request. In addition, you can also get a notification when somebody makes a new post to a blog you subscribe to. These alerts show up in the My Mail section of your profile, as shown in Figure 7-1.

New alerts

Figure 7-1:
Some new
alerts from
MySpace.

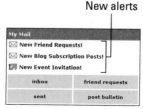

These alert notifications occur each and every time something happens to your profile. The only problem is that you have to be logged in to your profile to see them. It's obviously impossible to see them if you're away from the computer or not logged in. Rather than going through withdrawal, though, you have two ways to receive a virtual shout when something new happens.

Receiving e-mail notifications

Because you had to get an e-mail account to use MySpace anyway (for more on setting up an account, see Chapter 2), you might as well put it to work! This simple process will set MySpace up to use the e-mail address you entered when creating your MySpace account to e-mail you whenever you receive one of the following:

- ✔ A new message
- ✔ A new comment
- ✔ A new blog comment
- ✔ A new friend request

To set up e-mail notification of new alerts, follow these steps:

1. **On the main page of your profile, click the Account Settings link in the upper-left corner.**

   It's right next to your picture, as shown in Figure 7-2.

2. **When you get to the Change Account Settings window, make sure the check box next to Notifications is blank, as shown in Figure 7-3. If it is, you're all set.**

3. **When things start moving on your profile, you'll get all kinds of e-mails telling you what other people are saying to (and about) you.**

The Account Settings link

Figure 7-2:
The
Account
Settings
link.

The Notifications setting

Change Account Settings

| Home | Browse | Search | Invite | Film | Mail | Blog | Favorites | Forum | Groups | Events | Video | Music | Comedy | Classifieds |

Change Account Settings

NOTE: Changing your default email or name can make it hard for your friends
to find or recognize you on MySpace

[View My Profile] [Edit My Profile] [Cancel Account]

My Account Settings	
Email Address:	
Change Password:	- Change Password:-
Notifications:	☐ Do not send me notification emails -help-
Newsletters:	☐ Do not send me MySpace newsletters
Privacy Settings:	- Change Settings-
IM Privacy Settings:	- Change Settings-
Mobile Settings: New!	- Change Settings-
Groups Settings:	- Change Settings-
Calendar Settings:	- Change Settings-
Blocked Users:	- View List-
Profile Views:	- Reset Count-
Profile Settings:	- Change Settings-
Music Settings: New!	- Change Settings-
Away Message:	- View / Edit Away Message-
Preferred Site & Language:	www.myspace.com - English ▾
Time Zone Settings:	(GMT -08:00 hours) Pacific Time (US & Canada) ▾
	-Change-

Figure 7-3:
Check
this box
for notifi-
cations.

Remember the location of this check box in case you start getting too many e-mails. MySpace can move quickly, and you could find that you're getting more e-mail than you want. Check the box, and it will all go away. It's up to you. Also, if you change your e-mail address, be sure to update your MySpace account with the new address. For more on changing your e-mail address, see Chapter 2.

Getting notifications on your cell phone

My father has a cell phone, which is a sure indicator that the rest of the nation probably beat him to it. Given that it's such a widespread presence, it's no surprise that MySpace alerts are happily compatible with whatever phone and service provider you have. Through the magic of text message, you can keep up to date with everything that happens on your account.

At the time of this writing, the only wireless carriers supported by MySpace were Cingular and Helio.

To get notifications and alerts on your cell phone, follow these steps:

1. Click the Get MySpace Mobile Alerts link below your picture on the main profile page, as shown in Figure 7-4.

There is a separate link for advanced control over MySpace using Helio devices, and we'll look at that link later in this chapter.

The Get MySpace Mobile Alerts link

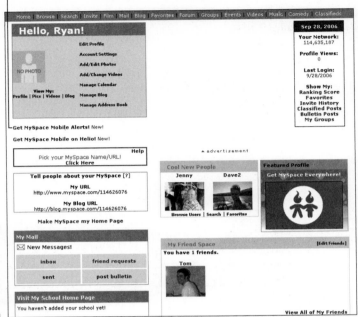

Figure 7-4:
The Get
MySpace
Mobile
Alerts link.

2. **The next page shows you all the notifications you can receive on your text-capable mobile phone, as shown in Figure 7-5.**

   All the choices here are checked by default, but you can uncheck any choice you want. Your choices are

   - Friend Request
   - Blog Comment
   - Profile Comment
   - Image Comment
   - New Message
   - Event Invite

3. **Click the Apply Settings button to begin the process.**

   Notice the fine print at the bottom of this page! MySpace won't charge you for this notification service, and that's mighty kind of them. Your service provider, however, probably won't be so generous. You'll get charged for these text messages, just as you would for any others. Check your plan (and your wallet) before you sign up for these alerts.

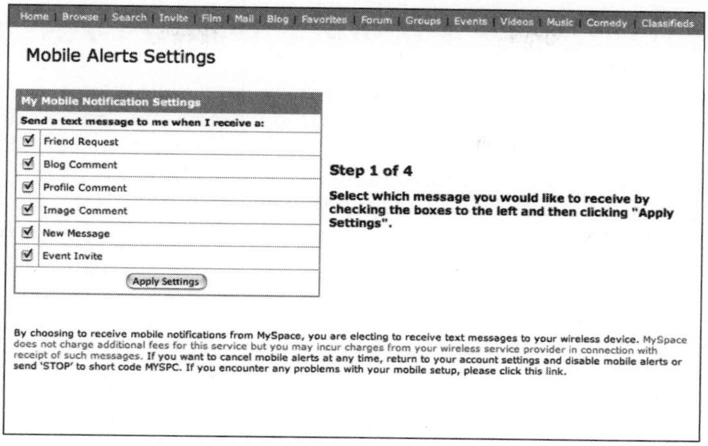

Home | Browse | Search | Invite | Film | Mail | Blog | Favorites | Forum | Groups | Events | Videos | Music | Comedy | Classifieds

Mobile Alerts Settings

My Mobile Notification Settings

Send a text message to me when I receive a:

☑ Friend Request

☑ Blog Comment

☑ Profile Comment

☑ Image Comment

☑ New Message

☑ Event Invite

(Apply Settings)

Step 1 of 4

Select which message you would like to receive by checking the boxes to the left and then clicking "Apply Settings".

By choosing to receive mobile notifications from MySpace, you are electing to receive text messages to your wireless device. MySpace does not charge additional fees for this service but you may incur charges from your wireless service provider in connection with receipt of such messages. If you want to cancel mobile alerts at any time, return to your account settings and disable mobile alerts or send 'STOP' to short code MYSPC. If you encounter any problems with your mobile setup, please click this link.

Figure 7-5: The My Mobile Notification Settings box.

4. **You'll be asked to enter your phone number and your wireless carrier (only Cingular and Helio are supported at this time), and then you'll verify your number through a text message.**

5. **When you've verified your number through the text message, you're ready to go.**

   Look for all the alerts for your MySpace account to come directly to your phone.

If you want to stop or reduce the text messages, go back to the Mobile Alerts Settings page and uncheck all the selections. When all the options are unchecked, click the Apply Settings button and they'll stop. You can also stop the messages from your cell phone by sending the message STOP to short code MYSPC.

Gotta Go! — Using Mobile Communication Devices to Access MySpace

So far, all the mobile interaction you've seen with MySpace in this chapter has been through simple e-mails or messages. However, there are other devices you can use away from your main computer to get you onto MySpace. Some use standard wireless Internet, and some are even built specifically for MySpace functions.

Connecting to MySpace with PDAs

Smart phones, also known as *PDAs,* are capable of working on the Internet, free from large computer towers and wired connections (and, in the case of some phones, even wireless hot spots). If your device can access the Internet remotely, chances are you can get MySpace on it. Be aware, though, that different browsers handle Web sites (including MySpace) differently. It might not look the same on your mobile device as it does on your desktop, and some of the functions might not work. Give it a shot, though — you should get good results on most devices.

Utilizing Helio

One manufacturer has taken a love of MySpace to dramatic new heights with their mobile devices. Helio handsets promise access to these MySpace functions:

- ✔ Photo bulletins
- ✔ Messages
- ✔ Pages of friends, family, and everybody else
- ✔ Adding new comments
- ✔ Adding new friends

Obviously, this device is tailored to work with MySpace directly, and its performance will probably exceed that of another smart phone. If you're in the market for a new phone (or your frenzy for the site is balanced with the budget for a new phone), you might want to check these out. Go to www.helio.com for more information on plans and devices.

I IM, DO U?

The instant message is a second voice for many today, and it's available nearly everywhere — which of course includes MySpace. The IM service Tom and company provide is limited to those who already have MySpace accounts, but that's easy enough to set up (for a refresher, head back to Chapter 2). Lets take a look at how to IM your friends with MySpaceIM.

There's a difference between using the Instant Message function in the Contact Box of a friend and using the MySpaceIM download. For more information on the Instant Message function, look at Chapter 5.

MySpaceIM only works on Windows machines using Microsoft's Internet Explorer. If you don't use these, you're out of luck. Anybody you IM must also use MySpaceIM.

Get it in your system

This program stands alone from the MySpace site, although it does work with profiles from MySpace. To use it, download the program from `http://myspace.com/myspaceim` and follow the instructions to set it up. It'll require the following information:

✔ The e-mail address you used to sign up for MySpace.

✔ Your MySpace password.

✔ Your MySpace username. If you already have one, it'll be entered automatically. If not, you'll be prompted to create one.

If you create a username at this point, your profile URL will change to

`http://myspace.com/yourusernameappearshere`

Remember that before you make a change.

If you've used instant messaging before, this won't seem much different from other programs. You'll be able to type messages in real time between two people using the program, and all the friends you have available for chat will be listed in the screen.

Adding Friends

Part of what makes MySpaceIM so convenient is that your Friends List is already created for you by MySpace. You just have to pick which ones you want to IM from your MySpace profile. The easiest way to make this happen is to drag your friends from their profile pages to MySpaceIM. Just click and drag on your friend's name (or main profile picture) from your browser to MySpaceIM. It'll be added automatically. You can also use the Add Friends wizard already installed in MySpaceIM.

To add Friends in MySpaceIM, follow these steps:

1. **Start MySpaceIM by clicking the Instant Message link in the Contact Box on the profile page of the person you want to add as a friend.**

2. **Click File, and then Add Friends.**

3. **Choose which friends you want to add.**

   If you know which friends you want to add, you can pick them individually. Click which ones you want in the separate window MySpaceIM brings up. You can also choose to add all your friends or just the ones in your Top Friends list.

4. **Now, just click your friends to send them a message.**

   Remember, though, that you both have to be logged in to chat.

Always changing

At the time of this writing, MySpaceIM was a *beta release* — it's still being tested and developed. That means that they're still working on it, and things are liable to change. In addition to instant messaging, the current version allows you to

- ✔ **Block unwanted messages and users**
- ✔ **Save your conversations**
- ✔ **Change the look of the MySpaceIM window**

Most of these functions are accessible under File➪Preferences, so go there once you've downloaded the program to see what's available. These are liable to change and expand as MySpaceIM evolves, so check MySpace often to see what's developing.

Doesn't play nice with others

You'll notice that MySpaceIM doesn't interact with instant-messaging services such as AIM, Google, or MSN. It also doesn't work with client programs like Trillian and meebo (which group the functions of other IM services together). The two selling points for MySpaceIM, in this case, are ease of use and interaction with the main MySpace site. The best use of this program is to keep in touch with your main MySpace friends.

Chapter 8

Staying on Schedule with MySpace

In This Chapter

▶ Creating events

▶ Inviting people to your events and managing RSVPs

▶ Managing your MySpace calendar

Go ahead and admit it — you're far too busy to manage your calendar without a little help. There's no shame in getting assistance from MySpace. Some of the tools available to you make it easier to work with than a paper calendar, and you never have to worry about accidentally losing your MySpace account the way you misplaced your PDA last month. Plus, because most of your friends have MySpace accounts too, you can set up invitations that help you keep all your planning organized. Lets see your old datebook keep up with that.

By the time you're finished with this chapter, you'll have an online reference that will manage your entire schedule. All of your important events and invitations will interact seamlessly, and you'll be able to access it from any computer with Internet access in the world. Pretty handy, eh?

Organizing Your Events

MySpace makes it easy to organize events outside of the digital realm, and your address book is already loaded with your friends on MySpace. It also helps you manage invitations you receive from others, you social butterfly. This section shows you how to create your own events and add events sent to you by others. These all go to one common calendar, which you can manage for yourself.

Getting the party started

Click the Events link at the top of your MySpace profile page, as shown in Figure 8-1, to get started.

The Events link

Figure 8-1:
The Events
link is the
first place to
go to create
an event.

In the MySpace Events window, you see the Events Links box in the upper-left corner of the screen. The Events Links box gives you four options:

✔ **Event Invites**

✔ **Events I've Posted**

✔ **Events I'm Attending**

✔ **Create New Event**

If you're relatively new to MySpace, you won't have anything in the first three options. Don't worry — these will fill up as more of your MySpace friends start sending out invitations. And there's no better way to let people know you're around than by throwing your own bash. Click Create New Event to have some folks over to your place.

Setting the stage

The Create an Event screen, as shown in Figure 8-2, contains several fields you'll use to describe your bash. Think of filling in this screen as just like writing out a paper invitation to somebody — minus the paper. You'll use the same information, but you have no cards or postage to buy. (Technology. Gotta love it.)

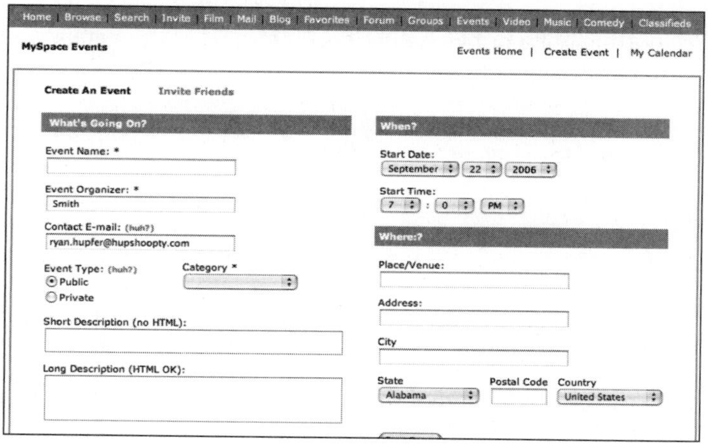

Figure 8-2:
Creating your first MySpace party.

Give your event a snappy and enticing title ("Free Pizza!" is always a favorite), and make sure your name and contact e-mail are correct. You'll have to decide now whether you want to make the event public or private. If you only want the friends you invite to see the invitation, click Private for the Event Type. If you want the world to know, leave it marked Public. Just remember — even those folks who don't get specific invitations could run across the invitation and decide to make their way to your event. Because you made the event invitation public, this wouldn't be considered rude or party-crashing. Manage your event invitations carefully.

You also have to pick a category for your event. The Category field gives those viewing your invitation a quick hint as to what the whole thing is about. Click the drop-down menu and pick the term that best describes your happening. There is a blank category entry in case none of the entries apply, or you could always just go with Miscellaneous. Be as specific as possible, though. Details are always helpful.

Picking a category is a required action — and you also have to specify the event name and event organizer. You won't be able to send an invitation without filling out these fields, but we figure you'll certainly want to add these and more. (Otherwise, how do folks know what it's about and who's throwing this shindig?)

Now give your event a short description. This should just be a few words that give a general idea of what your event entails. "Come watch movies at my place this Saturday!" is a good example — short, sweet, and to the point. You'll have the opportunity to get more long-winded in the Long Description field, and you can also include pictures and links there. For instance, you could link a photo of (say) the park where you're throwing the picnic, or an online map to the event's location. You could also get more creative — say, whip up an image of an invitation and insert it there.

If you're putting out a public invitation, be careful of the details you choose to include. It's probably not a good idea to give everybody with a computer and an Internet connection your address, phone number, or other information.

The HTML code for inserting an image is

```
<img src="(Insert Image URL Here)">
```

The HTML code for inserting a link is

```
<a href="(Insert Link URL Here)">Any descriptive text you
        want</a>
```

Now go to the top-right side of the screen and use the drop-down menus to set the Start Date and Start Time for your event.

Check to make sure your AM/PM choice is set correctly. You'd hate to have folks arrive half a day early or late.

Fill in the location of the event in the fields under the Where? section. Give the location a name such as "My House" or "Joe's Place," and fill out the actual street address from there. Now click Save Event button and you're ready to go. It should look like Figure 8-3 when you're done.

Your invitation's in the mail

After you've created and saved your event, you'll be asked to invite people. It wouldn't be a party without guests, would it? The Invite Friends screen, as shown in Figure 8-4, allows you not only to invite your MySpace folks, but those who aren't part of the site yet as well. It doesn't get much more convenient.

The Invite Friends screen first gives you the option to show your guest list to everyone (helpful if you want people to know who's coming, but it's your choice) and to requests RSVPs on the event page. These options are up to you — check them if you want to use them, or leave them blank if you don't. By default, these options are checked and enabled. You'll have to turn them off. You can also add some additional text in the Invitation Message field to have it included as part of (you guessed it) your invitation message. Something like "Check out my invitation — hope you can make it!" will work fine. You can also let people comment on your event on the event page if you want. An additional "Can't wait!" or "This will be fun!" can help entice folks to flock to your event. If, however, you don't need comments from everybody out there (or just want comments from those who have been invited), click the appropriate button for the Allow Comments By option.

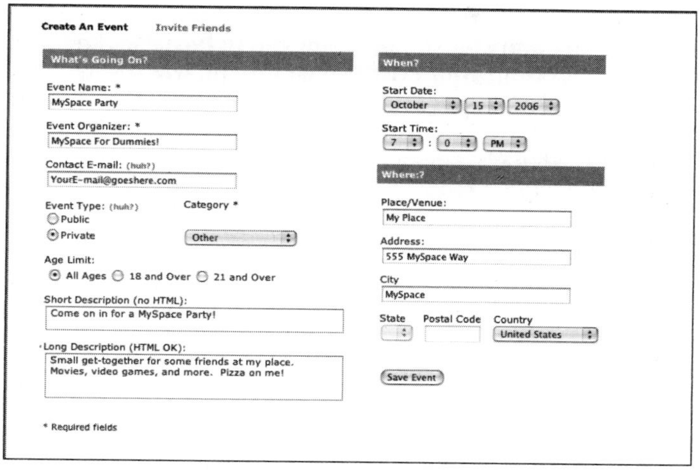

Figure 8-3: Your finished event.

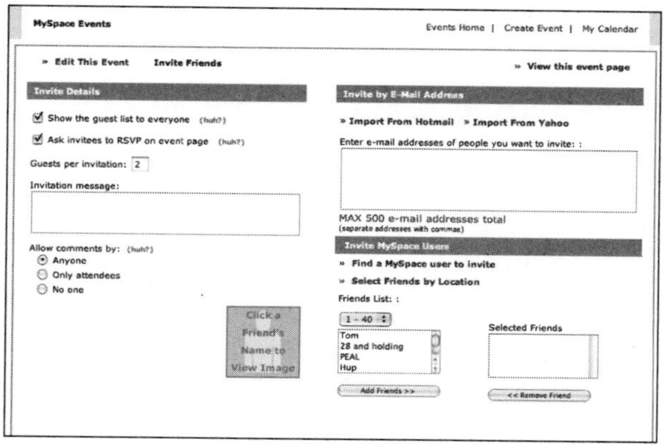

Figure 8-4: Inviting your friends.

To invite MySpace friends, just scroll through the list in the Invite MySpace Users section at the bottom-right of your screen, and then click Add Friend to send an invite to that person. If you click the wrong friend ("The Foreign Cinema Club" might not appreciate your *Terminator* movie marathon), click Remove Friend to take the name off your list. This doesn't remove the person or group as your friend; it just means they won't get an invitation to this particular event.

You should also check out two options just above your Friends List. The Find a MySpace User to Invite link will let you search for someone on MySpace who isn't already your friend and send that person an invitation. You can also group your friends by where they are located by clicking the Select Friends by Location link to access the Select Friends by Location box, as shown in Figure 8-5. After all, someone who lives out of state might not able to drop by this evening — and this approach saves you from having to search through all the out-of-state folks.

Just put in the city and state or ZIP code you're based in, and MySpace will sort out local folks from your Friends List for you when you click Find Friends. Pretty slick.

Changing your plans

Things change, and you may have to make some adjustments to your event as you go. If you have to alter your event plans, it's easy enough. From anywhere in MySpace, click the Events link at the top of your browser window (refer to Figure 8-1) to get to the main Events screen. From there, click the Events I've Posted link to see your events. It should look something like Figure 8-6.

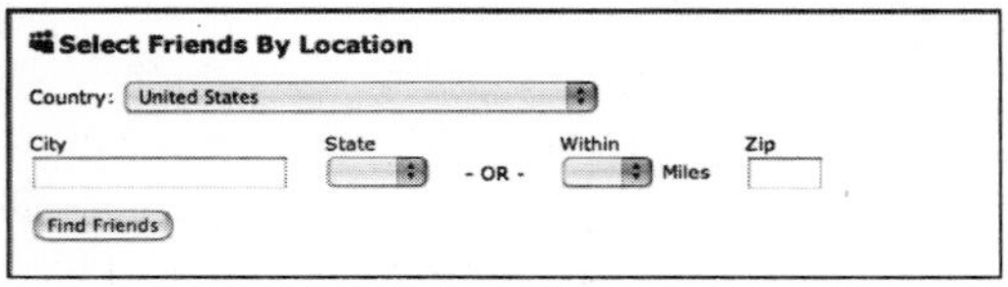

Figure 8-5:
Inviting friends by location.

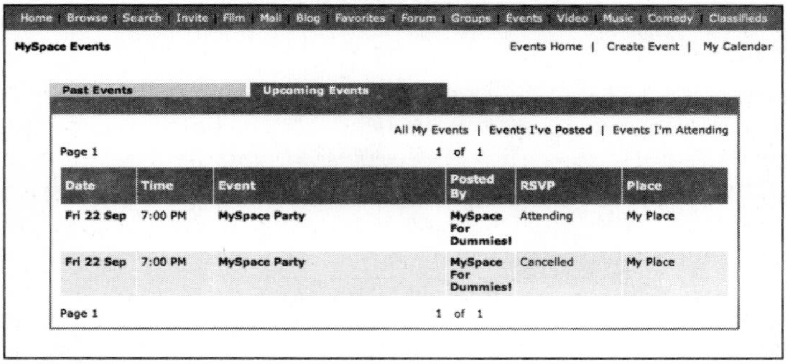

Figure 8-6:
Upcoming MySpace events.

Select an event from the list of Upcoming Events tab and you will be taken to the main page for your event, as shown in Figure 8-7.

From main page for the event, click the Edit Event link to change the event information. The fields will look just the same as when you created the event. You can also upload or change the image associated with your event, cancel the event, or invite more attendees by selecting the appropriate link on the event's main page. Choosing to cancel the event will mark the event as cancelled and, if you wish, send out an e-mail to those invited notifying that the plans are cancelled. Choosing to invite more people takes you back to the Invite Friends screen (refer to Figure 8-4), where you can add more friends or e-mail addresses. You can also click the Blog This link or the Bulletin This link in the Spread The Word . . . box to add your event invitation to your blog or bulletins, respectively.

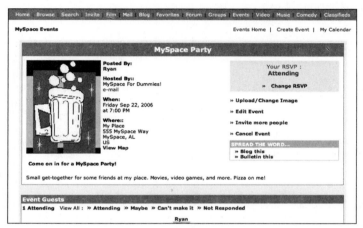

Figure 8-7:
Event page.

Adding your events to blogs and bulletins is a great way to make sure everyone knows what you're planning. Well, okay, it's probably best to avoid doing that if your event is marked private and/or you're planning to take over the world. A little judgment here.

Are you going to make it?

If you requested that somebody RSVP to your event, you can check responses on the main page for the event. At the bottom of the page is a list of event attendees. You can sort them by clicking the links for Attending, Maybe, Can't Make It, and Not Responded. This allows you to plan for who's coming — and gently remind those who haven't gotten back to you yet that you're waiting to hear from them.

This information will always be available to the event organizer (in this case, that's you). You can also choose to make it visible to others, as mentioned previously in the section "Getting the party started."

You're invited!

More than likely, you'll start getting invitations to events as soon as you pick up a few friends on MySpace. You'll have a bunch of your own friends on the site anyway, and you'll make new friends as you go on. You'll know when you get a new invitation when you see the alert shown in Figure 8-8 under the My Mail section of your home page.

Figure 8-8:
A New
Event
Invitation?
Oh, Happy
Day!

The New Event Invitation! alert

Click the alert to see what your new invitation is all about. You'll notice that
the link takes you directly to your Mail Center and your Event Invites box and
it will show you a list of invitations you've received, as shown in Figure 8-9.

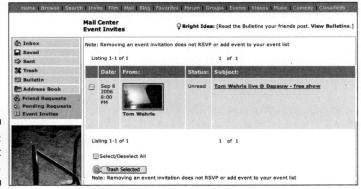

Figure 8-9:
An Event
Invitation.

Clicking an individual event invitation brings up a link to the main event page
and the simple greeting text, as shown in Figure 8-10.

Figure 8-10:
Reading
Your Event
Invitation.

If you want to see the invitation and all the details, just click the *Click here to see this event* button and you'll be able to see all the details, as shown in Figure 8-11.

If the sender has requested an RSVP, you can use the RSVP section to make your selection — and send along a short message as well. Whatever you feel is appropriate will work here. For the most part, MySpace invitations are casual and informal.

When you're done viewing an invitation, it'll be marked as read and the New Event Invitation! alert will be removed from your My Mail section on your profile page. You can always see the invitation again by going back to your Mail Center and selecting the Event Invites link.

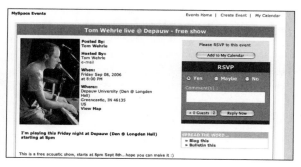

Figure 8-11:
Invitation
Details and
RSVP.

Using Your MySpace Calendar

If you're going to be sending and/or receiving a lot of event invitations, you'll need some kind of calendar to keep track of your busy schedule. Even if you don't choose to use MySpace's Event feature, there are times when an extra reminder can help. The point is, you'll need a calendar to keep track of every-thing — hey, just like the real world — and that's built into MySpace as well.

Making your calendar your own

To access the calendar, click the Manage Calendar link at the top of your pro-file page, as shown in Figure 8-12. Your calendar will pop up in the My Calendar window and it will show today's date, as illustrated in Figure 8-13. The default view is Day, but you can also choose Week, Month, or Year views by using the tabs at the top of the calendar.

The Manage Calendar link

Figure 8-12:
The
Manage
Calendar
link.

The View tab options

The Options link

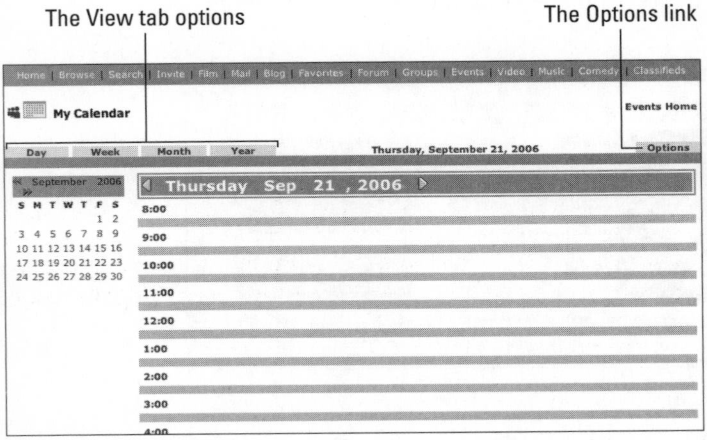

Figure 8-13:
Viewing
Your
Calendar.

Click the Options link (refer to Figure 8-13) to see how to modify your calendar. As you can see in the My Calendar Options box, shown in Figure 8-14, you can

- ✔ Choose to change your default view
- ✔ Specify whether your calendar is private, shared only with friends, or open to the world
- ✔ Declare the day of the week should begin on (sorry, Monday still has to come anyway)
- ✔ Set your workday hours

If your social calendar is just so crammed that you tend to lose track, you can also choose to have reminders of calendar events sent to you. These can be sent to you via MySpace messages or external e-mail — at any time from one to seven days before an event.

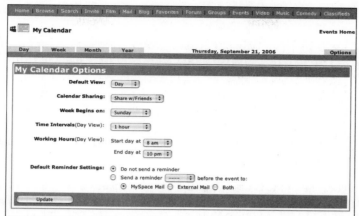

Figure 8-14:
Your
Calendar
Options.

I'll pencil you in

When you're ready to add an event to your calendar, just select the date on the main calendar to the left of the My Calendar page (take a quick look back at Figure 8-13) and click the time closest to your planned entry. The window shown in Figure 8-15 will come up, and you'll be ready to enter your information.

Filling in the info is practically a no-brainer:

1. **Give your calendar entry a title.**

   It could be anything from "Take the dog for a walk" to "Show up for your job interview, fool!" You can also assign a category from the drop-down menu just below the Title field. Your choices range from "MySpace Event" to "Bill Payment." (They think of everything, don't they?)

2. **Use the drop-down menus to set up the time and duration of the appointment.**

   If this is going to be a recurring event, you can also set the event to happen automatically over a period of time — set it to occur every other day, every week, the first Tuesday of every month, every thousand years (just kidding), whatever works for you. Just use the drop-down menus to make it happen.

3. **If you don't have reminders set by default, ask for one here.**

   Again, you get the needed notification via either your MySpace or external e-mail, or both. This calendar does whatever it takes to get you wherever you need to go (that information can be included in the calendar as well).

4. **Decide whether you want to share this information with others or not.**

   You have several options here:

- If you make it public, people viewing your page will be able to see what you're doing.

- If you're not absolutely sure you want people to know what you're up to ("Hey, Steve, I didn't know you were a fan of Disney on Ice!"), mark it private.

You can also choose to mark the time as busy or not. That way people will know, when they're scheduling their own events, whether you're available.

Click the Save button at the bottom of the page, and your event is entered, ready to rock.

 When your calendar is made public, everybody can see it. If you're a minor, it's a good idea to keep your calendar private and just tell your friends where you're going to be. If you're a parent, make sure the details of your child's calendar are private. MySpace keeps profiles for minors private by default, but this is an important step to follow as well.

Title:	[ ] (max. 80 characters)
Entry Type:	[Appointment ▼]
Date:	[September ▼] [21 ▼] [2006 ▼]
Time:	[12 ▼] [:00 ▼] [pm ▼]
Duration:	[1 hour ▼] [0 minutes ▼]
Repeating:	⦿ This event does not repeat.
	◯ Repeat [Every ▼] [Day ▼]
	◯ Repeat on the [First ▼] [Sun ▼] of the month every [month ▼]
End Date:	[September ▼] [21 ▼] [2006 ▼]
Reminders:	⦿ Do not send a reminder
	◯ Send a reminder [——— ▼] before the event to:
	◯ MySpace Mail ◯ External Mail ◯ Both
Location:	[ ] (max. 80 characters)
Street:	[ ]
City:	[ ] State: [▼] Zip: [ ] Country: [United States ▼]
Notes:	[ ]
	(max. 120 characters)
Sharing:	[Share w/Friends ▼]
Show as Busy:	[No ▼]

Figure 8-15:
Creating a
New Event.

But wait, there's more!

Any events you schedule or accept can be added to your calendar automatically. MySpace does a good job of integrating the various functions of these tools, so you don't have to worry about missing an appointment. There's a link to your Events page in the top-right corner of the My Calendar screen (refer to Figure 8-13), and there's a link to the Calendar in the top right corner of the My Events screen (refer to Figure 8-2). Furthermore, when you RSVP for an event, look for the Add to My Calendar button (refer to Figure 8-11) to instantly add the event. No messy cut-and-paste jobs here — it's all taken care of!

Chapter 9

Getting In with the In-Crowd

- -

In This Chapter

▶ Joining and creating MySpace groups

▶ Posting and replying to classified ads

▶ Participating in online forums

▶ Joining communities based around your school or work

▶ Letting others know what you think about your professors

- -

*J*oining MySpace is a great way to meet different people with interests similar to yours. Just because they're in Hawaii doesn't mean you can't talk about your favorite albums or movies or books. You can search for other folks on the basis of their hobbies and favorite things individually, but you can also look for groups of people who enjoy what you do. In fact, you can do more with these groups than you can alone. There's strength in numbers!

Understanding MySpace Groups

MySpace users can form *groups* that link people with common interests together. Take a look at the groups already available on MySpace (shown in Figure 9-1) by clicking the Groups link at the top of your MySpace page.

Quite a huge list, isn't it? There are literally hundreds of thousands of groups for you to look at and possibly join. These groups are based around everything from neighborhood locations to schools to religions to the occasional supper club. You should be able to find something in here that will appeal to you.

Lets narrow down this overwhelming mass to something a little more manageable. Lets say you're interested in music (pretty safe bet if you're like most of us). You can either click the Music link on the Groups page to sort out all the music groups available, or you can enter the type of music you're interested in (oh, I *do* hope it's polka!) in the Keyword field at the bottom of the screen.

Figure 9-1:
The master
list of all
MySpace
groups —
impressive,
eh?

Let's just see what comes up when you click the Music link. You'll get a screen that looks like Figure 9-2.

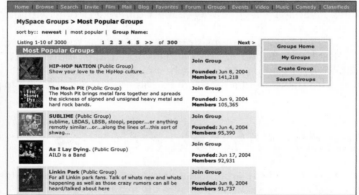

Figure 9-2:
A sample
viewing of
MySpace
music
groups.

In this case, MySpace brings up the 3000 (!) most popular MySpace music groups. You can sort through these groups by clicking the number of the page you want to move to at the top of the list, or just click Next to get to the next page in line. You can also sort out groups by the newest formed or the alphabetical listing of groups by clicking Newest or Group Name, respectively.

Joining up

Let's join a group and see what it's all about (not exactly the official MySpace motto, but close enough). Click the Join Group link next to one you're interested in. After confirming that you do want to join this group, you'll be admitted as a member and taken to the group's main page, as shown in Figure 9-3.

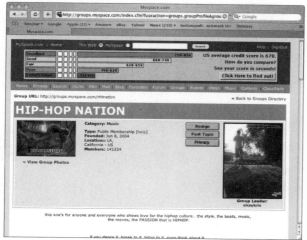

From here, you can look at profiles for all those who are part of your group. Contact them, chat, communicate — it's what MySpace is all about! You can also see a forum where you can discuss issues (we discuss forums in the section — you guessed it — "Taking a Look at Forums," later in this chapter) and a bulletins section. By clicking the View All Group Bulletins link, you can see the messages that the group members have sent to everyone on the membership list. You can also send your own bulletin from here by clicking the Post Group Bulletin link.

You're all here because you have common interests. It's better to keep group bulletins related to the reason the group exists. You don't want to annoy your new friends with messages they're not interested in.

Starting your own

Out of all of those groups, you should be able to find something you're interested in. Still, there's the remote possibility that your interests aren't represented on MySpace, or maybe you just want to set up a private group for you and some friends. The list of groups on MySpace is always growing, and there're no reason you shouldn't start your own — which you can do by following these steps:

1. **On the main Groups page (refer to Figure 9-1), click the link in the top-left corner of the screen that says Create Group.**

   You see the Create a Group box, as shown in Figure 9-4.

Figure 9-4:
Creating
your own
group.

2. **Give your group a descriptive name.**

You want the name to sum up the group you're starting in a few words. MySpace also requires you to pick a category for your group to fall into. Although you may have several interests represented within the group, there should be a single category it best fits into. For example, half your group's members may swear the other half's cars couldn't stand up to theirs in a race, but they can all agree that they love automobiles — so that's the category for your group: automobiles.

3. **Specify who gets to join your group.**

From here on out, you get to exercise a little control:

- **Decide whether you'll let just anybody join by clicking Yes or No for the Open Join field.** Yes means the door is open — anybody wanting to join is automatically accepted. This can be a great way to bring in people you might never hear from otherwise, but you'll never know exactly who is going to show up. This can make for uncertain groups interactions, especially if someone is just looking to cause problems. No means that you invite each and every member to the group. You'll only get those you want in the group, but that can be a limited number if you don't meet a lot of people. It also means you'll have to manually approve everybody who wants to join, which can take some time. (Think about this carefully before you make a decision.)

- **You can choose to hide the group from uninvited eyes.** Not only will people not be able to join without your approval, but they won't even be able to see that the group exists. This works best if

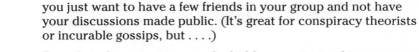

you just want to have a few friends in your group and not have your discussions made public. (It's great for conspiracy theorists or incurable gossips, but . . . .)

Even though your group may be hidden or private, things you post on MySpace (and the Internet in general) don't always stay private or confidential. Somebody in your group could show somebody else, or your screen could be seen by someone else if you're posting in a public place such as a library or coffee shop. Always be careful with the information you put anywhere on the Internet.

4. Specify what you want to let the members do while they're in your group.

Here's where you get to decide

- Whether members can invite others in (otherwise, those decisions are all up to you)

- Whether your forum is made public

- Whether members can post bulletins or images

- Whether the material in your group is acceptable to show to those under 18

5. When MySpace asks, provide a general location for the group (including city and country) and a description of the group.

Keep in mind what the long and short descriptions are used for:

- The short description is shown to anybody who happens to be looking at the public listing for the group.

- The long description is reserved for those who are actually looking at the group's main page.

- You can only post pictures, links, and other HTML-related information in the long description.

6. Enter the URL for your group. It should follow this format:

```
http://groups.myspace.com/(yourgroupnamehere)
```

Using this address, you'll be able to get directly to your group's page — as will anybody else.

7. Click the Create Group button.

Your new club is officially formed!

Managing your group

So now what? You've got a club and maybe a few members. Lets see how you can get your club started and get others participating.

Inviting others to join

Click the Groups link at the top of your profile page, select My Groups from the menu in the upper left side of the page, and click the name of your group. You should notice a Moderator image just below your picture. Congratulations on your new title!

In the top-right of your page, click the Invite Others link, shown in Figure 9-5. You can select people off of your Friends List to invite, or you can search for other MySpace users to bring in. After they accept (hey, why not be optimistic here?), they'll be able to see your group and participate in the bulletins, forums, and pictures your group hosts (provided you've activated those options).

The Invite Others link

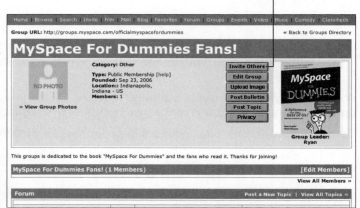

Figure 9-5:
Use the
Invite
Others link
to grow your
group.

Posting pictures

There's a section for posting images if you think your group might want to see them. If you're in a car group, post some pictures of your latest trip to the dealership. A music group might appreciate seeing your snapshots from a concert. Let your imagination run wild. You post images here the same way you do in your personal profile (for more information, see Chapter 10), and your group can also have a default image in the same way your profile does. If you're interested in posting pictures to your group, click the Upload Image link on your group's main page.

Posting a bulletin

People in your computing group might want to hear about the sale they're having at an online site, or your Italian movie group would probably like to know about the film festival going on right now just down the road from you. Send out periodical updates about your group and the members, too. This keeps everybody in the loop and aids discussion about the topic your group formed around. To post a bulletin for your group, click the Post Bulletin link on your group's main page. For more on bulletins, see Chapter 5.

Posting a topic

If you've got the urge to post a topic for your group, just click the Post Topic link on your group's main page. This command sets up a discussion topic in your forum. Group members can post about that topic, and you can get a dialogue going from there. We'll talk more about this in the section "Taking a Look at Forums," later in this chapter.

Keeping your group focused

If your group is just a bunch of friends trading stories, jokes, and pictures, you've already found your focus. Enjoy! If it's something a little different — say, a group of book fans — try to keep the discussion focused on those matters. If there seems to be not much purpose or focus within the group, people tend to lose interest — and then they stop checking back in. The title of "Moderator" means it's your responsibility to guide the discussion and activities along. You don't have to be heavy-handed about it, but a little effort to keep things coherent doesn't hurt. Just make sure the group gets the gentle direction it needs — and you can let the members take it from there.

You can also go back and change the settings of your group at any time by clicking the Edit Group link on the group's main page. Only you, the Moderator, can make these changes.

Utilizing the Classified Ads

MySpace can be a resource in connecting people with jobs, apartments, and the odd comic book you'd never thought would show up in your lifetime. These classified ads work just like the ones in the back of your local newspaper, with a few key exceptions:

- ✔ They're free to post
- ✔ Anybody in the world can read them
- ✔ You can get an instant response from anybody regarding your item or service

In this chapter, you'll figure out how to post your own ad and get it out to the hundreds of thousands of MySpace users. You'll also learn how to answer these ads safely and effectively, so that both sides are happy with the transactions. Best of all, there's no newspaper to recycle when you're done. Advertise away!

Browsing the ads

Click the Classifieds link at the top of your MySpace profile page to get started. There's a huge list of available categories, as well as links for posting your own ads, as shown in Figure 9-6.

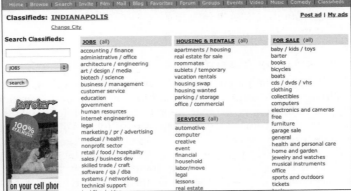

Figure 9-6:
The
MySpace
Classifieds
screen.

The ads shown will automatically default to your hometown for your convenience, but you can click the Change City link to see other available listings. This can be helpful if you're moving to a new city and need to see some available apartments.

Again, the Classifieds screen allows you to sort out ads in much the same way you did with Groups — either by entering a keyword or selecting a category. Clicking a top-level category from the drop-down-menulike Cars For Sale will show you all the entries in that category; clicking Motorcycles will only reveal those bikes that appeal to the daredevil in you. You could also type **Harley** in the keyword field, use the drop-down menu below that field to select Cars For Sale, and click the Search button to narrow down your search even further. After you've clicked the Search button, your results will be displayed in a screen similar to that in Figure 9-7.

Okay, we know a Harley isn't a "car" — but sometimes you just have to play along with the categories as they are. Take a look at those drop-down lists to get a feel for what usually shows up in the category you're searching. It's also possible somebody will put the item you're looking for in the wrong category. Checking around may help you find it.

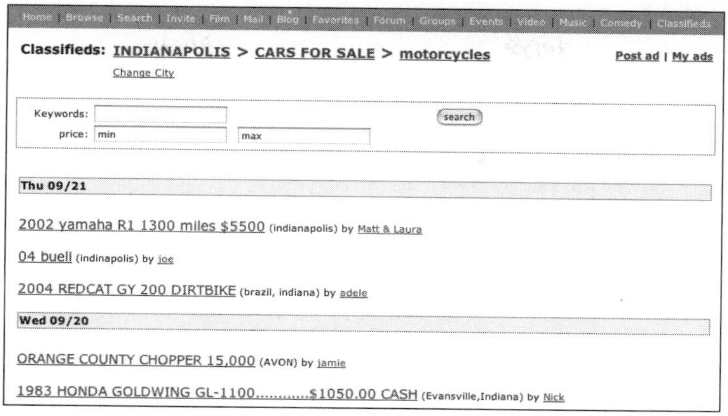
Home | Browse | Search | Invite | Film | Mail | Blog | Favorites | Forum | Groups | Events | Video | Music | Comedy | Classifieds
Classifieds: INDIANAPOLIS > CARS FOR SALE > motorcycles
Post ad | My ads
Change City
Keywords:
price: min
max
search
Thu 09/21
2002 yamaha R1 1300 miles $5500 (indianapolis) by Matt & Laura
04 buell (indinapolis) by joe
2004 REDCAT GY 200 DIRTBIKE (brazil, indiana) by adele
Wed 09/20
ORANGE COUNTY CHOPPER 15,000 (AVON) by jamie
1983 HONDA GOLDWING GL-1100...........$1050.00 CASH (Evansville,Indiana) by Nick

Figure 9-7: A list of MySpace classified ads.

Click the ad you want to see, and go from there. The ads should include a firm or negotiable price, a description of the item, and contact information from the seller. If it's something you're interested in, go ahead and contact the seller. MySpace hosts the ad, but it's not an auction service along the lines of eBay — it's up to you to make it work.

Be careful when contacting sellers; take precautions that enable you to see or receive the item in question before you send money. As often as not, you'll be dealing with strangers — and while MySpace is a pretty friendly place, you don't want to be ripped off!

Posting an ad

Time to get rid of some old clothes or that ugly coffee table? You can post a free classified ad on MySpace! Just click the Post Ad link on the main Classified page and then fill in the information on the screen, as shown in Figure 9-8.

Take note that there are a few guidelines MySpace requires ads to follow. Pay attention to these, and your ad will stay up for all to see. Disobey the rules, and it'll be deleted. These guidelines are designed to prevent people from posting the same ad in multiple categories or posting the same thing several times in a row and cluttering the screen. It also prevents people from posting adult content or scams. Use the drop-down menus to select the correct category and subcategory for your item (that coffee table, for example, would fall under For Sale and Furniture), and enter the price range you're looking for and the neighborhood or city you're located in.

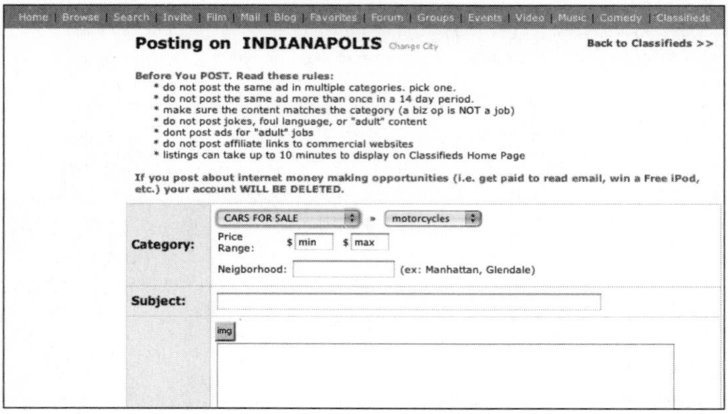

Figure 9-8:
Posting an
ad in the
MySpace
Classifieds.

Now, enter a descriptive subject ("**TAKE MY COFFEE TABLE!**") and type a description of the item. You can also upload a picture of the item for buyers to check out. Click the Preview link to see what your ad will look like, and then either click Edit to change it or Post to see your ad made public.

People looking at your ad can contact you through your MySpace profile. You can add other contact information to your ad if you want, but keep anything you don't want people to know about you out of the ad.

Managing your ads

By clicking the My Ads link on the Classifieds page, you'll see a list of all the ads you're posted. From here, you can click each ad to modify or delete it. It's best to take ads down after the sale has been conducted to avoid clutter and confusion down the line. It's also a good idea to change ads that have been up occasionally to attract new interest. If you're selling a service, reword the ad to attract new attention through different keywords. You may also lower or raise the price of an ad as you go. In any case, make sure the information in your ad is always current. It will benefit both you and the buyer immensely.

Replying to ads

Each ad is linked to a MySpace profile, so the easiest way to respond to an ad is to click the seller's profile from the ad and send that person a message. If they've included other contact information in the ad, you can also try that. Just include a brief mention of the ad and your interest, and wait for a reply. Don't be obnoxious by sending several messages or demanding a reduction in price. If the seller is open to negotiation, he or she will usually say so in the ad — and if the seller says the price is firm, don't be a pain by trying to dicker anyway.

Taking a Look at Forums

Without getting deep into Roman history and a bunch of politicians arguing over democracy and toga styles, a forum is basically a place for holding discussion and debate over the issues of the day. In this case, though, you don't have to go to some stone ruins and learn Latin. An electronic forum lets you post your messages online and allows others talk about them from there. It can be a great way to learn and discuss things important to you in a public place — without actually having to drive or fly or organize a big meeting (so it can also be a great way to save gas). Okay, it's not a real-time discussion, but it does make possible some conversations that might not get the chance to happen otherwise.

Explaining forums

If you've seen what forums look like at the bottom of the Group pages — and that clicking the Post Topic link on your Group page will make an entry on those forums — you've got the gist of it. That's basically how forums work. They contain a series of discussion topics, and group members can post replies to those topics (and other replies, and replies to those replies). Eventually, discussion topics can go on for several posts and pages.

Note, however, that forums are not limited to groups. Click the Forum link at the top of your profile page to see other topics that are available to all MySpace users, as shown in Figure 9-9. The forum controls will work similarly in both the Group page and your profile page — but in this case, we focus on the main forums found when you use the link on your profile page.

Let the discussion begin! Pick a forum topic that interests you and check out the discussions going on. For example, lets look at the Computers & Technology forum, shown in Figure 9-10.

It just makes good sense to *read* a few posts on a particular forum before you toss your two cents in. If you can get a handle on the discussion beforehand, you're a lot more likely to say something relevant when you do post. But you knew that.

There are four different folders for this forum. Let's just keep it straightforward and choose the main Computers forum, which takes us to the screen shown in Figure 9-11.

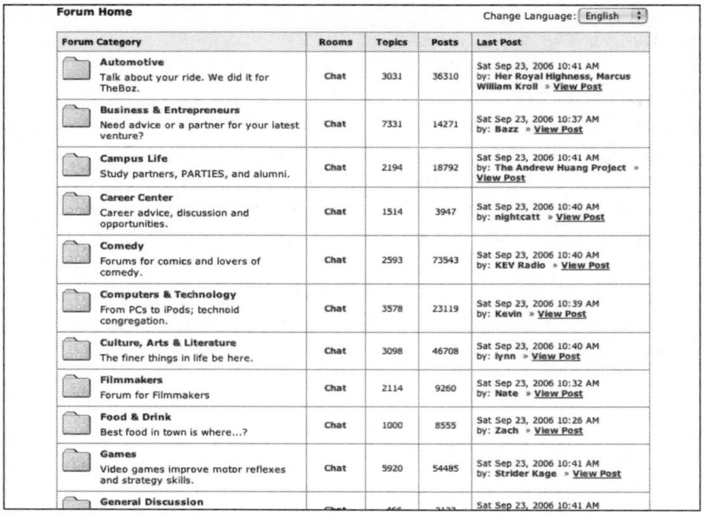

Forum Home

Change Language: English

Forum Category	Rooms	Topics	Posts	Last Post
Automotive Talk about your ride. We did it for TheBoz.	Chat	3031	36310	Sat Sep 23, 2006 10:41 AM by: Her Royal Highness, Marcus William Kroll » View Post
Business & Entrepreneurs Need advice or a partner for your latest venture?	Chat	7331	14271	Sat Sep 23, 2006 10:37 AM by: Bazz » View Post
Campus Life Study partners, PARTIES, and alumni.	Chat	2194	18792	Sat Sep 23, 2006 10:41 AM by: The Andrew Huang Project » View Post
Career Center Career advice, discussion and opportunities.	Chat	1514	3947	Sat Sep 23, 2006 10:40 AM by: nightcatt » View Post
Comedy Forums for comics and lovers of comedy.	Chat	2593	73543	Sat Sep 23, 2006 10:40 AM by: KEV Radio » View Post
Computers & Technology From PCs to iPods; technoid congregation.	Chat	3578	23119	Sat Sep 23, 2006 10:39 AM by: Kevin » View Post
Culture, Arts & Literature The finer things in life be here.	Chat	3098	46708	Sat Sep 23, 2006 10:40 AM by: lynn » View Post
Filmmakers Forum for Filmmakers	Chat	2114	9260	Sat Sep 23, 2006 10:32 AM by: Nate » View Post
Food & Drink Best food in town is where...?	Chat	1000	8555	Sat Sep 23, 2006 10:26 AM by: Zach » View Post
Games Video games improve motor reflexes and strategy skills.	Chat	5920	54485	Sat Sep 23, 2006 10:41 AM by: Strider Kage » View Post
General Discussion				Sat Sep 23, 2006 10:41 AM

Figure 9-9: The main forums page.

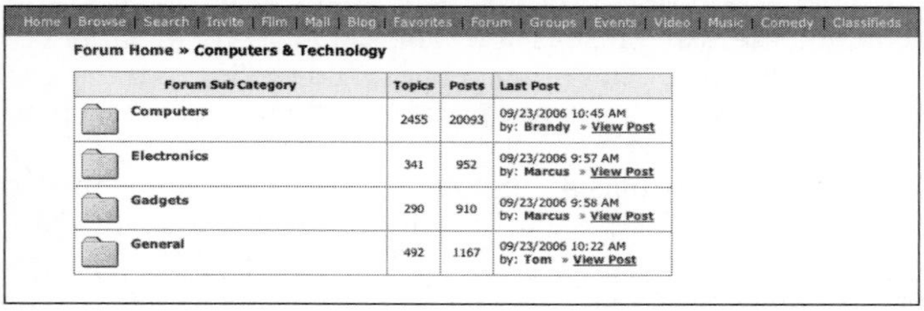

Forum Home » Computers & Technology

Forum Sub Category	Topics	Posts	Last Post
Computers	2455	20093	09/23/2006 10:45 AM by: Brandy » View Post
Electronics	341	952	09/23/2006 9:57 AM by: Marcus » View Post
Gadgets	290	910	09/23/2006 9:58 AM by: Marcus » View Post
General	492	1167	09/23/2006 10:22 AM by: Tom » View Post

Figure 9-10: The many subcategories of the forum.

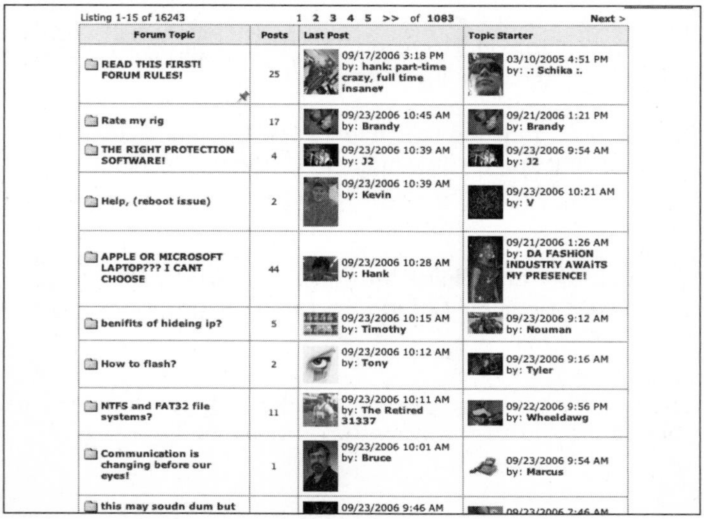

Listing 1-15 of 16243 1 2 3 4 5 >> of 1083 Next >

Forum Topic	Posts	Last Post	Topic Starter
READ THIS FIRST! FORUM RULES!	25	09/17/2006 3:18 PM by: hank: part-time crazy, full time insane♥	03/10/2005 4:51 PM by: .: Schika :.
Rate my rig	17	09/23/2006 10:45 AM by: Brandy	09/21/2006 1:21 PM by: Brandy
THE RIGHT PROTECTION SOFTWARE!	4	09/23/2006 10:39 AM by: J2	09/23/2006 9:54 AM by: J2
Help, (reboot issue)	2	09/23/2006 10:39 AM by: Kevin	09/23/2006 10:21 AM by: V
APPLE OR MICROSOFT LAPTOP??? I CANT CHOOSE	44	09/23/2006 10:28 AM by: Hank	09/21/2006 1:26 AM by: DA FASHION INDUSTRY AWAITS MY PRESENCE!
benifits of hideing ip?	5	09/23/2006 10:15 AM by: Timothy	09/23/2006 9:12 AM by: Nouman
How to flash?	2	09/23/2006 10:12 AM by: Tony	09/23/2006 9:16 AM by: Tyler
NTFS and FAT32 file systems?	11	09/23/2006 10:11 AM by: The Retired 31337	09/22/2006 9:56 PM by: Wheeldawg
Communication is changing before our eyes!	1	09/23/2006 10:01 AM by: Bruce	09/23/2006 9:54 AM by: Marcus
this may soudn dum but		09/23/2006 9:46 AM	

Figure 9-11: The Computer forum.

Here's where you actually see the topics being discussed. You'll see the topic that's received the most recent reply at the top — and you can scroll through the topics in one of two ways:

✔ Choosing page numbers from the top of the list

✔ Clicking Next at the top of the page

When you see something interesting, click the topic's name and you're taken right to that topic, as shown in Figure 9-12.

Figure 9-12:
A sample
topic.

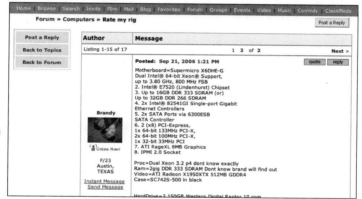

From here, you can engage in a discussion with the poster or anybody else who has replied to the original topic. Just think of it as reading a bunch of notes and leaving a note of your own that furthers the discussion. It's not the easiest way to hold a conversation, but it can go farther than normal conversations because it doesn't have to happen in real time or within the confines of a building or a phone call. You can have time to think, research, and respond.

If you want to post a reply to a message, just click the Post a Reply link on the left side of the page or the Reply button in the message itself. Type in your message, click Post Reply at the bottom of the page, and you're ready to go. If you want to back out, just click Cancel. Also note that you can click the Quote link, which includes the original text you were replying to in your post. This can help keep the discussion clear and focused. If you don't quote the text, there's no guarantee that your reply will show up near the post you were commenting on, and things can get confusing.

If you want to start your own topic, click the Post Topic link on the forum's page and enter the title and text of your topic. It's as simple as posting a reply, but you're the one starting the discussion.

Check around the forum for topics that are similar to the one you want to discuss — before you post a new topic. This little bit of discreet prep work will help keep things organized and helpful.

It's easy to get angry and say harmful things when you're not actually face to face with the person on the other side of the argument. Discussions can sometimes get heated, but it's best to remain polite and remember that it's just an online conversation and MySpace is supposed to be fun. Don't get too heavy with it — or take it too seriously.

Why should we use the forums?

We've already seen how to post topics and replies on these discussion forums. But why would you want to? There are several reasons these online discussions can be helpful. Let's take a look at a few:

- **Opinions:** Forums are a great chance to express opinions and viewpoints on topics that are important to you. No matter what your interests, from politics to knitting, you've got a viewpoint. Express it! Just be sure to do so in a polite and respectful manner, and be prepared to discuss it. After all, you're telling your opinions to people around the nation — possibly around the world — and there will always be people who want to agree or disagree with you. That's the great thing about online discussions. You might never know what these people think — and they might not get a look at what you think — without these forums.

- **Like interests:** There'll always be someone who knows as much or more than you about certain topics online. Imagine getting to pick that person's brain about things you like but might have never heard about before. You could discover things you never knew before or pick up tips about creating that perfect song or painting or hot rod. Hanging around forums with people interested in the same things means you'll learn and share more. You'll also make contacts with people who could help you with activities related to MySpace. Just because you're making contact electronically doesn't mean the contact has to disappear suddenly; it's entirely possible to share friendships with these people.

Chat versus forums

On the main page of the forums, you'll see a Chat link next to each main category. Whereas the forums are a series of topics and replies meant to be viewed days and weeks from now, the Chat function is real-time conversation, as shown in Figure 9-13. These discussions won't be saved, but then, you'll be talking to people live — it's a lot more immediate than leaving a note.

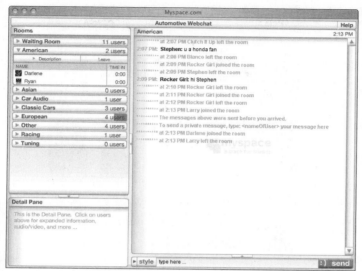

Figure 9-13:
A chat
room.

There's a main Waiting Room and different "rooms" for specific discussions. Just click the room you want to go to and select Join. Anything you type in the bottom field will be sent to everyone in the room, but you can click some-one's name to send a message to just that person. Feel free to introduce your-self and talk about whatever's appropriate to the room. This conversation moves fast, so be prepared to stick around. If you just want to say something and come back to a discussion later, it's probably best to stick with a forum.

Make sure your message goes only to the person it was intended for. Sending private information to everybody in a chat room is a classic newbie mistake — it can be seriously embarrassing.

School and Work Communities

Depending on where you work or go to school, there may already be a com-munity for you on MySpace. When you first created your profile, you were asked to enter your occupation and any schools you attended. Those groups will appear at the bottom left of your profile, and you can click them to see any community available to you. Lets take a look at a school profile, such as the one shown in Figure 9-14.

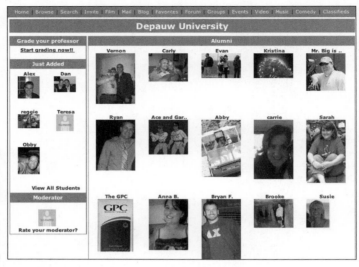

Figure 9-14:
An example
of a school
commu-
nity — just
one of many.

This community is just like any other group on MySpace, except it's centered around your current or former school. Here you'll find a list of people who also attending or are currently going to your school, and there's a forum of topics related to that institution. You can link up with old classmates or discuss how things are going at your school. There are also sections for people looking for roommates, apartments, and textbooks. This is a great place to link up with current students or alumni.

Rate Your Professor

You may be salivating at the thought to bash a former or current teacher right now, but it's important to remember why this function is here. Students have always given other students going into classes a little advice about how to deal with their teachers — and general evaluations on classes in general have been around for a long time. This is just a place to do it electronically. It's important to be truthful and fair here — you'd want the same information, honestly offered and (hopefully) reliable, if you were *asking* about a professor, wouldn't you? It's also good to remember that professors and teachers are people too (what a concept!) — and they could be reading your comments.

In your school profile, look at the top-left of the page for the Grade My Professor section and click the Start Grading Now! link. You'll see an alphabetical list of the professors listed at your school, as shown in Figure 9-15.

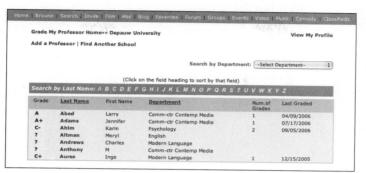

Figure 9-15:
The
alphabetical
list of
professors.

You have several options from here:

- To search by the last name of the professor, click the letter at the top of the list.

- To search by department, click the drop-down menu marked Search By Department.

- If you don't see your professor listed, click Add A Professor at the top-left of the screen.

- If you're in the wrong school, click Find Another School.

Each professor has an average grade next to his or her name, as well as the prof's department, the number of grades, and the date the last grade was issued. Read what other students have to say, and click the Grade This Professor link to add your own grade. You'll be asked for the class you took from the prof, overall comments, and a grade for each of the following categories:

- Lectures

- Homework

- Tests

- Fairness

- Grading

- Accessibility

These grades are averaged together with those from other people reviewing the professor, and compiled for an overall profile on this teacher.

Be respectful and truthful. This can be as good of a resource as you make it.

Part III
Customizing MySpace

The 5th Wave   By Rich Tennant

"What do you mean you're adding video clips to your profile on MySpace?"

In this part . . .

It's not called MySpace for just any old reason. It is indeed *your* space. This white-and-blue-and-silver color scheme is certainly pleasant, but it's kind of boring and it has to go. First thing you need to do is put up a cool picture of yourself. Maybe get that one your friend snapped while you were laughing — the one your friends say looks most like you. Then grab a song to add to your page. Just one click and you can add that Green Day song you like. Or one from your cousin's band.

That's a good start. Now let's add your favorite football team's logo as a background, change the font to something cool, and rearrange things so your Friends List is at the top of the page. There — now, that's a MySpace page to show off.

Directions for doing all these things — or turning your own ideas into MySpace reality — follow. Read on and happy customizing.

Chapter 10

Your MySpace Photo Album

MySpace is a great place to show off your favorite photos. From simple self-portraits to vacation photos to what happened at the party last night (okay, *some* of what happened at the party), you can put just about everything you want on MySpace for public display. You can also use your page as a place to host your images for use on other sites as well. Let's get you ready for your close-up!

MySpace does require users to register before they can see photos on your profile page.

Getting Your Pictures Ready for MySpace

Any picture you've got on your computer, digital camera, cell phone, or other device can probably be shared on MySpace (and any content within reason, which we'll get to in a minute). There are just a few considerations to take into account before you start putting your images up on the site. When you clear all these hurdles, you'll be ready to go.

Using the correct file format

MySpace only recognizes two image-file formats. These just happen to be the most common formats used on the Internet, though, so you should be okay. Your pictures should either be GIFs or JPEGs — that is, each one must have the file extension `.gif` or `.jpg` after the filename, because files in those common photo formats need the least space to store. Other formats, such as `.tif`, `.bmp`, or `.png`, will have to be converted to a GIF or JPEG before you try to upload your images.

MySpace recommends using a program called IrfanView, available at `www.download.com`. This program will help resize and reformat your pictures into a usable picture on MySpace. You can also use commercial programs like Adobe Photoshop, Macromedia Fireworks, or the GIMP (`http://gimp.org`) to change your images. Finally, most digital cameras come with software that allows you to manipulate your pictures. Use whatever feels easiest to you.

To convert your picture into a nice, compact `.gif` or `.jpg` using IrfanView, follow these steps:

1. **Open IrfanView.**

2. **Click File in the top menu, select Open, and navigate to your image.**

3. **Click Open to open the file.**

4. **Now click File and select Save As, as shown in Figure 10-1.**

   You can keep the filename the same or change it, but you must select either `.gif` or `.jpg` in the Save As Type drop-down menu.

5. **Click Save.**

Figure 10-1:
Converting your picture to the correct file format.

Making sure you have the right file size

MySpace requires that your pictures are less than 600K in size. *Size,* in this case, refers to the *overall file size* — how much storage space it takes up on a computer — not the actual length and width of the picture. The basic 600 kilobytes should provide plenty of room for your snapshots. If your pictures exceed 600K, use photo-manipulation software or IrfanView to get them down to an acceptable file size. You can also try setting the *dpi (dots per inch)* of the photo to 72. That should make a huge difference in your photo's file size.

To get your picture into the correct file size using IrfanView, follow these steps:

1. **Open IrfanView.**
2. **Click File in the top menu, select Open, and navigate to your image.**
3. **Click Open to open the file.**
4. **Click Image in the top menu bar and select Resize/Resample.**
5. **Set the DPI at 72, and change the length and width of the picture to smaller values, as shown in Figure 10-2.**

   Make sure the Preserve Aspect Ratio box is checked, as this will keep your pictures from looked stretched-out or unnatural.

6. **Now click File and select Save As.**

   You can keep the filename the same or change it, but you must select either .gif or .jpg in the Save As Type drop-down menu.

7. **Click Save.**

Figure 10-2: Giving your picture the correct file size.

Naming your photo file

Keep the file name simple — and it's okay to run the words together. Something like Dayatthebeach.jpg will work just fine. MySpace will have problems if you try to use spaces — or, for that matter, symbols such as dashes or dollar signs. Change the name if you have to before uploading the picture.

Your images must be either .gif or .jpg files before they can find their way onto MySpace. Make sure you use those extensions when you're naming your photo file.

Adhering to the content policy

The Internet is home to all manner of strange, beautiful, shocking, and downright disturbing images. MySpace will have none of that, thank you. The site bans adult content on its servers, and you can lose your account if you violate the policy. Before you post your picture, determine first whether it falls in the PG or R category. More than likely, an R rating will cause problems. MySpace will also delete any pictures that include contact information (such as a phone number, address, or Web-site URL); think about that for a minute and you'll see the wisdom of it.

You can't use a home computer to host pictures you intend to be viewed on the Internet. To be seen by others, the pics have to be on MySpace or another Web site.

Finding Places to Host Your Images

There are other places to host your pictures on the Internet beyond MySpace. *Hosting sites* exist solely to give your digital images a home on the Internet so you can hotlink to them on other Web sites, like MySpace or other forums, and send links to friends and relatives ("Oh, those wedding photos are so BEAUTIFUL! When are you giving me grandkids?"). You upload photos from your computer to these sites (usually after registering for an account) and use their links to send out your photos. Please read each site's agreements and policies carefully — most of these accounts will have differences between free and paid hosting solutions; some limit the amount of data they'll let you transmit (the capacity that geeks call the "bandwidth") on a monthly basis, depending on the option you've chosen.

What to add, and what not to add

MySpace profiles are associated directly with you, and what you put on the site is a direct reflection on yourself. You're the only one in control, after all. Therefore it's important to remember that what pictures you put up on your site can come back to haunt you if you're not careful. It's great to post pictures of your friends and the fun times you have with them, but posting pictures of illegal activities can get you in trouble — not only with MySpace, but with the law. Keep in mind that anybody browsing around MySpace can see your profile. Anybody. Think about what potential employers or relatives can see, and you've got a decent test as to what picture you should put up. Just because it's on the 'Net doesn't mean it doesn't affect you IRL (in real life).

Two of the most popular sites are Flickr (`http://flickr.com`) and Photobucket (`http://photobucket.com`), although other sites are out there. Take the time to investigate these services, and you'll find one that works for you. These are great alternatives to MySpace — especially if you're going to be posting large quantities of photos or sending them to people (there must be a few) who don't use MySpace.

Beam Me Up! — Loading Your Photos on MySpace

When you're sure your photos are ready to be pushed forth on the unsuspecting world, it's time to upload them. This is a simple process that transfers a copy of the picture from your computer to MySpace. A few clicks, and you're on your way.

To load your photos on MySpace, follow these steps:

1. **Click the Add/Edit Photos link in the top-left corner of your main page, as shown in Figure 10-3.**

   You can find this handy link right next to your profile picture (in case you want to punch up the charisma).

2. **Click the Browse button found next to the text field in the Upload Photo box (as shown in Figure 10-4) and find the picture you want to upload from your computer.**

   If you've got the urge to type, you can type the address of the picture by hand.

The Add/Edit Photos link

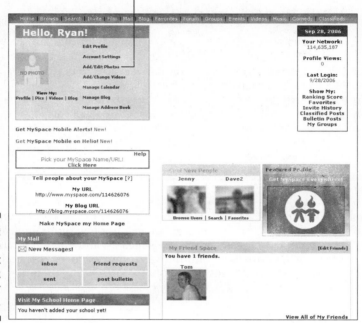

Figure 10-3:
The
Add/Edit
Photos link
on your
profile page.

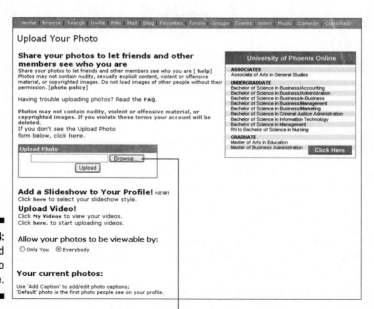

Figure 10-4:
The Upload
Your Photo
page.

The Browse button

3. **When you've found the photo you want, click the Upload button and you're done!**

   This uploads your picture to MySpace. That's it. Your picture is now available under the View My Pics link on your main profile page. If you get an error message, check to make sure your image follows the rules outlined in the section "Getting Your Pictures Ready For MySpace," earlier in this chapter.

Managing Your Photo Page

Great! Your photos are uploaded — now what to you do? You've got a few options from here, and you can do it all from the Upload Your Photo screen that you used to upload your pictures in the first place. First, choose whether you want to have your pictures viewed by the public or keep them private. You make that decision by choosing the appropriate radio button, as shown in Figure 10-5.

Note that the selection you make with this button apples to all your photos. Choose wisely.

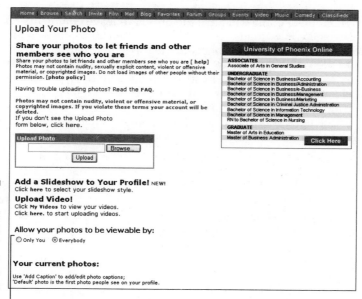

Figure 10-5: Determining who can view your MySpace photos.

The Allow Your Photos To Be Viewable By: options

All of your photos will appear under the upload field, and they all have the same options:

- **Set as Default:** Only one picture can be the default photo at a time. This photo is the one that shows up in the upper left corner of your profile when anybody views it. This is usually a picture of you, but you can feel free to use others if you choose.

- **Add Caption:** Each photo can have a short caption attached to it to give people a little context — what it is, where it was taken, or the intended attitude. (Think "Me at the beach" or "Do these clothes look funny?" as good examples.)

- **Add to Ranking:** You can also only have one photo at a time added for ranking. If you feel like throwing your images into a popularity contest, click the button under that photo. People can then vote on your image, and you can see what people think. Click the Ranking Score link in the top-right corner of your profile page to see the results.

- **Delete:** If a picture has outlived its usefulness, just click the Delete button underneath the picture, and it'll be gone. You'll be prompted to confirm your decision. Use this if you just want to clear a little space, too.

You can do some other things with your MySpace photos as well, such as viewing and editing comments from other MySpacers or creating a slideshow:

- **Comments:** People will have the option to leave comments on your photos if you've made them public. You can view these comments by clicking the View My Pics link in the top-left corner of your profile page and then clicking a photo. You'll see a full-size version of your photo and any comments that have been left, along with the profile name and default profile of the user that left the comment. If you like the comment, do nothing. If you don't like it, there's a small Delete link next to the comment, as shown in Figure 10-6. Click it, confirm that you want to delete, and the comment is gone forever.

- **Slideshow:** No, don't run in fear or dread the thought of Aunt Mildred's vacation photos. This slideshow just puts together a constantly moving presentation of all your uploaded photos. Why have just one static photo when you can exhibit all of your work in full color and motion? Click the Slideshow link on the Upload Your Photos page you use to upload photos, as shown in Figure 10-7.

You'll be presented with two choices of styles, along with code examples of each. One style scrolls your photos from right to left, whereas the other gives you larger views and a more random display of photos. Just copy and paste the code into your main profile. (MySpace recommends that you put it in your "About Me" section, but you can put it anywhere that allows HTML.) Your pictures will show up there in live and living color.

Figure 10-6:
Deleting
unwanted
photo
comments.

Comment
June 11, 2006 11:44 AM
Ben and I like this photograph a lot. Great eye for lighting and composition.
Delete
June 5, 2005 12:55 PM
I absolutely love the setting. Would have probably shot in there for hours. Great contrasts.
Delete

Figure 10-7:
The
Slideshow
link allows
you to add a
slideshow to
your profile.

Home | Browse | Search | Invite | Film | Mail | Blog | Favorites | Forum | Groups | Events | Video | Music | Comedy | Classifieds

Upload Your Photo

Share your photos to let friends and other members see who you are
Share your photos to let friends and other members see who you are [**help**]
Photos may not contain nudity, sexually explicit content, violent or offensive material, or copyrighted images. Do not load images of other people without their permission. [**photo policy**]

Having trouble uploading photos? Read the **FAQ**.

Photos may not contain nudity, violent or offensive material, or copyrighted images. If you violate these terms your account will be deleted.
If you don't see the Upload Photo
form below, click **here**.

Upload Photo

[Browse...]
[Upload]

Add a Slideshow to Your Profile! NEW!
Click **here** to select your slideshow style.
Upload Video!
Click **My Videos** to view your videos.
Click **here.** to start uploading videos.

Allow your photos to be viewable by:
○ Only You ⊙ Everybody

Your current photos:

Use 'Add Caption' to add/edit photo captions;
'Default' photo is the first photo people see on your profile.

The Slideshow link

What hath MySpace pictures wrought?

Since the birth of MySpace, people have been posting their own images on the site. However, a few types of images have taken hold, becoming unique fixtures of MySpace. Their very appearance signals a MySpace origin — giving it a context beyond the actual content of the photo. Lets take a look at a couple of examples.

By far, the most common MySpace shot is the "Point the camera at the mirror" self-portrait. You've got a digital camera and a MySpace account, but apparently nobody else is around to take a picture of you. Just stand in front of the mirror, point, and shoot. Voilà! Not only do you have a new default picture, but everybody knows you're on MySpace!

For some strange reason, men seem to just throw their shirts off as soon as they know a MySpace picture is being taken. Bare-chested males are a common feature, apparently wanting to show off their amazing muscle definition (or not caring if it isn't there). This tactic seems to have backfired, though; most women I know find the pictures either cheesy or disgusting. But good job on the workouts, guys! Now put a shirt on!

Some MySpace profiles don't even feature an actual photo. You can pretty much guarantee that once an animated GIF achieves some popularity or recognition on the Internet, it will pop up as the default picture on many, many profiles. They'll go away eventually, but for now you're witnessing a mini-trend.

Finally, there's the far-too-posed shot. Whether it's the glamour shot from the mall or the PERFECT black-and-white photo you took in the cemetery, most of these themes have already been explored. If you're looking for a good default photo, just be yourself and look natural. Or, what the heck, go ahead and put on the lion suit. Whatever works for you. Just keep your shirt on. Seriously.

Chapter 11

Sound and Movies

● ●

In This Chapter

▶ Finding songs and video to use on your MySpace Page

▶ Adding songs to your profile

▶ Uploading your own video

▶ Adding video to your profile

● ●

*O*ne of the quickest — and easiest — ways to add some sparkle and flash to your MySpace page is to include some audio and video. Whether the files start automatically when you pull up the page for the first time or are stored in a separate section of your profile, MySpace has several places for you to store your favorite song or that hilarious video of your little cousin singing "Tequila" with pantyhose on his head.

This chapter shows you how to place audio and video directly inside your main profile page, so that it's readily available to anybody who comes across your profile. You'll also be able to rate and comment on other's videos, and let them do the same to yours. Think of it as the world's largest private screening.

Adding a Profile Song

Tons of bands put songs up on MySpace, primarily to help spread the word about the music they're bringing to the world. You're not going to want to spend more than a few seconds around some of it, but other artists might capture your attention. Or you may run across the perfect song for your mood that day and you want to share. This section shows you how to add that music to your profile.

Planning your setlist

First, you have to find the song you want to use. Most of your favorite bands will already have a MySpace page with music on them, so it's just a matter of finding the right address. The band's MySpace address could be posted on their main Web site, or you could search for the name of the band using either the MySpace search engine or one like Google.

You can also start exploring your friends and the friends of those friends (their MySpace sites, anyway) for bands that just sound right. Part of using a social network like MySpace is finding new and different peoples and groups, and this is a great example. By exploring different profiles, you could find a song or band you've never heard on the radio — that turns out to be the best thing you've heard all year. Take a risk!

Putting on the hits

When you find the perfect musical accompaniment to your profile page, look for the Add link next to that song on the site's jukebox, as shown in Figure 11-1.

You do have to be logged in to your MySpace account at this point to add or change your song.

The Add link

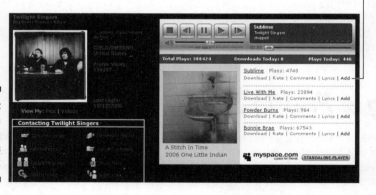

Figure 11-1: Adding a song from a band's jukebox.

When you click the Add link and confirm your entry, the song is added to your profile page *just like that* — and it'll be played every time someone views your page. No mess, no muss, no fuss. The song appears as a small player (as seen in Figure 11-2), just below your profile picture. And you're not stuck with the song forever, either. If you run across another song you want to put on your profile, just click the Add link next to it. You can only have one song linked to your profile (unless you're in a band and you have your own MySpace Music Player — to find out more about creating a MySpace Music Player, see Chapter 14), but you can change it as many times as you want. The one button on the player allows you to pause or continue playback of the song. Have fun!

Figure 11-2:
The song player as it appears on your profile page.

The Internet is changing all the time (but you knew that). MySpace is no exception. So check the song occasionally to make sure the link is still active. When a band removes a song from their page, your link will die — and you'll be left with an empty player. When that happens, its time to go looking for some new tunes.

Adding Video to Your Profile

There are a few ways to add video to your profile, and depending on the way you choose, your video can show up in several places within your profile. It's now just as easy as adding a song and you actually have more control over the process. Also, anyone can upload video to their MySpace account, which means you can upload your own video and not have to worry about linking to somebody else's profile.

Finding video

This process is basically the same as finding songs for your profile (see the section "Planning your setlist," earlier in this chapter. Just go out and look for it! Some users have video uploaded to their profiles, or they'll have links on their pages. Go out and see what's available.

Click the Videos link under your picture on your profile page and the next thing you see is the main video page. There's a field for searching out videos by keyword, as shown in Figure 11-3. Just type a few words into the field that pertain to what you're looking for, and then click the Search Video button. You'll get a list of videos matching your terms, and you can pick and choose from there.

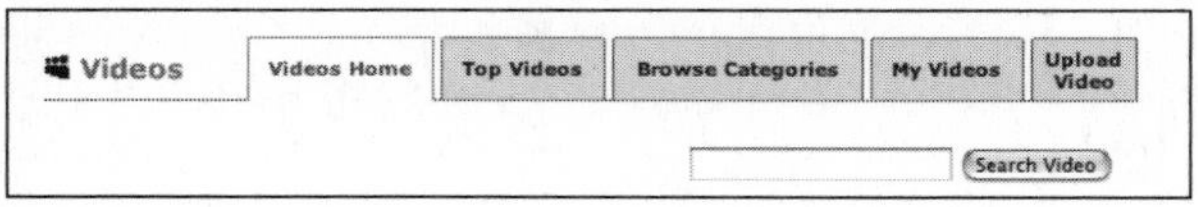

Figure 11-3:
Searching
for videos
on
MySpace.

Videos | Videos Home | Top Videos | Browse Categories | My Videos | Upload Video

Search Video

There's also a tab for Top Videos, which are videos MySpace users have rated highly, and a tab for Browse Categories, where you can look for videos based around a general subject. Need sports video? Click that category. Feeling adventurous? Click Weird Stuff. It's up to you.

Unlike audio, you don't have to restrict yourself to MySpace videos when you're looking to trick out your profile. Look at any video hosting service, such as YouTube (www.youtube.com), and you should be able to find something you can use. These services will also include search fields, so look up the keywords for your videos there as well. The key is finding the code you can *embed* into your profile. If you find a video on MySpace, the code will be located beneath the video, as shown in Figure 11-4.

Figure 11-4:
Embedded
video code
provided by
MySpace.

Video code from MySpace

If you find a video on YouTube, the code will be located to the right of the video, as shown in Figure 11-5.

This code is important, as it represents the link from that video to your profile. Look at the section "Putting on a show," later in this chapter, to see how to put this video in your profile.

Video code from YouTube

Figure 11-5: Embedded video code provided by YouTube.

Using your homemade movies

If you have video of your own to put up, MySpace provides space for that. You must have the video on your computer, but plenty of digital camcorders, cameras, and even cell phones have the ability to put digital video on your hard drive. From there, you're just a few clicks from sharing it with the world.

Click the Videos link under your picture on your profile page. You'll see a series of tabs, and the last one on the right will read Upload Video. Click that tab, and you'll see the page shown in Figure 11-6.

Give your video a title and a brief description. You'll also choose whether to make your video public or private and whether you'll agree to the MySpace terms and conditions. Public means the video will be indexed and appear in search results and category lists. Private means that your video will only be available from your profile, and it won't show up in searches. Click the link to Terms and Conditions to read them, and realize that you can't post video unless you agree. Finally, click the Next button for the next page.

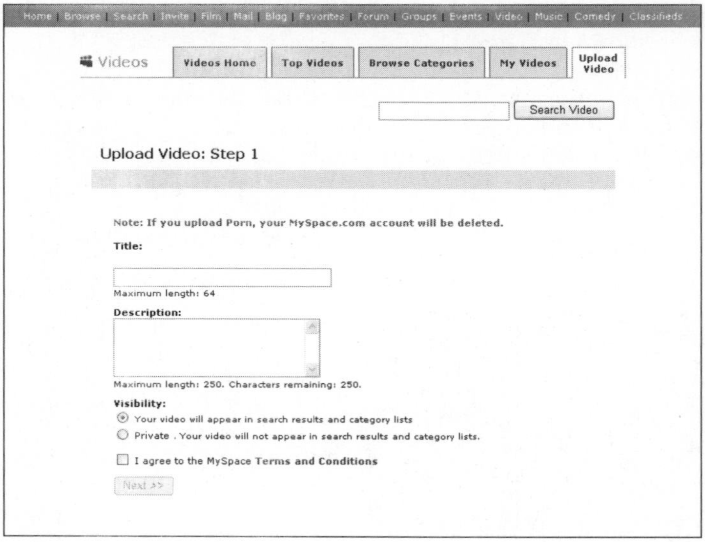

Figure 11-6:
The first
page in the
video
upload
process.

It's written in bright red on every page, so it must be important. Posting porn video will get your account deleted without warning, notice, or even a wave. (Okay, you've been made aware. 'Nuff said.)

Step 2 of the process, as shown in Figure 11-7, helps label your video for easy searching. Check any categories that apply to your video, and type in as many keywords as you can to describe your clip. Start with the basics, such as "dog," and work your way up to things like "Pug," "playing," and "laundry." The more descriptive your terms, the more likely it is that searches will turn up your clip. Click the Next button to go to the next page.

If you marked your video private, categorizing your video won't apply as you've already pulled it from any searches.

The final step of the process looks like a cat got loose on your keyboard and played for awhile, hitting keys with whimsical randomness. In actuality, these jumbled-up messes of letters, as shown in Figure 11-8, are the types of video files that will be accepted. Loosely translated, it means MySpace accepts most digital video formats — including those associated with Microsoft, Apple, and most mobile devices. The only restriction is that the file sizes can't be larger than 100MB.

Click the Browse button to find your file on your computer, and after you find it, click the Upload button to transfer the file. Depending on the size of your file and the speed of your connection, this can take anywhere from a few seconds to several minutes.

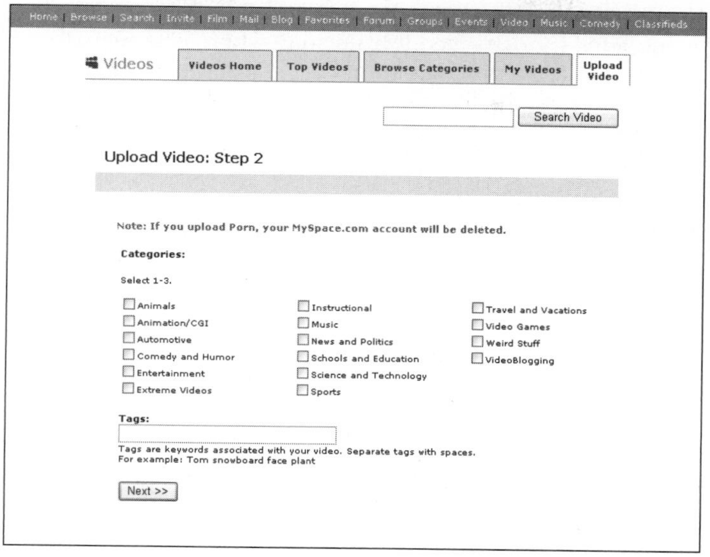

Figure 11-7:
Categorizing your video.

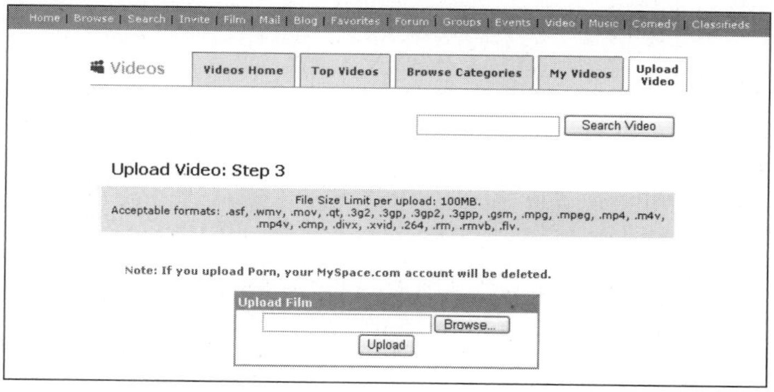

Figure 11-8:
The last step — uploading your video.

Putting on a show

If you've uploaded your own video (see the previous section), it's already a part of your profile — you can find it by clicking the Videos link under your picture on your profile page, and then selecting the My Videos tab. This means anybody clicking the Videos link on your page can view the videos you've chosen.

Although people looking at your MySpace profile can find the videos by selecting your Videos link, they might not always take the time. If it's something you want them to see immediately upon loading your page, you can embed the video in various sections of your profile.

Start by cutting and pasting the embedding code from your video, whether you've uploaded it or snagged it from somewhere else (usually another MySpace location or a video-hosting site). Click the Edit Profile link next to your picture on your profile page and you'll see text fields for several of the sections on your profile, as shown in Figure 11-9. Basically, any of these are fair game for your embedded videos.

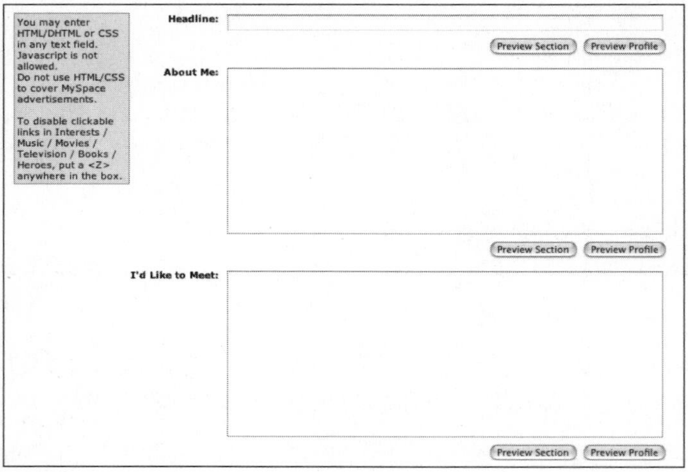

Figure 11-9:
Choosing where to embed your video.

If you've run across a video of a hero of yours (say, a rock star or Pittsburgh Steelers RB Willie Parker making the longest run in Super Bowl history), you could include it under the Heroes section of your profile. For Interests, you might include video of your kids playing. There are many options, and you're only limited by which fields accept HTML coding (see Chapter 12 for more information about HTML and customizing profiles).

Video can stretch out sections of your profile, depending on how wide or long it is when it shows up on-screen. To make sure everything still looks okay before you post the video, click the Preview Section button under the field where you've added the video.

If even just one letter or number is missing from the embedded code, it won't work. Be sure you highlight the entire section of code when you cut-and-paste it into your profile.

Videos on your profile — made easy

In their never-ending quest to make things easier, MySpace also lets you add video to your profile the same way you add songs. Under each and every video MySpace has on their site, you'll see a link under it that says Add to My Profile. Click that link, and it's added automatically to your home page. You can also remove it by logging in to your profile and clicking the Remove from My Profile link under that video. Simple, isn't it? Now everybody can pass along the video of your brother injuring himself on the screen door. Bob Saget never had it so good.

This function differs from embedded video in two very important ways. Although you can embed video in any text area in your profile, video added by this Add To My Profile link will appear only in the creatively named Video Place just above your Comments section. Second, you can embed as many videos as you can tolerate in your profile. Your Video Space can only feature one video at a time. Choose wisely.

Reviewing and commenting on videos

In addition to viewing the videos on other users' profile pages, you also get the chance to give some feedback about what you're seeing — and to link those videos to other locations. Just use the options available under the video, as shown in Figure 11-10.

You can click the MySpace icons on the left to give the video a rating between 1 and 5 (5 being the most worthy). You can also click links on the right to perform the following actions:

- **Add to My Profile:** This command can sometimes be unreliable. It might be better to manually embed the video (see the previous section, "Putting on a show").

- **Bulletin This:** Allows you to bulletin the video, which sends out a bulletin with links to the video.

- **Blog This:** This option works just like the bulletin option — it allows you to blog the video, which creates a blog entry on your profile and links it to the video.

- **Save to My Favorites:** This saves the video to your My Favorites section on your Videos page.

Unless you actually host the video yourself, it's always subject to the whims of the person who's giving it virtual real estate, and it could disappear at any time. More than likely, it will be available for awhile, and you can safely blog about it or put it in your favorites. Check back every so often to make sure the video is live, though, and delete any dead links. It's less frustrating for you and your readers that way.

Figure 11-10: Commenting and rating videos on MySpace.

Rating the video   Options for commenting

Easy ways to edit and post video

Believe it or not, you've probably got a video editing facility on your computer right now. Even if you've never done it before, it's easy enough to make some simple changes to your video and put a decent looking edited product up on the Internet. Both Microsoft and Apple include basic video-editing programs in their operating systems, and manufacturers often bundle basic versions of video-editing software with their digital cameras. These cameras connect via a USB or Firewire cable, which are basically two different ways to move data at high speeds between computers and another device. Newer computers will be able to handle either connection, and your computer should automatically recognize the device after it's plugged in. From there, follow your manufacturer's instructions for moving the video from your device to your computer. This process is known as "capturing" the video.

Microsoft uses a program called Windows Movie Maker, and it allows you to cut out sections of video, change the order of those sections, insert basic transitions such as fading in and out, and add a soundtrack. For example, you may want to put just a part of the home movie you took on MySpace. Cut out the extra video at the beginning and the end of the section, fade in at the beginning, fade out at the end, and put your uncle's favorite song underneath it all (why does he like Barry Manilow so?). You've got a presentation ready to go.

Apple does much the same thing with its iMovie program, which is part of the iLife suite distributed on most new Macs. The controls differ from program to program, but each is extremely user-friendly and links well with your outboard gear, such as cameras or other video recorders. You can also add still pictures to your video and determine how long those pictures stay up, creating an automatic presentation.

When you've got a finished product, you'll want to save it in a format suited to the Internet. Your goal is to save the video at a decent file size — remember, MySpace only allows videos of up to 100 MB to be posted — while still keeping the image clear and crisp. If you're working on a PC, you'll want to save your video as a Windows Media file, or `.wmv`. If you're working on a Mac, you're going to use a QuickTime format (`.mov`). Other formats include Real and MPEG4 files. Each compresses the video down to a manageable size, allowing it to be uploaded to file services such as YouTube or MySpace.

These basic tools will get you on your way, but there's so much more to look at it. Adobe offers pro level editing capabilities with Premiere, whereas Apple offers Final Cut. You can also use programs such as Adobe's Flash, After Effects, or Apple's Shake to create animation and motion graphics. There's no limit to what you can do if you keep investigating this field. It's deep, but there are many rewards. If you want to delve deeper into creating, editing, and publicizing your digital video, consult *Digital Video For Dummies* by Keith Underdahl, available from Wiley Publishing.

Chapter 12

Customizing Your MySpace Page

....

In This Chapter

▶ Changing the look of your MySpace page

▶ Learning what you can and can't change

▶ Writing your own changes in HTML

▶ Using profile editors

▶ Using safe mode to evaluate your changes

....

*B*ecause your MySpace page is basically your own little piece of the Internet, you should think of it as your own place — yours to change or customize to match your own personal style and personality, like an apartment. You obviously can't paint the virtual walls or lay down some sassy virtual throw rugs, but you can change the way your page looks to those who stop by to have a look. Your changes can range from tasteful enhancements to radical modifications, depending on your mood and skill. Ultimately, the look should reflect a little bit of what you like and what you're about.

If your MySpace page is your virtual apartment, consider this to be the "Do-It-Yourself" chapter. We won't touch on replacing plumbing or refinishing hardwood floors, but we will cover all the basics to quickly and painlessly get your space in ship shape so you'll be comfortably hosting guests before you know it.

Customization Restrictions on MySpace

Just about everything you see on your MySpace page can be changed or altered in some way. With just a little extra work, you can change the appearance and sound of your

 ✔ Background

 ✔ Text

 ✔ Different fields in your profile

 ✔ Background audio

There are some things MySpace won't let you change, though. The same basic information (About Me, Comments, and so on) has to appear in every profile. You can reorder those fields in limited ways, but they're always going to be there.

Furthermore, MySpace checks your profile for inappropriate or pornographic images and other disruptive content. Finally, MySpace doesn't want you using code to cover their advertisements or inserts on your page. They have to pay the bills somehow, and they're throwing the party. If you don't want your account to be deleted or changed, it's best to follow house rules and keep it in line.

First Things First

Lets take a look at where all the customizing takes place before we jump into actual coding and start making changes. If you've already created your MySpace profile, you've seen the Profile Edit screen (shown in Figure 12-1) before. You can reach it again by clicking the Edit Profile link next to your picture in the top-left corner of your MySpace profile page. It's the same series of text fields you use to enter your personal information. While you were typing in all that text, you probably didn't know it contained so much power, did you?

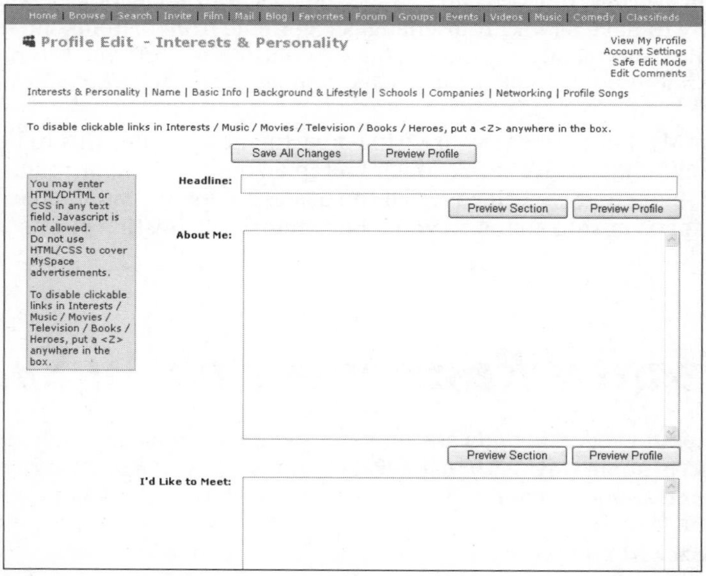

Figure 12-1:
The Profile
Edit screen.

Whenever you make a change to a section, you can click either the Preview Section or Preview Profile button to see what your page will look like before any changes are saved:

- ✔ Use the Preview Section button if you just want to see exactly what was changed.

- ✔ Use the Preview Profile button to see how your change fits in with the entire profile.

Notice the message to the left of the page that mentions using CSS, HTML, and DHTML in any text field. Those are acronyms for the commands that change the look of your MySpace page. It may seem like gibberish right now — and yeah, okay, it'll look like gibberish even when you're done — but that gibberish is your way of telling MySpace what you want your page to look like. There are two ways of going about customizing your profile:

- ✔ You can do it yourself if you're already pretty handy with techno-gibberish.

- ✔ You can use an automatic profile editor to do the lion's share of the techie work for you.

The following sections cover both methods for customizing your profile.

Doing It Yourself

Putting in your own code means you have complete control over what goes into your profile, and you can tweak every aspect of it to your liking. *HTML, or HyperText Mark-up Language*, and *CSS, or Cascading Style Sheets*, are the languages that form the basis of the vast majority of the Web pages you see on the Internet. As you can imagine, getting them under your belt (even a little) gives you a lot of power. Just look at those Web pages and you can see what's possible.

How long did that take you?

As you might expect, then, it can take quite a while to learn how to create your own HTML and CSS coding. It's one thing to understand that HTML outlines the form and content of each Web page and that CSS provides that page with a series of directions on how to lay itself out. But it's a different matter to actually learn the commands that make all that stuff happen. It's a subject that goes far beyond the scope of this book — especially because several books have already been dedicated to it. For in-depth looks at HTML and CSS, get hold of *HTML 4 For Dummies* by Ed Tittle and Mary Burmeister and *CSS Web Design For Dummies* by Richard Mansfield. Both are available from Wiley Publishing.

Well, hello HTML! Tag — you're it!

Even though HTML and CSS coding are topics that extend beyond this book (and into territory known only to geeks), fear not — we won't leave you high and dry without at least a little background. HTML is basically a series of commands called *tags* that tell Web browsers how the data should look when people load it and it shows up on their computer screens. Most of these tags have already been provided for you by MySpace, but there are additions you can make.

For example, here's how to change the color of the font in a text field to red instead of plain old black. Type the following command into the beginning of any text field on the page:

```
<font color="red">
```

Here's what you're telling the browser to do:

- ✔ The angle brackets < > around the command tell the browser to treat this as a command and not to show the actual text to anybody looking at the page.
- ✔ The `font` command tells the browser what is being changed, and `color` defines the exact attribute being changed.
- ✔ The quotes and the color name define the exact change being made.

After this command runs, only the text in that particular field will be colored red, making it stand out from the rest of the page.

If you want to change more, you can add some *tables* in to your text fields. Tables are ways to organize your text into columns and rows. Everything in the table goes between these two tags:

```
<table>
</table>
```

Each row goes in between these tags:

```
<tr>
</tr>
```

And each cell of table data (which can be text or a picture) goes in between these tags.

```
<td>
</td>
```

The first tag tells the browser where something begins; the second tag tells the browser where it ends. A table with two rows and two columns might look something like this:

```
<table bgcolor="red">
<tr>
<td>hi</td>
<td>there</td>
</tr>
<tr>
<td>what's</td>
<td>up></td>
</tr>
</table>
```

If this table was entered into the I'd Like to Meet field of the Profile Edit screen, it would look something like Figure 12-2 on your MySpace profile page.

Figure 12-2:
A basic
table in a
MySpace
section.

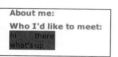

Notice how there are two rows and two columns, as defined by each set of tags. Notice also how this really basic example doesn't look too great. HTML is highly customizable, but it takes some effort to get it looking right. You can change the background color (notice the bgcolor tag in the above example), the width of the table lines, the space in between the lines and the data, and much more. But there's no such thing as a free lunch; you're going to have to do your research to get all this cool stuff to happen.

Each tag must have a *closing tag* (basically the same tag with a / in front of it), or the browser won't read it properly. The lack of a closing tag can cause problems viewing your page or cause it to have some unexpected results. Check carefully before you publish your page to MySpace! Refer to the section "First Things First" (earlier in this chapter) for more on previewing your changes before you save them.

Two other helpful tags you can use will allow you to insert images and hyperlinks to other locations on the Internet. To insert an image, use the following code:

```
<img src="http://URLofyourimagehere.jpg">
```

As implied, you'd put the address for your image in the appropriate section, but everything else should remain the same. There's no closing tag here, but what the heck — computers and languages wouldn't be the same if there wasn't a little confusion.

To add hyperlinks to other locations on the Internet, use the following tag:

```
<a href="http://www.yourfriendssite.com">Your Friend's
          Site</a>
```

The first part actually defines the link, while the text in the middle is what actually shows up. This will give anybody who looks at your MySpace page a direct, clickable link to what you want them to see.

Cascading style sheets (CSS) get their name because they come at the beginning of the document and their commands "cascade" down through the entire page. The style part applies to the sheet, telling the browser how to interpret each element it comes across. For example, you can tell it to change the width or length of certain tables and define different types of text to change in the ways you specify. Okay, it's beyond the scope of this book to address these elements (we're more about the fun than the work of MySpace anyway), but at least you'll be familiar with the concept when we look at it in the "Taking the Easy Way Out" section, later in this chapter.

Adding HTML

You can add your own HTML anywhere there's a text field. Furthermore, the HTML added in that text field applies only to that text field, so you can change the attributes in each field to look different, or you can use the same code over and over again to make things look the same. Cutting and pasting text in this instance can be your friend. Here's a quick review:

- On a PC, highlight the text you want to copy by clicking and holding the mouse button, dragging the cursor over the text you want to copy, and pressing Ctrl+C on your keyboard.

- On a Mac, do the same thing but use Command-C to copy the text. Move the cursor to where you want the text to appear and press Ctrl+V (or ⌘+C and ⌘+V if you're using a Mac) to make it appear there.

If you're using cascading style sheets, that information is posted in the About Me field of your page. Your specifications are applied to all fields on the Profile Edit screen — which is why that info needs to go in at the beginning of the page.

Copying and pasting HTML in and out of your profile is a common practice. If somebody has already written it and you want a similar view, go ahead and copy it into your text fields (just don't try to take credit for somebody else's work — that's an Internet no-no). However, make sure you know *exactly* what's going into your profile. If you don't know what you're doing, it's possible to cause a lot of problems by copying and dropping in some malicious code you didn't know was in there.

You're safe now

Everybody makes typos, so it's easy to mess up a little bit if you're typing out your own HTML in your MySpace profile. Furthermore, anybody can forget a tag or a bracket — causing the whole page to vomit out of your browser as an unintelligible mess. (Well, yeah, we've done that a few times ourselves.) That's why MySpace includes a Safe Edit Mode link at the top-right side of the Profile Edit screen, as shown in Figure 12-3. If your HTML editing has hosed your entire page, click this link to get a look at your page without letting it recognize the HTML tags you've inserted — that way, if you see something wrong, you can go ahead and change or delete it.

The Safe Edit Mode link

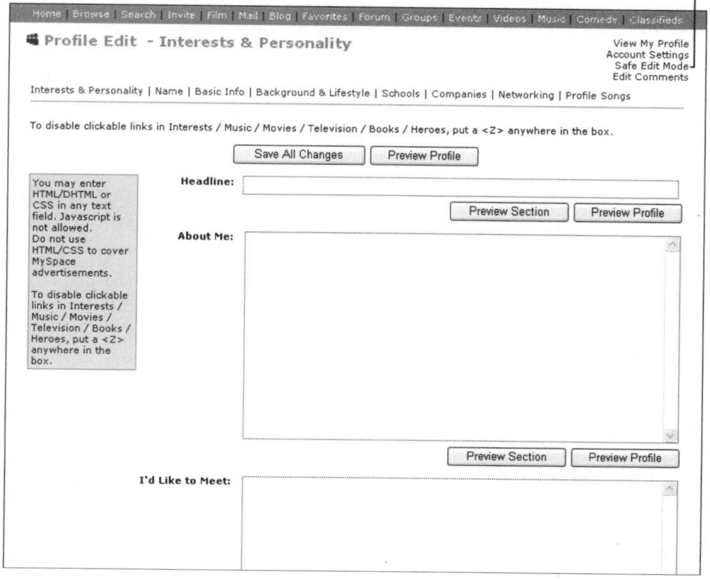

| Home | Browse | Search | Invite | Film | Mail | Blog | Favorites | Forum | Groups | Events | Videos | Music | Comedy | Classifieds |

Profile Edit - Interests & Personality

View My Profile
Account Settings
Safe Edit Mode
Edit Comments

Interests & Personality | Name | Basic Info | Background & Lifestyle | Schools | Companies | Networking | Profile Songs

To disable clickable links in Interests / Music / Movies / Television / Books / Heroes, put a <Z> anywhere in the box.

[Save All Changes]   [Preview Profile]

You may enter HTML/DHTML or CSS in any text field. Javascript is not allowed. Do not use HTML/CSS to cover MySpace advertisements.

To disable clickable links in Interests / Music / Movies / Television / Books / Heroes, put a <Z> anywhere in the box.

Headline:

[Preview Section]   [Preview Profile]

About Me:

[Preview Section]   [Preview Profile]

I'd Like to Meet:

Figure 12-3:
Use the Safe Edit Mode link to review and correct your coding.

Online resources

Okay, we've probably emphasized that HTML and CSS coding are big projects to take on for newcomers — but don't let that dissuade you from looking at what's possible. The Internet is one big repository of knowledge (and stupid pictures), so that makes it a logical place to look for information on how to learn about these languages.

Many Web sites set out directions and helpful tutorials on how to use these tools. One of our personal favorites is Webmonkey, located at www.webmonkey.com. In addition to a library of projects divided among categories such as Design, Authoring, and Multimedia (as well as quick references to HTML and style sheets), you can find front-page articles that keep you updated on tips and trends in working with the Web.

Remember that you're not the only one just starting out; don't feel bad about looking for help. Webmonkey even has sections for beginners and advanced users, so you can find something that matches your skill level. Starting at the beginning is the only way you're going to learn. If you have more specific questions, just Google it and see what pops up. You might find the answer — and you might also find something that takes you in a totally different direction.

If you want more interaction, feel free to look up some online forums that deal with HTML and CSS. These operate a lot like the forums on MySpace, so you should be on familiar ground there. Remember to look around the forums first and see whether anybody has asked your question already before you jump in and try to reinvent the wheel.

It can also be valuable to go back and edit any comments somebody else has left that cause problems in your profile. For example, you may need to get rid of an exceptionally large embedded video somebody left you that's causing your page to load s-l-o-w-l-y.

If you notice anything strange going on with your MySpace page after you've made changes, viewing your page in Safe Edit Mode should be your first option. Go back and check to make sure you typed everything in correctly, and make sure it does what you think it should do. If it doesn't respond, delete it and see whether that fixes the problem.

Can we ask you a question?

The Internet Quiz is a very common feature on MySpace profiles — in part because it gives you an entertaining way to tell people about yourself, and also because the sillier and nonsensical the survey is ("What kind of foreign sports car are you?"), the more fun it is. These surveys usually include code at the bottom that let you share the results of the survey with the world. It's similar to the embedded code we used to put videos on your page in Chapter 11. Just cut and paste the code into a MySpace text field (such as the About

Me field) to show the results, as shown in Figure 12-4. In this figure, the code tells the rest of the world that the user is an evil pumpkin — just as if the world truly needs this news.

Figure 12-4:
An exam-
ple of
embedded
Quiz Code.

```
<center>
<table width="410" border="0" cellspacing="0"
cellpadding="0" style="border: 1px solid black;">
<tr><td align="center" style="font-weight: bold;
font-size: 12pt;">YOU ARE "EVIL PUMPKIN"</td></
```

Copy each and every character in the code, or else it won't show up correctly.

Taking the Easy Way Out

So did everybody who has a cool, customized MySpace page devote the time and energy necessary to become familiar with HTML and CSS in order to per-fect their online profile? Hardly. The truth of the matter is that a few people took the time to learn not only HTML and CSS, but also some programming that allows them to put together MySpace page generators. You click a few options, copy and paste the code into your profile, and before you can say, "What does this thing do?" you, too, have a customized MySpace page. It's not magic — it only seems that way.

If you were to type MySpace Page Generator (or some variation thereof) into Google and get the results, you'd see a huge variety of sites that offer you the option to customize your profile. Most of them are based on a series of text fields and check boxes that apply to different parts of your profile. Lets take a look at one example — the popular Thomas Myspace Editor (as shown in Figure 12-5) found at www.strikefile.com/myspace. 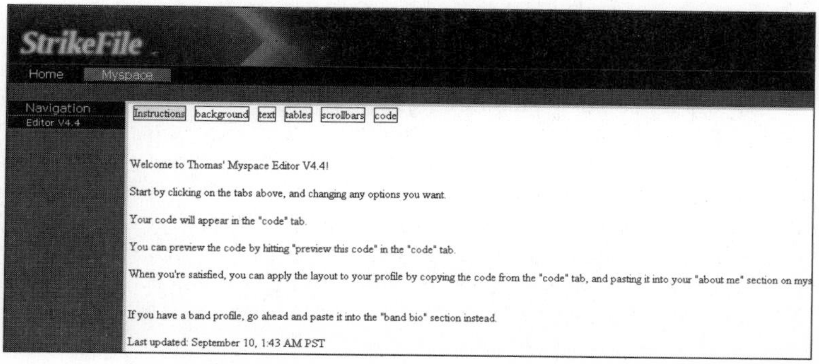

Figure 12-5:
Using the
Thomas
Myspace
Editor to
customize
your page.

StrikeFile

Home   Myspace

Navigation
Editor V4.4

Instructions | background | text | tables | scrollbars | code

Welcome to Thomas' Myspace Editor V4.4!

Start by clicking on the tabs above, and changing any options you want.

Your code will appear in the "code" tab.

You can preview the code by hitting "preview this code" in the "code" tab.

When you're satisfied, you can apply the layout to your profile by copying the code from the "code" tab, and pasting it into your "about me" section on mys

If you have a band profile, go ahead and paste it into the "band bio" section instead.

Last updated: September 10, 1:43 AM PST

On the first page of the editor, you're given the instructions for using the site. After you read 'em, click the background button where you're asked to choose what you want to do with the background of your page, as shown in Figure 12-6.

Figure 12-6:
Editing the
profile
background
in the
Thomas
Myspace
Editor.

You can choose either a solid color or a background image. When you start telling the image what to do, you can also choose what position the image should occupy, whether it should scroll with your MySpace page as it moves (or remain in place), and whether it will tile (repeat) across or down the page. That's already a huge amount of control you have — and we've only taken a look at one part of the editor!

Any pictures you want to use for your background have to already be loaded to a hosting service. You can upload them to MySpace and then use them as a background from there once you have the direct link.

After you've made your background edits, click the text button at the top of the page. This screen allows you to alter page attributes like text, links, and headings, as shown in Figure 12-7. There's a huge amount of control here as well — as you choose what you want to modify, more options become available. Some of the options are grayed out, but they'll become active when you choose to modify them.

Clicking the Tables button at the top of the page takes you to the screen in which you can work on the tables and borders in your MySpace page, as shown in Figure 12-8. This affects mostly the text and colors inside each section of your page.

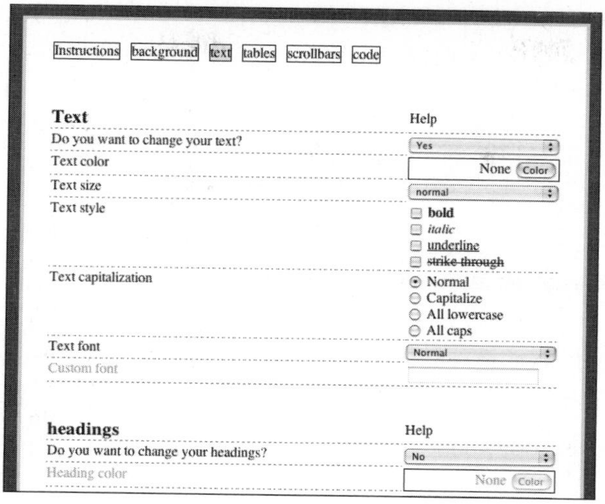

Figure 12-7:
Editing your
text's
appearance.

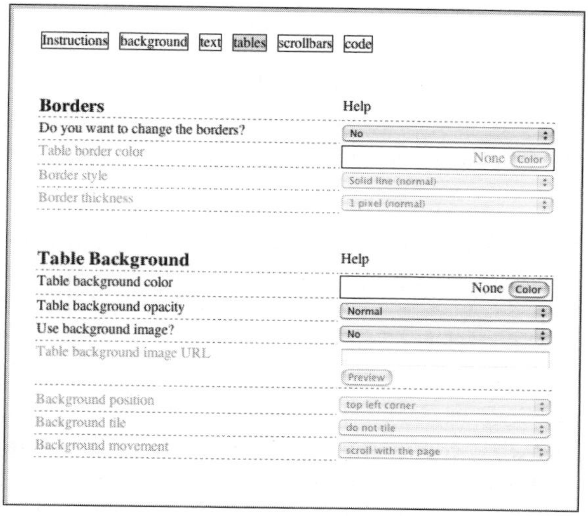

Figure 12-8:
Editing your
page's
tables.

Select the scrollbars button for the screen where you can modify your scroll-bars and how they appear, as shown in Figure 12-9. Again, you have several options available to you, so don't be afraid to experiment and change what you see here.

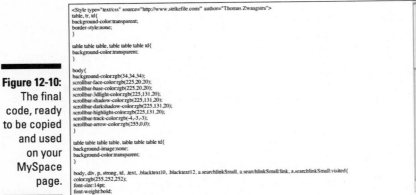

Figure 12-9:
Editing the
scrollbars
on your
page.

After you've made all your choices, click the Code button and a window
opens with your browser, as shown in Figure 12-10. Copy this code into your
About Me field on MySpace's Profile Edit screen and save it. You're ready to
go with your custom profile!

Figure 12-10:
The final
code, ready
to be copied
and used
on your
MySpace
page.

You can also preview what you've put together before you copy it into your
page, just to be sure you're getting what you want. To do so, click the Preview
This Code button, shown in Figure 12-11.

Hopefully the page you put together doesn't look too bad, although you may
find you want to go back and change some of your choices. That's the great
thing about profile editors — and about changing the code on a MySpace
page in general. Nothing is ever permanent.

You'll notice that most of these generators include some sort of tag they use
to publicize themselves, along with a link to their site so you can see what
generators the other MySpace profiles come from. There's always going to be
something new and different out there, so keep looking.

Finding the right profile editor

There's no easy ranking service for MySpace profile editors, and there are more and more coming along every time you look. So how do you choose which one you want to use on your profile editor?

The first thing to do is to look for examples of the types of profiles you want to use. Referrals are a great source of information, so don't be afraid to ask other users what works for them. Again, custom editors will more than likely include their name and location in every profile they edit.

You'll also have to decide whether you want to use a complete pre-made layout or customize your own. After you've seen what other people can do with their profiles, you might feel more comfortable making your own. Nothing you put in the code (except for the tags the profiles might leave on your page as their way of signing their art) will affect the text you put in

describing yourself. And it could always be removed or changed.

From here, you're free to explore the possibilities. There are a few things to keep in mind, though:

- ✔ Red text on black background might seem like a good idea, but it hurts the eyes. Ow. Stop that.

- ✔ Busy backgrounds also hurt the eyes. Consider something a little more user-friendly.

- ✔ Flashing text or pictures are annoying. If you like people, don't do it.

- ✔ Whole songs are okay, but repetitious loops can be annoying. Especially if they belong to a crazy frog or a ringtone or something. Stop that as well.

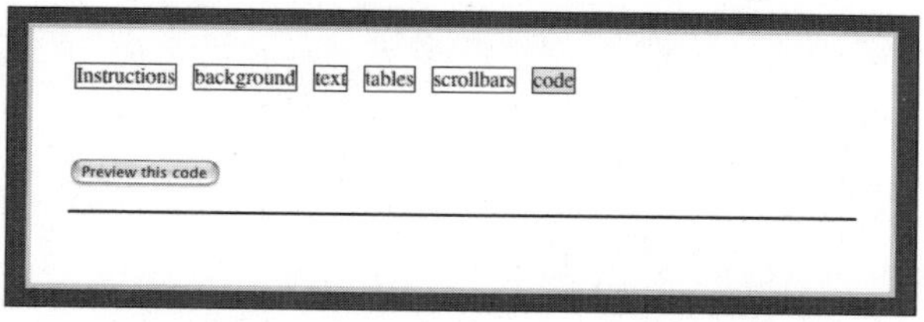

Figure 12-11:
The Preview This Code button allows you to check your changes before applying them to your page.

Part IV
Capturing Your Audience

"So far our presence on MySpace has been pretty good. We've gotten some orders, a few inquiries, and nine guys who want to date our logo."

In this part . . .

Wow, there are a lot of people out there in MySpace-land. We know there are over 100 million profiles. How many real people do you think are behind all those profiles? 25 million? 50 million? Geez, even if it's only one million, that's a lot of people. If you can sing or tell a joke, this would be a great place to show your stuff.

In fact, MySpace does let you take the online stage in front of all those people by using the site. With special tools for musicians, filmmakers, and comedians to share their talents, it's an ideal launch pad for the next superstar career.

Of course, with so many people using MySpace, it's also a perfect way for marketers to get the word out about a cool new product, a movie release, or a concert announcement to a lot of people at once. This part explores some ways talented artists and marketers are using MySpace.

Chapter 13

Marketing the MySpace Way

Marketing is all about finding your audience and ways to connect to them so they know what you have to offer. In theory, its goal is to present information that allows consumers to decide what products and services they need as they go about their daily lives — at work, home, and everywhere in between. Recent research suggests that you will be exposed to an average of 5,000 marketing messages each day. Well, it's an expected part of the evolution of media that marketers will find ways to use any new outlet — especially one as popular as MySpace — to reach, connect with, and cultivate their audiences.

As the MySpace population escalates into the hundreds of millions, it shouldn't come as a surprise that businesses and brands are finding ways to access these people. Beware — this world is different from the forms of mass media (television, newspaper, magazines, and so on) that have become the delivery systems for *most* of those 5,000 daily messages. People now expect to be reached in many different ways — and on MySpace in particular, there is a direct connection that goes both ways. If you don't want to hear what other community members have to say about you, it's really best not to ask. But if you're prepared to take that risk and make contact, the rewards can be great.

It's no longer about mass media. It's "me" media. It's about personal connections — and the people you want to talk to get to decide whether they want to hear what you have to say. It had better be relevant, because you only get one chance to make a "friend."

Whether you're hoping to market yourself or your business, or even just bracing yourself to be marketed to on MySpace, this chapter will get you prepared.

The Ultimate Online Social Community

It's only natural to be drawn to other people with whom you find a connection. You had a lot in common with the group of kids you ran with in school — the clothes you wore, the way you spoke, the music you liked, the city you grew up in. As you grow older, that continues. You join a church, participate in recreational activities, and get involved with civic organizations that allow you the opportunity to surround yourself with others with whom you feel an allegiance. Ultimately, we all seek to feel understood — and who understands us better (or is more fun to be with) than the people who have similar interests and passions?

The beauty of MySpace is that it tears down the geographic and societal barriers that were previous hindrances to finding these people. A decade ago, you might have been able to find only one other person within your circle of friends and acquaintances who shared your secret passion for carving pelicans out of soap, or swing dancing, or even eating your favorite brand of candy bar. Today there's an ever-expanding resource for connecting and communicating with an entire community of chocolate-chomping, swing-dancing soap carvers (or whatever it is you love in this world).

True, from a concept level, the idea of an online social community is fairly straightforward. Such virtual gatherings basically give you the opportunity — and the capability — to find that needle in the haystack with a click of your mouse. Bottom line: Creating connections and communicating to the masses has become easier than ever before.

The idea of an online social community, such as MySpace, is not a new one. There have always been small groups of people scattered across the Internet who use online forums, message boards, and other online-community tools to interact with people with similar interests. However, these types of communities were usually very niche-oriented (musicians, artists, pet lovers, and so on) and their members were much more Web-savvy than your average day-to-day Web user. What MySpace has done, in a very short time, is create an online community that has gained acceptance by all types of users, from all types of backgrounds and interests — the musicians can find a huge number of other music lovers, pet-owners can find scads of other folks who are into the same breeds they are, you name it.

Regardless of who you are looking for, MySpace brings it all together under one roof. This is what makes it extremely attractive as a marketing tool. Some of the reasons for the incredible growth of MySpace are hard to pinpoint. Being at the right place at the right time comes into play, as does the cumulative power of the people. MySpace has grown because the people who love it draw other people to it — it's a prime example of self-perpetuating "viral" growth. There is longevity in what has been created, but the explosive growth follows the path of some of the most significant "fads" or pop-culture reference points of all time (well, *recent* all time anyway). The following list contains a few of the more obvious reasons for MySpace's unbelievable success:

- ✔ **Founded on bands and celebrities:** When MySpace first hit the Internet scene, the majority of the members were bands and celebrities who were intrigued by how MySpace could potentially create a new way for them to connect and interact with the people most important to them — their fans. The more these bands and celebrities promoted their MySpace pages, the bigger their fan base and the MySpace community grew. MySpace was a perfect tool for creating a grassroots-level channel directly to those fans that wanted a way to connect. The rest, as they say, is history.

- ✔ **Ability to customize:** MySpace may not have been the absolute first in the market among online social communities, but it has definitely become the biggest and most widely recognized. Another major contributor to this success has been the way MySpace engages its users' creativity: They can customize nearly every part and piece of their own personal spot in the MySpace world. MySpace users number in the millions, but every single one can turn his or her profile into a personal statement that truly reflects a distinct identity.

  MySpace has always given users the ability to add videos, photos, text, background images, and any color of the rainbow to their profiles, which makes MySpace truly feel like a reflection of who you are. Many Web sites have been created with content created specifically for use on MySpace pages, which is a testament to the fact that users are constantly looking for the latest and greatest stuff to add to their profile pages.

  You can read all about how to customize the many different parts of your MySpace profile in Part III.

- ✔ **Easy-to-use interface:** Whether you're a major computer geek or a mother of three without enough time to sit still at a computer, MySpace has created an interface that's intuitive and easy to use. This allows anyone and everyone the opportunity to access and use MySpace.

- ✔ **Communication options:** MySpace gives you several ways to connect with people using tools such as e-mail-like messaging, instant messaging, blogs, bulletins, event invitations, audio and video players, and much, much more. These different tools make it easy for any newbie to hit the ground running when they first register, while still giving the more Web-savvy users the freedom and flexibility to mix, match, and customize the tools at the same time. So whether you're on MySpace for fun or you're there strictly for business, you can tailor it to your own needs.

✔ **It's free:** One of the things that has drawn users to MySpace is the fact that it costs the user absolutely nothing to use it. Yep, you heard right — it's free — and that it's packed full of tools — also free — that you can use right away to communicate with the masses. Those features make MySpace a very attractive alternative to forking over the cash to create a Web site of your own. Even major bands and movies have realized that they have direct access to their target audience through MySpace — compare that to trying to create yet another Web site outside the social hotspot. If you have gone to a movie lately, it's likely that you've seen the domain MySpace.com pop up somewhere on the big screen during some of the previews. No accident, that.

✔ **It's where the people are:** MySpace has been growing exponentially lately — and that means if you don't have a MySpace profile, you are "like, totally out of the social loop." The more people who sign up, the more people hear about it and the faster the community grows. It's cyclical, baby. MySpace is like a runaway train that is gaining speed and momentum every second, with no slowing down in sight anytime soon. This means you need not only to get into the MySpace mix socially, but (for many companies and organizations) professionally as well. After MySpace hit a few million members, there was no turning back — which means you can no longer expect the users to come to you (unless of course, you're on MySpace). Now the sheer numbers of users are having an effect: Even the people who had initially vehemently opposed being on MySpace have grudgingly made profiles. After awhile, they're starting to find they like it. And when everyone you know is connecting in a certain way, maybe there's something to it. If you want to find out what that potential advantage is, you have little choice but to join the fray.

As you can see, MySpace created the right community for the right audience at the right time with the right tools — which has made it the 800-pound gorilla in the world of online social communities. So, does this whole MySpace community offer enough market potential that you should get involved in it? That depends. In the next few sections, we lay the groundwork for a good, hands-on sense of who should jump into the MySpace marketing world, the pros and cons of marketing to MySpacers, and some strategic advice if you decide that this is the way to go. Are you ready for a little bit of MySpace Marketing 101? We think you are.

Deciding if MySpace Is the Right Place

Unlike more traditional marketing and advertising venues — and, to a lesser degree, even your standalone Web site — MySpace is a living and breathing environment. Well, not literally, but you get what I'm saying: It changes and responds and can't be taken for granted. So, in order to get the most out of marketing on MySpace, you have to make a continuing commitment. Tossing up a profile page, walking away, and leaving it out of sight and out of mind can cause significant damage to your brand or business among the MySpace crowd.

MySpace is about connection and communication, and that means it's a two-way dialogue. Your audience will have questions. They will have comments. They will be boisterously supportive, but they might also be outraged. It is your responsibility to treat your marketing efforts on MySpace with great care. That said, consider your audience. If they are on MySpace, maybe you should be, too. But check first. If you're selling life insurance, MySpace may not be as immediately profitable as it would be if you were selling designer T-shirts.

Evaluating the MySpace audience

When deciding to involve yourself or your organization in the sometimes wacky world of MySpace, you should first ask yourself if the MySpace audience is the audience that you are wanting to connect with. The MySpace community currently skews towards the younger, Web-savvy demographic, but with over 100 million registered users — and its popularity constantly growing — it becomes more and more traditional. No wonder older people are joining as well. But no matter who the target demographic is, once people join the MySpace community, they tend to make it one of their most-visited stops on the information superhighway.

The ability to build an audience

Whether you're a poet trying to get feedback on your latest haiku or a multi-million-dollar company intent on pitching your new product, you will always have the same end goal in mind — building an audience. Well, building the audience is really just one piece of the puzzle. As you're building your audience, you also need to be interacting with them, engaging them, keeping them interested with what you have to offer, and motivating them to act. It's basically a double-edged sword — just as you now have the capability to communicate easily to an audience in MySpace, your audience can just as easily choose not to listen. This is a major shift from the traditional mass-media methods of disruptive advertising and marketing that we're all so used to seeing.

The MySpace corporate invasion

When MySpace first started, most of the more well-known corporations were very hesitant to make the jump to MySpace. After all, it represented an enormous shift in the way they communicate. If they were to reach out on MySpace, they would be forced to "let go" of quite a bit of control and realize that people would be able to say whatever they wanted — and millions of others would be able to read it. However, as the community grew and grew, many have changed their minds not because they wanted to, but because they had to. MySpace is like a virtual shopping mall that's packed with millions of people — younger people with money, the ones these companies need to get in front of if they want to be successful. So, for starters, here's a list of a few corporations who have officially made the move to MySpace — and a look at how they're utilizing this new marketing medium:

✔ **Burger King** (www.myspace.com/burgerking), Friends: 220,000.

Burger King, the creator of the Internet phenomenon known as the Subservient Chicken, is at it again on MySpace. The Burger King himself is the main character on Burger King's profile, but they haven't stopped at that. Burger King was the first company to partner with MySpace to distribute free and pay-per-download content on MySpace. The content they're pushing, of course, already has an audience — episodes of the super-popular television series *24.* Two episodes are free to download; any other episode is $1.99 and can be downloaded directly from the Burger King profile. This is just another way that companies can leverage the MySpace platform to give them fresh and interactive experiences that can create connections to their brands.

✔ **Dell** (www.myspace.com/makeuswork), Friends: 8,000

Dell has created a profile on MySpace that feels just like it came out of a Dell brochure. Besides a few cool-looking graphics, Dell hasn't really implemented the medium of MySpace to its full potential. There is also a "Tell us to:" piece you can use to tell a Dell worker set his hair on fire or arm-wrestle a dinosaur (virtually), or build you a Dell (virtually or for real). It's a great start, but Dell could do much, much more.

✔ **Honda** (www.myspace.com/hondaelement), Friends: 43,000

Honda has really pushed its Element SUV on MySpace — no surprise there, because a younger demographic usually buys this particular vehicle. Their profile has run a MySpace background contest called the "Embrace MySpace Contest," where MySpace users could create and submit a background image to be featured on the Honda Element's profile page. Honda has also created a profile page specifically for Gil, the "I pinch" crab featured on a few of their commercials at www.myspace.com/crab. The newly famous crustacean currently has over 100,000 friends — and someone just commented "gil... will you please pinch me!!! I NEED TO BE PINCHED!!" It seems the MySpace community likes him. (You go, Gil. Ow.)

✔ **Wal-Mart** (www.myspace.com/walmart), Friends: 10,000.

Wal-Mart is the MySpace new kid on the block. After first attempting to create its own version of MySpace for the back-to-school audience, Wal-Mart has now made the jump into the world of MySpace proper. The Wal-Mart profile allows people to vote on their favorite music, electronics, and dorm-room essentials.

✔ **Wendy's** (www.myspace.com/wendy square), Friends: 80,000.

Wendy's has used its MySpace profile specifically to promote its cartoon mascot, the Wendy's Square (named "Smart"). You can learn all about Smart on this profile page and you can also download a set of "Beadicons," which are small images of Smart that show him with different emotions, such as Shocked, Bored, and Foot in Mouth. This attempt by Wendy's is a very non-corporate way to work their brand into the MySpace world — and so far it seems to be working.

The concept of picking a billboard next to a busy highway or running your commercial during that new, popular sitcom, just hoping that people will see it, isn't going to fly for the new MySpace generation. You're dealing with a very fickle audience and a consumer-driven medium where the members have more control than an impatient guy with a remote — and you are attempting to work your way into their world, so be careful. Through MySpace, the audience decides whether they want to hear from you at all — thus the ones who *do* choose to listen to what you have to say are much more receptive to what you're telling them — and incredibly valuable, because they also tell their friends.

This idea of building yourself an audience isn't a new one, but the methods and best practices for doing so have changed. It's definitely not something to fear — just like anything else that's new and dynamic, it'll take time to get used to. And don't worry — no one really has all of the answers yet, so don't be discouraged if your first online marketing campaign doesn't work right out of the gate. One of the main keys to success in building up an audience is consistency — and this environment not only rewards trying new things, but keeping at it. You'll figure out what works best for you with some committed effort and experimentation.

New rules, new expectations

With the growth and acceptance of high-speed Internet connections, the Web has quickly become a major player in the world of marketing. Major advances in online communication and multimedia technologies have made things possible on the Internet today that were just crazy ideas a few years ago. The very nature of the medium allows for personal, one-to-one connections that are unlike any previous interaction with the forms of mass media that have dominated advertising so far. This type of connected environment is what turned a once-small (and relatively unknown) online community into the MySpace that we know today — not only a community, but an audience and a potentially demanding market in its own right.

But with innovation comes greater expectations — and today's users expect more from the Web than any other group of users the Internet has ever seen. Marketing has become highly interactive and the ability to give the masses the content they're looking for and wanting has become easier — now you just need to make sure that you're giving them what they want, when they want it, and how they want it. The Internet has become a gigantic consumer-driven playground — and if you want to get involved, you had better be ready to let them play. There are a few things that will be very different when looking at marketing in the world of MySpace compared to marketing in the "traditional" sense. You should definitely be aware of and prepared for these differences, but by no means should you be scared of them. Even so, here's a practical list of things that you should be ready for as you start marketing the MySpace way:

- **Don't just sit there:** So, you finally decided to carve out your own little space in the MySpace world and you are officially ready to get this marketing party started. You will quickly realize that by just having your own space doesn't mean that you now have a presence. Whether it's running a TV commercial, posting a billboard, or placing an ad in your local newspaper, traditional advertising and marketing has always been a set-it-and-forget-it process. But the new online spaces like MySpace demand participation — you must be prepared not only to market to the community, but also to become a living, breathing member of it. MySpace rewards those who are proactive — and will easily ignore those who are not — so get to it!

- **It's a two-way street:** MySpace is all about give and take. If you want people to communicate with you and become more aware of your talents, products, or services, you had better start getting in touch with them. It also never hurts to give the members of MySpace stuff to "play" with. Use your space in a way that encourages interaction and engagement — after all, that's what MySpace was created for. Also, don't treat MySpace as just another Web site. Utilize and take advantage of the tools that the masses are already used to responding to and make it as easy as possible to interact.

- **Take the good with the bad:** Someone once said, "Be careful what you wish for, because you just might get it." Well, MySpace has given marketers that direct, open channel to their end users — the one they've always dreamed about — and now that it's open, they should be prepared to hear the voice of the people . . . which isn't always complimentary. If you run a TV commercial, you might get some feedback from a few people in passing who have seen it on the air — and (depending who they are) they might even tell you the truth about their reactions. Now, on the other hand, if you run an online video via MySpace, anyone with a MySpace account will be able to give their opinions — instantly. Those may be good, bad, glowing, ticked off, or incoherent — but you'll be getting true opinion of the masses (at least the MySpace masses). Just make sure you're ready to hear it.

✔ **Learning to "police" your space:** One of the things that marketers have feared the most when it comes to MySpace and other online social communities is the fact that the members have so much more control than ever before. What do you do if one of them posts a terrible comment or a pornographic picture on your profile page? The fact that the user now has an open conversation with your brand has to be taken very seriously. Knowing how to set up your profile in a way that allows you the control you're comfortable with — while still allowing enough interaction from the members of MySpace that they feel involved — is the key to effective online marketing. This idea of controlling users' interaction with your space — for the sake of your image and that of your brand — is known as *policing*. Users' expectations — when it comes to interacting with your brand — are only going to become greater as online communities continue to make our world smaller and nearly everything more accessible. Just make sure you're up to speed on how to deal with it.

If you keep all of these in mind as you are stepping foot into the MySpace scene, you should be prepared for some of the things that might otherwise catch you off guard. Also, remember that MySpace is still fairly uncharted marketing territory — and the whole concept of marketing to online social communities is something many people are still having to figure out as they go along. Just make sure you don't get too frustrated as you begin your journey — this is just the beginning of a phenomenon that will most likely be around for a long, long time — and even the pros are uncertain of what to expect.

Real-World Marketing versus MySpace Marketing

MySpace has basically rewritten the rules on how a marketer can reach his or her audience. And it's about time; the traditional methods that most marketers use are showing less impact and fewer results than ever. Part of this ferment is due to the sheer number of messages we receive on a daily basis — and part of it is because we don't spend our time in the same ways we did just a few years ago. Television provides so many options that even the popular shows gather much smaller ratings than they did a decade ago. Newspaper circulation is dropping at an alarming rate. And magazines are becoming attuned to niche audiences — read: markets — in order to survive. Although many marketers are hanging on to these time-tested advertising methods, others are focusing on new and innovative ways to connect. Lets take a look at how MySpace is contributing to the changes.

The first part of each bullet item summarizes the way marketers have always done it — and the second part is MySpace's version of how it can be translated into the online world. (Now, pay attention — there might be a quiz after this.)

- ✔ **Passing out flyers:** Behold the almighty flyer — it's pure and simple promotion. As the ultimate grassroots way to communicate your message, the flyer is about as up-close and personal as you can get with your audience. No wonder yard sales, concerts, sporting events, and clothing sales use this time-tested method as a way to get people up to speed on what's going on. Okay, online doesn't entirely replace hard copy — there will most likely never be a day when flyers aren't used — but certain MySpace tools can give you the same result with a lot bigger audience, a lot less effort, and no printing costs.

  MySpace's version: You comment as many of your friend's pages as you can, displaying an eye-catching image along with the when-where-and-how-much info about your next must-see performance with your punk-rock band, The Preppy Misfits. That simple comment links back to your profile — where they can hear your music and check out pictures from your last few shows. You also decide to create a snazzy-looking bulletin that you send out to your Friends List, where it will definitely catch their attention. Then you sit back and wait for the flood of feedback — which is, according to the comments you're getting, looking great. Rock and roll lives on — and you saved a few bucks' worth of printing and a few trees' worth of paper. All is well with the world.

- ✔ **Running a TV commercial:** TV commercials have long been a way to get a marketer's message out to the masses. The problem is that traditional commercials are definitely not the *cheapest* way to tell your story — and they are strictly a one-way marketing technique; it's hard to target the message accurately, and even harder to get feedback on it. There is no guarantee that the people you want to talk to are even tuned in — but if your goal is to reach the masses, television is the established way to go. If you have thousands of dollars on hand — and a whole lot of hope that you can guess when your audience is watching what shows — then maybe TV is the channel (sorry about that) for you.

- ✔ **MySpace's version:** You know in your heart that you own the greatest restaurant in your town. The people who have eaten there love it and can't get enough of it. The only problem is that everyone else in your town *doesn't* know this and you need to get the message out. You grab a camera and start creating your own videos about why anyone would have to be nuts not to stop in for a bite to eat. You get your cooks on camera, you get your satisfied customers on camera, you even interview your mom about why your restaurant is great and you put that on camera. Before you know it, you have a couple great videos posted on your MySpace page that you start spreading the word about. You send the clips to the customers you interviewed — you send them to people who have never heard of you before — and you send them to (of course) your mom. Those people enjoy the videos almost as much as they enjoy your restaurant, so they pass them along to their friends, co-workers, and members of their softball team. The whole thing snowballs like compound interest till *the word is out* on your restaurant — and the only problem you have now is where to seat all your newfound (and hungry) friends.

✔ **Developing a street team:** From a marketing perspective, it always helps to locate and assemble a loyal group of people who are dedicated to your brand and to what you are doing. That's especially valuable when they are so loyal that they become a powerful marketing channel in their own right. These groups, usually known as *street teams*, utilize word-of-mouth marketing to communicate their messages. You've seen these people handing out free samples, trying to get you to sign up for contests, and posting flyers on college campuses. Well, word of mouth has always been one of the most powerful forms of real-world marketing — and with MySpace, word of mouth can be extended to a whole new level.

✔ **MySpace's version:** Lets say you really want to let people know about your company's new MP3 player, the mePod. You have begun to notice that several people have already bought it — and can't say enough great stuff about it in the comments and messages they've sent to you. Okay, stay with us here — you live in California and only one out of about 15 of these extreme mePod fans are from California too, but that doesn't matter with MySpace. You begin to message them all, wherever they are, telling them about how you want them to start a virtual mePod street team that would help preach the mePod gospel from one end of MySpace to the other. You entice them by putting them in your Top 8 friends, adding their pictures to your profile, and by hooking them up with tickets to the mePod-sponsored national tour of that can't-miss band they all love so much. You also mail them all a version of the new itsy-bitsy mePod that doesn't hit stores for another six months. They become rock stars (more or less) in their world, and they're doing some effective promoting that's really working. Before you know it, your Friends List has doubled in a month and sales for the mePod have never been better. Mission accomplished. Pat yourself on the back.

✔ **Creating a T-shirt:** Wearing a T-shirt with a company logo or message on it is a very personal and powerful way for people to communicate their brand loyalty. This type of "real" marketing is priceless for your brand because it shows that the person wearing the shirt is proud to tell the world that they think of you or your organization. It's very honest — the person wearing the shirt has the ultimate decision on whether to wear it, and other people realize and respect that. In fact, people will line up and work themselves into a tizzy just to earn a free T-shirt, even if they never wear it. This very personal and loyal type of marketing can be easily translated into the MySpace world as well. Just make sure that if your audience wants to show their loyalty to your brand, they can do it digitally — and that you've given them the means to do so.

✔ **MySpace's version:** You can't believe that your movie is actually getting ready to hit theaters soon — and now you need to get the word out about your video creation because you know it has blockbuster potential. You create a profile on MySpace that allows the millions of MySpace users to add different versions of your movie trailer to their own profile and download new movie-themed backgrounds for their profiles, and you encourage them all you add your movie's profile to one of their coveted "Top Friends" spots. You also decide to let members of the community download raw video clips of the movie so that they can make their own versions of your movie trailer: Let the mash-ups begin. Soon MySpace is overflowing with digital odes to your movie, and you decide to showcase your favorite five user-generated movie trailers on your profile page — heck, you might even show them at your premiere screening. The MySpace masses are engaged completely in your movie — and it eventually gets them up and moving to fill up the theaters. A blockbuster . . . how sweet it is.

Measuring Your MySpace Success

To most of its millions of registered users, MySpace is a place that is entertaining, amusing, and a great way to burn some time while bored at work. But, to a marketer it could mean creating potential opportunities to grab the attention of a demographic that isn't really known for sitting still. MySpace, however, with it's marketing potential and possibilities, isn't an easy place for a marketer to fit in. Just like any other marketing initiative, to be successful you must plan to budget certain resources when marketing in the MySpace world and, when this type of planning and resources are used, there must also be a way to gauge success.

Being able to state what would mean marketing success for you or your organization on MySpace — clearly defining the goal — is the first order of business. Do you want to create more awareness of your product or service? Maybe you want to drive users to a Web site outside MySpace where they can make online purchases? Do you want the members of MySpace to buy tickets to your next event? Maybe you just want feedback on the last song you posted? These are all things that you could potentially accomplish by utilizing MySpace. Giving some thought to what would spell "success" for your MySpace marketing efforts is an essential first step to take before anything else. From there, it's pretty straightforward . . .

Find your people. Get their attention. Listen to what they have to say. Keep them happy. And have fun doing it, for goodness' sake.

X-Men: The Last Stand— A MySpace success story

Already a litany of success stories surrounds the bands, brands, comics, and movies that have had phenomenal market success through their efforts on MySpace. Even before Fox's parent company, News Corp., purchased MySpace for $580 million, they had been experimenting with it as a lucrative marketing option. Two weeks before the opening of *X-Men: The Last Stand*, Fox posted a MySpace profile specific to the site. Within hours, they had 50,000 friends. By the time the film opened (as the #5 biggest opening ever, with more than $102 million in domestic ticket sales), there were 2.3 million "friends" on the profile, making it the most popular profile on MySpace.

Successful marketing takes a meaningful message to the right audience. The MySpace audience may not be right for every business, but for those who find their target market on MySpace, be prepared for an experience like no other. You can create more loyal fans than you've ever imagined, but you'll have to earn — and keep — their trust and their support. After all, any great relationship is based on quality communication and mutual understanding.

The figure included here shows you some of the *X-Men 3* MySpace profile. As you can see, it uses the medium very well — and at the time of this writing people were still interacting with it.

Chapter 14

Rockin' in the MySpace World

We've all heard the "discovery" stories of our favorite musicians. The idea that anytime, anyplace, you just might get noticed for your talents by someone who actually has the power take you to the next level is an alluring dream. While that still happens, in these days of fragmented markets, record labels love to look for new acts that are as close to a "sure thing" as they can find. They want talented musicians, but they also want them to have an existing audience of rabidly passionate fans. No wonder the industry is catching on to MySpace — a destination like no other for bands who are trying to build an audience, maintain their fan base, and share their sound with the world. Geographic boundaries are fading — and the audience is listening. Now, more than ever, you have the capability to gain exposure, book gigs, promote the new album, and talk to your fans — regardless of whether they listen to you in your own garage, at their cousins' weddings, or in a sold-out stadium.

Music — the Foundation of MySpace

How does an online community go from an idea to what has become the MySpace phenomenon in just a few years? One word — music. When MySpace got its start in the sunny state of California, it was initially pitched to musicians as a way to gather fans and expose their music as never before. Before anyone quite knew what was happening, word spread about this new online tool. Many musicians were swearing by it, and as more and *more* musicians moved to MySpace, their fans, of course, followed. MySpace created a whole new way for musicians and fans to connect. After just a couple of short years, MySpace has become the most popular online hangout for millions of people and at its core, it's all thanks to the one thing that everyone loves in one form or another — music.

When you buy a guitar, it doesn't come with a publicist. Drum kits don't have managers or booking agents living inside them. If you signed something when you bought a microphone, chances are pretty good that it was an extended warranty, not a lucrative recording contract. The talent and the tools are just the start. The years of musical training or generations of musically-inclined genes (or those that favor creative and poetic wordplay) are the reason you'll create beautiful music — but none of that guarantees you an audience. There is a whole other series of commitments and responsibilities that come with being a musician. For many bands, MySpace easily opens doors, organizes information, and introduces them to an entire world of potential fans. That can be a solid start.

Want to hear some music from that band your daughter is talking about? Click. Want to share with your friends about the most amazing song you've ever heard (this week)? Click. Want to tell a musician that his or her lyrics feel as if they were written for you? Click. Want to add that song you've been humming all week to your own profile page? Click. It's all at your fingertips, and it's all just a click away.

Basically, MySpace owes its popularity to the musicians who wanted to get their music out to the public using some easy tools. Some of the things that drew the musical masses to MySpace are relative no-brainers:

- **It's FREE:** The only thing better than awesome online tools for an up-and-coming band are free and awesome online tools. Anyone can jump on MySpace and create an online presence for their music free of charge, which has made MySpace a very attractive way for musicians to promote their tunes. If MySpace had charged bands to register an account from the beginning, MySpace might have never extended out of its California roots. But, luckily, it is 100% free to use, which has made millions of bands very happy.

- **Easy to use:** With its easy-to-use and straightforward interface, MySpace has made even the least Web-savvy musicians into powerful online-promotion powerhouses. Adding show dates, music, pictures, and band information is a piece of cake, and it shows. It's one reason that (increasingly) you'd be hard put to find a band that hasn't staked a claim in the MySpace world.

- **MySpace Music Player:** The MySpace Music Player is by far one of the greatest standard features on any MySpace music profile. After registering as a musician, you can upload a limited number of full-length songs in MP3 format onto MySpace. After the songs are uploaded, any user who stumbles upon a musician's page can easily listen to all that exciting new music — it's instantly streamed though the MySpace Music Player. Before MySpace hit the scene, a musician needed a little bit of cash and know-how in order to stream music on the Web, but now, thanks to the MySpace Music Player, it's never been easier.

✔ **Where the fans are:** Prior to MySpace, musicians had to drive potential fans to their specific Web sites — which is never an easy task, especially when you're just starting out and not many people know your music yet. But now, considering that there are 100+ million users on MySpace, it's much easier to get them to visit your Web space. More and more musicians are getting asked the question, "Are you on MySpace?" by those who dig their music.

Also, musicians who book out-of-town gigs in that not-so-well-known venue can now let the locals know they're coming. With a few searches and Friend Requests, an audience could potentially be created in no time. Heck, they might even be able to find a sofa here and there for the band members to sleep on.

✔ **An online musical standard:** For musicians with pro aspirations, it's quickly becoming less of a convenience and more of a necessity to have a music profile on MySpace. If a band has high hopes of getting its music "out there," they had better have a few songs uploaded on the MySpace Music Player. Why? Because the MySpace music profile has quickly become the online musical standard for Web users. The users of MySpace have become very familiar with how music is played on the music profiles, which gives a great opportunity to any musician who utilizes all that MySpace has to offer.

✔ **Equal opportunity:** Not only has the MySpace music profile become a powerful promotions tool for up-and-coming musicians, but it has also made its way into the worlds of the most mainstream musicians as well. A local bluegrass band in Kentucky uses the same exact MySpace platform and tools to promote their music as Coldplay and U2 do. Even though MySpace is still considered the new kid on the block when it comes to music, it has probably become the largest equal-opportunity musical clearinghouse in the world.

As you can see, there are many reasons why MySpace is a perfect fit for all types of musicians. By developing a new channel between musicians and their fans, MySpace has not only created a way for the masses to listen to music — they have provided an opportunity for the creation of the meaningful conversations and feedback that surround it. MySpace has created the ultimate online fan experience.

Getting Your Music onto MySpace

The Battle of the Bands is approaching. This year, your band has what it takes to win the whole thing. Great songs, an impressive stage show, pyrotechnics, and more. You've designed some flyers and you've asked all your friends to show up, support your dream, and vote for their favorite (as long as it's you). There must be a better way to help get the word out: a better way to connect to the new fans you've earned once you're there. You're prepared to do what it takes to get the adoring masses the information they need — quickly and easily.

So you think that it's time to give MySpace a taste of your musical talents, eh? Fortunately, getting your MySpace music profile up and running isn't too tough. The first thing that you need to do is register a music profile on MySpace. This process is very similar to creating a personal MySpace page, but with a few small differences. Tune that guitar of yours, turn up your amp, and follow these steps to take your first step towards MySpace music stardom:

1. **Go to the MySpace.com homepage and click the Music link, as shown in Figure 14-1.**

   Registering on MySpace as a musician is different from registering a personal MySpace page. By clicking the Music link in the main MySpace navigation, you will be taken to the main MySpace Music page. Don't be surprised if this area becomes very familiar as you make increasing use of your MySpace music profile. It's where most of your musical MySpacing will begin.

   Most musicians register a personal MySpace page as well as a music profile. This allows them to manage their personal friends with one and utilize the other as mainly a promotional tool for their music. As many people say, it's a great way to "separate business from pleasure."

The Music link

Figure 14-1:
The Music link on the MySpace home page takes you to the main MySpace Music page.

2. **Click the Artist Signup link in the main MySpace Music navigational links.**

   The Artist Signup link is at the top of the page on the far-right side of the MySpace Music navigation links. This link takes you to the Musician Signup window.

3. **Fill out all required information and click the Sign Up button.**

   Fill out all the required information on the Musician Signup window, shown in Figure 14-2. Make sure to check the box that lets MySpace know that you agree with their Terms of Service and Privacy Statement.

4. **Complete your registration and click the Continue button.**

   After filling out your initial registration information and clicking the Sign Up button, you're taken to the Registration Completion window. In this window, you need to finalize the following:

   - **Your MySpace URL:** This is where you enter the MySpace URL that you intend to promote to anyone you want to attract to your MySpace page. Make sure that this site reflects you, your music, and your musical interests that your fans can relate to. You will be able to edit this later if needed, so it's not set in stone. (That's okay. Music isn't, either.)

     Keep this bit of online wisdom in mind: The shorter the address, the better.

   - **Genre(s):** There are three drop-down lists that let you select what genre(s) your band falls under. Whatever you select here will be what you're listed under on MySpace. It will be displayed on your music profile — and it will be searchable by the millions of MySpacers after you set it.

   - **Web Site:** If you already have a Web site established outside of MySpace, you can add that in here.

   - **Current Record Label:** If you're one of the lucky few who are already signed to a label, add it proudly here — and make all the unsigned bands jealous. This information will be displayed on your music profile as well.

   - **Label Type:** There are three choices in this drop-down list; Unsigned, Major, and Indie. If you aren't sure which one you are, you're probably unsigned. This is a great first step in doing something about that.

5. **Add a Profile Picture, Invite Friends, and Upload Songs.**

   Your MySpace music profile is now created. MySpace now gives you the options of adding a profile picture, inviting friends and uploading songs. You can either fill some of these options out or skip them for now. At the very least, you should probably add a profile picture. This can be done by clicking the Browse button, locating a picture on your hard drive, and clicking the Upload button.

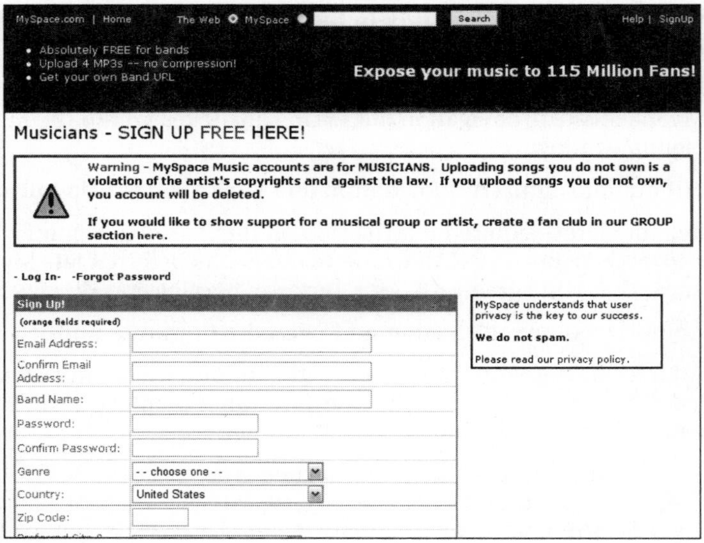

Figure 14-2:
Filling
out the
Musician
Signup
window is
the first step
in creating
your
MySpace
music
profile.

At this point, your Music profile is very similar to a personal account — with a few important differences. The following section helps you get your music profile playing music to the masses in no time.

MySpace Music Profile Options

So, your MySpace music profile is now officially registered and you're ready to get your music up for the world to see, um, *hear*. The following list of options will help you make the most out of your music profile — in almost no time — so you can start spreading the word about your music as soon as possible.

As stated earlier, many of the options on a MySpace music profile are the same as the options on a personal profile. If what you're looking for isn't covered in this section, be sure to check out Part III for detailed information on customizing other non-music-related profile options. Either way, it's good practice.

The main difference between a MySpace music profile and personal profile is the Edit Profile window. When you edit a personal profile, you have the options for entering in and managing all kinds of personal information such as your favorite television shows, movies, what town you grew up in, what high school/college you attended, and others. In a music profile, you're asked to enter information that is specific to you as a musician. This information includes Upcoming Shows, Band Details, Basic Band Info, Song Uploading & Management, and Band Listing Info.

To get to your music profile's Edit Profile window, click the Edit Profile link that is located just to the right of your profile picture on your MySpace home page. The Edit Profile link is the very first link at the top of the list of links, as shown in Figure 14-3. The following sections discuss the various aspects of your music profile so you can get the most out of your MySpace page.

The Edit Profile link

Figure 14-3: By clicking the Edit Profile link, you can manage all things music for your profile.

Upcoming Shows

No matter how much of a fan base you build online, it's not going to do you much good if you don't give them a chance to see you live and in all your harmonic glory. Book a gig. Then, book another. Sell out a venue. Keep your fans in the loop and aware of every one of your dates via MySpace. It's the perfect way to put your info up and send it out. If you're going to make it big, you must expand awareness of every show you play. You are your biggest promoter.

The first tab in the Edit Profile window is named Upcoming Shows. This is the place where you add, delete, and edit the details of any shows you'll be playing in the near future. To enter your act's upcoming show, follow these steps:

1. Enter in Show Date and Time.

Fill out the date and time of the upcoming musical masterpiece that you'll be playing. You can click the calendar icon to make your date selection a little easier.

2. Enter in Venue and Cost.

If you actually want some people come to your show, it's probably a good idea to let them know where you're actually playing and how much it's going to cost them to get in once they walk in the door.

3. Enter in show location information.

Enter in all show location information that you can. This location info can be searched by other MySpacers who might be looking for a show to check out.

4. Enter a Description.

Are you going to be solo? Should people wear orange tube socks? Is there a great place to park that only you know about? Things like these would be great to add into the description so the people who end up coming to your show know everything they need to for maximum enjoyment. The better time they have, the more likely they are to love your band and come to the next show, and the next, and the next . . .

5. Click the Update button.

After you've filled out everything that you want, click the Update button. This will then take you to the Preview Show window, as shown in Figure 14-4.

6. Click the Save Show button.

If the preview looks good, click the Save Show button and save the show for good.

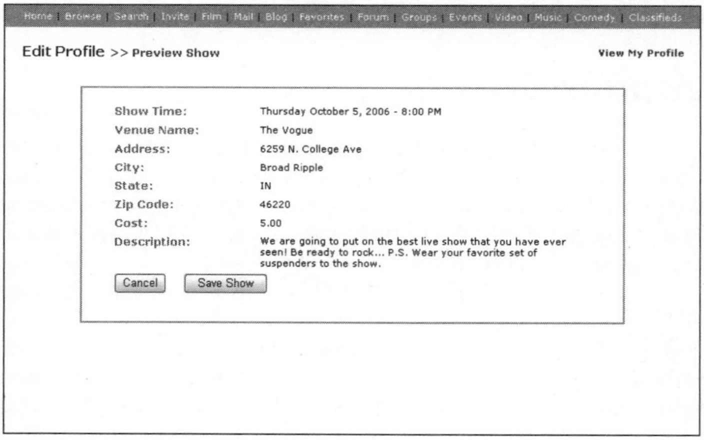

Figure 14-4:
The Preview Show window gives you one last look at your upcoming event before you save it.

After you save the show, it will be listed under the upcoming show form so you can edit or delete it if needed. After you've added the gig to your Upcoming Shows list, the show will be displayed in two places. One place it is now displayed is in the Upcoming Shows box on your MySpace home page (your private administration page), as shown in Figure 14-5.

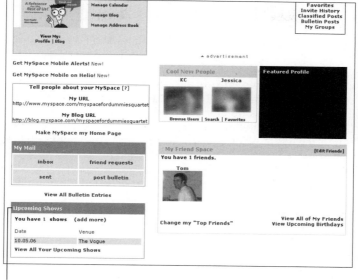

Figure 14-5:
After saved, the Upcoming Show can be seen on your MySpace Home Page.

The Upcoming Shows box

The other place that the show is displayed is on your public MySpace music profile (the page that the public will see) in the Upcoming Shows section, as shown in Figure 14-6.

The Upcoming Shows section

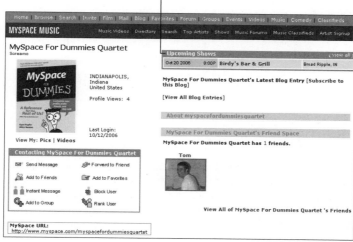

Figure 14-6:
The Upcoming Show is also added to your public profile page.

Band Details

The Band Details section is where you can enter in all the wonderful information that you feel the general public should know about you or your band. This section is split into specific segments that are designed to give people a better feel for what type of band you are and what type of music you play. After it's entered, all this information will be displayed on your public music profile for the world to see. It's a good idea to fill out as much of this as possible — that way, if someone who has never heard of you before stumbles upon your piece of the MySpace world, your new visitor will get a good understanding of what you're all about.

As seen in Figure 14-7, there are several sections that make up the Edit Band Bio window. Each section has an Edit button so you can go in and modify any information that you entered, whenever you feel the need to do so.

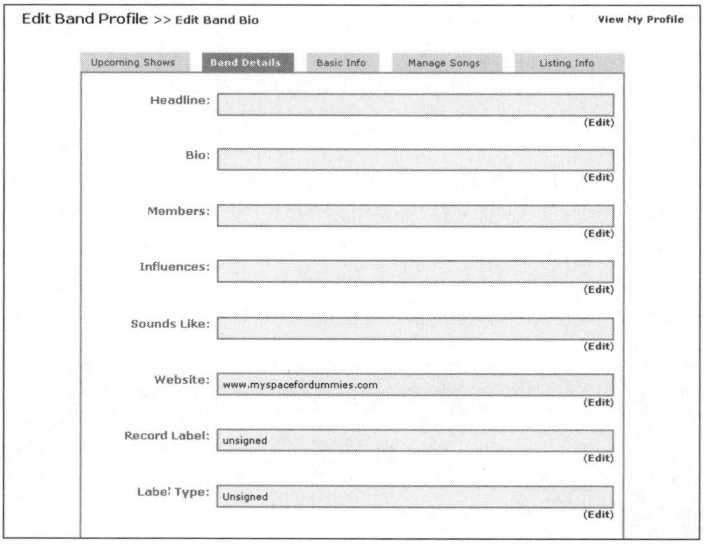

Figure 14-7:
The Edit Band Bio window is made up of eight sections.

The sections that you can change are as follows:

✔ **Headline:** The Headline is the quoted text that appears next to your profile picture on your public profile. This is something that most people will read when they find your MySpace page, so the more clever, the better.

✔ **Bio:** Every band or musician has a story. This section lets you tell it. Where did you come from? Where do you want to go? Why music? These are all questions that you can answer in the Bio section. Feel free to add pictures and links to give it even more depth.

✔ **Members:** Who makes up the band — what are their names, what do they play, who are their favorite performers? Let everyone in on this information — and more — in this section.

✔ **Influences:** Many musicians started playing in the first place because other musicians inspired them at some time in their lives. Did someone ever inspire you — how about two or three musical heroes of yours? If so, feel free to add them in here. This is a great place to add links for additional information on your influences; don't expect the general public to know musicians as well as you do.

✔ **Sounds Like:** "If you like *blank*, you will definitely dig our music." If you've ever said this, fill in this section, putting whomever you're using as a role model in the *blank*. It's always good to relate your music to a more well-known band so people can get a better feel for what type of music you play.

✔ **Web Site:** If you have another site that's outside the MySpace world, type it in here so your fans can check it out. MySpace is a great tool for driving online traffic to other Web sites — so don't be afraid to use it that way.

✔ **Record Label:** Every musician wants a record label, but few actually have one. If you're one of the lucky few, fill out this section with a big smile on your face.

✔ **Label Type:** There are three choices for this section; Unsigned, Major, and Indie. Pick whichever one fits, and go with it.

Just as with a personal profile, HTML and CSS style sheets can be used in these different sections. This can help you add a more branded and engaging look to your music profile page, which could help draw more attention to your music. Refer to Chapter 12 for more the nuts and bolts of changing the look of your profile page to match your image.

Basic Info

The Basic Info tab is pretty straightforward. It's where you can edit your band's name and location information. It's no secret that bands often go through many changes as they move along — even the most successful ones — and if you just happen to feel the urge to give your band a different name, this is the place to make that change.

Manage Songs

Allowing those who come to your music page the ability to instantly listen to your songs through the MySpace Music Player is one of the major benefits of setting up a MySpace music profile. When you're ready to upload a few of your tunes so all the world can hear all that hard work you put in behind the recording mic, the Manage Songs tab is where you need to be. The steps to add a new song are as follows:

1. **Click the Add link in the Manage Songs window.**

   When you first click the Manage Songs tab, you will be taken to the Manage Songs window. There are two links that will get you on your way to uploading your first song to MySpace. You can click the Add link in the Add Your First Song text box, or you can click the Add a Song link in the Current Songs heading in the upper-right corner of the Manage Song window, as shown in Figure 14-8.

The Add links for adding a song

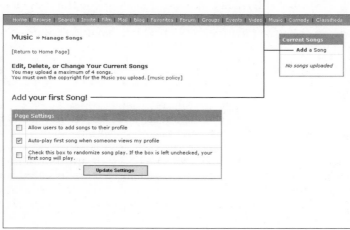

Figure 14-8: To upload your first song to MySpace, click one of the two Add links in the Manage Songs window.

2. **Enter in all song details and click the Update button.**

   After you click the Add link, you will be taken to the Edit Song Details window, where you can add in all the information about the song you're about to upload. Enter in the Song Name, Album Name, Album Year, Record Label, and Lyrics. If you're in a hurry, you can skip most of this stuff for now — the only required field that you must fill in is the song name.

There are two option check boxes at the bottom of the Edit Details window that you should pay attention to. These two check boxes are options for how users can interact with the songs that you upload to the MySpace Music Player. The two options are

- **Allow users to rank this song:** By checking this option, your fellow MySpacers will not only be able to listen to your songs, but they will also be able to rank them from a scale of 1-10 and comment on the song as well. This gives your fans a chance to let you know exactly how they feel about your tunes.

Checking this box can open up a great channel for feedback from listeners — just be sure that you're ready to hear it.

- **Allow users to download this song:** If you want to give your listeners the option to download your song from the MySpace Music Player, you should check this option. Most bands that are signed to a label don't use this option because they obviously want their listeners to buy their music. But, if your main goal is to just get your music out there for as many people to hear as possible, why not let your listeners download it?

One of the great things about this option is that your songs are hosted by MySpace — so theoretically a song of yours could be downloaded a million times and you wouldn't have to pay for one cent of bandwidth costs. MySpace is there to take care of all that. Pretty nice of them, eh? (Of course, whether *you* make any money from all that downloading is a whole other issue.)

3. **Upload the MP3 file of your song.**

   After you've entered in all your song information and clicked the Update button, you will then be taken to the MP3 upload window, as shown in Figure 14-9. This is where you upload the MP3 file of the song you wish to add to your MySpace Music Player. It's a simple process:

   a. Click the Browse button and locate the MP3 on your local hard drive.

   b. After you find the MP3 you're looking for, select it and click the Upload button.

   This uploads your MP3 to MySpace so it can be streamed from the Music Player on your MySpace music profile.

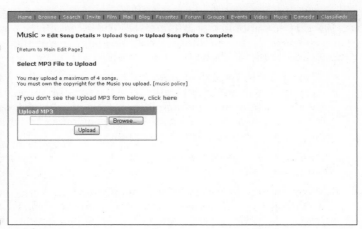

Music » **Edit Song Details » Upload Song » Upload Song Photo » Complete**

[Return to Main Edit Page]

Select MP3 File to Upload

You may upload a maximum of 4 songs.
You must own the copyright for the Music you upload. [music policy]

If you don't see the Upload MP3 form below, click here

Upload MP3

[_____] [Browse...]

[Upload]

Figure 14-9:
The MP3 upload window is where you can upload your music files to your MySpace Music Player.

An MP3 file (short for MPEG-1 Audio Layer 3) has quickly become the standard for digital music over the past few years. It is by far the most popular and widely used audio format on the Internet today. Although there are many different types of audio file formats, MySpace only allows MP3s to be uploaded to their music player. If you want to learn more about digital music and MP3s, check out *WindowsXP Digital Music For Dummies* book by Ryan Williams (Wiley Publishing, Inc.). It covers how to create, manage, and distribute audio in a digital world. For MySpace, stick with MP3s.

4. Upload an image for your song.

After you upload the MP3 file for your song, you then have the option of adding an image for the song as well. This is all done through the Upload Song Photo window that you're taken to after your MP3s upload is completed. You can add a different image to each song that you upload and don't worry, if you want to change these images later, you can. You can add an image now if you like — or you can click the Skip for Now link and add it later. To add an image, you have two (probably very familiar) things to do:

a. Click the Browse button to select an image from your local hard drive.

b. After you've selected the image, click the Upload button to add it to your song.

If you see a pattern emerging here, you're on to something.

5. Upload additional songs.

After you upload the MP3 file for your song, you then have the option of adding an image for the song as well. After you've finished with the Upload Song Photo window, you wind up back at the main Manage Songs window. At this point, you can add another song if you like. There are just a few things to remember at this point:

- MySpace allows you to upload four songs to your MySpace Music Player, so feel free to add more if you want.

- After you add a song, MySpace will process the MP3 so it can be streamed via your Music Player.

- The amount of time for this whole process to finish its business depends on the amount of MySpace traffic during your upload and the size of your MP3 file.

- As MySpace is processing your newly uploaded musical masterpieces, there will be a red Processing message under the image of those particular songs, as shown in Figure 14-10. This lets you know that MySpace is working on getting those particular files up and running on your music player.

After the Processing message is gone, your music should be streaming on your public MySpace profile.

Figure 14-10:
Once uploaded, the Processing message lets you know that MySpace is working on getting your songs added to your MySpace Music Player.

The Processing message

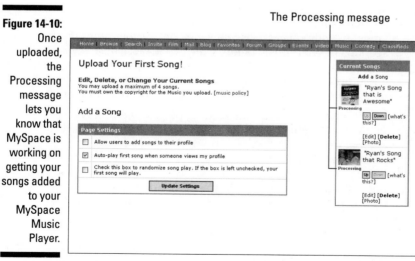

6. **Choose your Page Settings.**

Now that you've uploaded your songs to MySpace, they will be added to your MySpace Music Player so anyone who comes to your music profile can listen to your tunes. With this addition of music to your profile, you now have a few more options that you can choose to modify regarding the songs you've posted. These three options are listed as check boxes on the main Manage Songs window under the Page Settings heading. Here's what these options do:

- **Allow users to add songs to their profile:** Any MySpacer has the option to add any song that is posted to MySpace to his or her personal profile — but only if the artist explicitly allows it by checking this box.

  By clicking the Add link under a song that's listed on a musician's MySpace Music Player, as shown in Figure 14-11, any user can add your song to their MySpace profile.

  By allowing other MySpacers to add your song to their profiles, you're giving your fans (and other people who like your music but may not want to rip your shirt off) the chance to promote your tunes to whomever happens to visit their personal MySpace pages. Note that this option is unchecked by default; if you want it, check it.

- **Auto-play first song when someone views my profile:** If this option is checked, your MySpace Music Player will begin to play your songs as soon as someone opens up your music profile. Many musicians like this option; the idea is that when a potential fan lands on your space, those new ears get to hear at least a few seconds of your music before they can leave. These few seconds could be enough of a listen to keep them around a little longer and could potentially result in your gaining a newfound fan — which is never a bad thing. No wonder this option is checked by default.

- **Check this box to randomize song play. If the box is left unchecked, your first song will play:** This option is basically the MySpace Music Player's version of shuffle. If you want one song in particular to play every time that someone visits your profile, leave this unchecked. Many bands like to randomize their songs because they don't want a frequent visitor to hear the same thing over and over with every visit (that's thinking like a visitor — pretty savvy). But if you want to make sure everyone hears the song you think is destined to be the next huge hit single, leave this option unchecked — and let your future blockbuster play on. This option is unchecked by default.

The MySpace Music Player   The Add link

Figure 14-11:
By clicking the Add link, MySpace users can add any musician's songs to their own profiles.

Listing Info

If you're reading this and you're a musician, you know how quickly a band can break up, change members, switch genres, and modify their name. If you or your band decide that you should now play jazz instead of rockabilly — or you've added some hip-hop to your act — you can make sure that your MySpace music profile reflects it. Your Listing Info window allows you to change/add additional genres to your music as well as change your MySpace music URL. If you're starting to suspect that the URL `MySpace.com/ CrazyDinosaurUncles` doesn't quite fit your folk-music groove, no problem: You can change that URL with a click of a button in the Listing Info tab. Keep that folk music rocking!

MySpace — a Music Fan's Paradise

There are thousands of bands putting music into the MySpace world and millions of people eager to consume it, creating an unparalleled distribution environment. With so many choices about the music you can hear and where and how you consume it, it is truly an amazing time to be a music fan. Certain music-related elements have been around since the beginning of MySpace, but when it comes to music, there's always something fresh and new lurking up MySpace's digital sleeve. It's a part of what continues to fuel the phenomenal growth and success of this online community.

In the following sections, you will discover some of the ways that the millions of MySpacers can currently interact with music on a day-to-day basis, as well as some things that are coming up just around the corner. It's safe to say that everyone likes to involve music in their lives in one way or another — and with MySpace, getting your musical fix has never been easier.

The almighty MySpace Music Player

If you want to pinpoint one of the things that drove musicians to MySpace by the truckload, you need to look no further than the MySpace Music Player. The MySpace Music Player — shown in Figure 14-12 — has been a feature of MySpace from the beginning. By now, it's become the most popular way to listen to music online. The MySpace Music Player gave musicians an outlet to the masses — offering an even playing field for any band that used it, no matter how obscure. Who needs radio play when you could (potentially, anyway) have *millions* of people listen to your song on MySpace? With MySpace, any band has a shot at building up an astronomical audience of listeners — and it all started with this somewhat simple streaming music player. Brilliant.

Figure 14-12:
The MySpace Music Player is one feature that benefits musicians as well as their fans.

Though the bands and musicians love the MySpace Music Player, the fans on MySpace love it even more. A band's MySpace Music Player gives any potential fan an instant taste of what the musician has to offer. No downloads, no payment, and no hassles. Giving power to the people has never been so hip.

So what makes up this seemingly simple music player? Check out the following list:

- **Instant access:** You want to hear the music now? You got it. The MySpace music player gives anyone the opportunity to listen to that potential-next-breakthrough band instantly. The proof is right there — and you "so totally" knew them before they went mainstream and sold out.

- **Interaction and feedback:** So you *really like* that song, huh? Or maybe you *really can't stand* that song. Either way, you now have a platform for voicing your opinion to the rest of the MySpace community. The MySpace Music Player has a rating and comment system that lets you voice whatever opinion you want to, when you want to. The musician also has the option of allowing song downloads through the MySpace Music Player — making you potentially only one click away from having your own copy of their must-have MP3.

   Also — if you've always wondered what that band was *actually* singing in that one song you can't seem to get out of your head? The MySpace Music Player has a Lyrics option too, so wonder no more — it's all spelled out in black and white.

- **Easy to distribute:** No longer do you have to send songs via e-mail instant message so your friends can listen to that new song you just discovered by that band no one's heard of yet (but you figure everybody will know about real soon now). Just send them the band's MySpace URL and they'll be listening in no time.

- **Standalone Player option:** If you just can't seem to get enough of that new band, but you don't want to hang out on MySpace at work all day (even if you'd like to), just click the Standalone Player button that's on each MySpace Music Player. You'll then have your own personal jukebox full of your band's goodies that can float over even the harshest of Excel spreadsheets during your workday.

- **Ability to add songs to personal profile:** Any song that you can listen to on a musician's MySpace Music Player can potentially be added to your personal MySpace page as well. You can do this handy bit of magic by clicking the Add button below each song — it's just that easy. And it's a great way to show your friends your new favorite song — while also adding a little bit of personality to your page.

Top Artist listings

Everyone enjoys music — but lets face it, we don't have the time nor the energy to constantly keep up with which bands are hot at any given moment. MySpace has realized this, and has created something that might just help you keep up with the who's who of the MySpace music world. This simple, yet powerful MySpace music feature is the MySpace Top Artists listings. These listings are a quick and easy way to find out who's making some serious noise on MySpace. Think of it as the MySpace version of the Billboard Top Ten.

You can check out the Top Artist listings by first clicking the Music link in the main MySpace navigation, and then by clicking the Top Artists link in the main music navigation links.

When you've got the Top Artists window on-screen, as shown in Figure 14-13, you can then sort the Top Artists by several different criteria such as Country, State, and Genre. Want to see who the hot, local rock musicians are in Indiana? Just select United States, Indiana, and Rock, click Update and see who comes up. The Top Artists are also separated into columns depending on whether is the band is unsigned, indie (independent), or signed to a major record label.

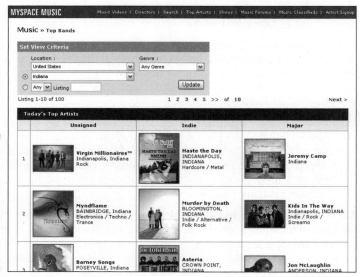

Figure 14-13:
The Top
Artists
window will
help you
keep up
who's hot on
MySpace.

The Top Artists are ranked depending on the play that their MySpace Music Player is getting, so it is a true view of what the millions of MySpacers are currently listening to. This is different than the Featured Artists on MySpace, which are dictated by the MySpace powers-that-be.

Music Videos

As numbers and airtime for music videos on television continue to drop, the popularity of music videos on sites such as MySpace is quickly picking up the slack. Music videos on MySpace Music are getting more and views every single day and they have become the easiest way to see your favorite main-stream musician doing their thing. Unlike television viewers, MySpacers no longer need to "tune in" at certain times to catch a glimpse of the latest and greatest music videos (and hope the good ones are on the air). They can now get the videos they want, when they want them, in a place where they're already spending their time.

If you want to go watch a few videos, click the Music link in the main MySpace navigation, and then click the Music Videos link in the main music navigation. This will take you to the MySpace Music Videos window, as shown in Figure 14-14, where you can watch the most popular videos or search for a particular artist, song, or genre. All your favorite music videos are now at your fingertips — it's a beautiful thing.

Figure 14-14: With MySpace Music Videos, watching your favorite artists has never been easier.

Finding live shows

With MySpace, it has never been easier to find new music you love, catch the details about local shows in your area, and even get in touch with others who have similar musical tastes. So, if you live on a farm in Iowa but can't get enough Cajun Zydeco music, you'll still be able to keep your finger on the pulse.

With the incredible number of bands that are constantly writing updates, posting their tour schedules, and relying on MySpace to promote and distribute their music, you're going to have a hard time finding a better resource for getting information on live music on the Net. You want to find the next reggae show within 20 miles of the town you live in? No problem. Looking for a local hard-core rock show for some stress relief during your business trip? Piece of cake. With the Shows search feature that's included in the MySpace Music section, your next live music show is just a few clicks away.

Want to give the shows search a shot? Click the Music link in the main MySpace navigation, and then by clicking the Shows link in the main music navigation. When you get to the main Shows search window, as shown in Figure 14-15, you simply add in a ZIP code, a maximum distance for the search to cover, and the genre of music you want to find. Click the Sort button and every live show within your requested area will be shown. The shows are sorted by date and you can click the band or venue for more show information.

Figure 14-15:
The MySpace shows search allows you to easily find shows by location and genre.

The future of music on MySpace

Music serves as the poster child for digital convergence. As media has found its way to digital format, and shortly thereafter, the Internet, the way in which we enjoy our favorite tunes has forever changed. MySpace is continuing this evolution and helping millions of fans experience music they love.

Although MySpace has been very innovative up to this point when it comes to giving the public new and fresh ways to interact with music, without constantly adding new features and tools, MySpace could lose its very valuable audience of musicians. So how does MySpace keep the millions of people constantly coming back for more? Don't worry, they've got a few things up their sleeve that could potentially begin to redefine how you listen to, distribute, and buy your favorite tunes. MySpace has gathered the audience, and now it's time to give this audience what they want, when they want it, and how they want it. Here are a few new and innovative things that have either just hit the MySpace world or that are coming soon:

- ✔ **Cingular's Mobile Music Studio:** If you haven't noticed, ringtones are everywhere. You hear them at work, at the mall, and (unfortunately) sometimes in a movie theatre. At the moment, most of these ringtones are produced by big-time music labels — and (no surprise here) are songs played by mainstream artists. Well, MySpace has decided to shake up this model a bit — behold the Cingular Mobile Music Studio. Now any musician who has a few songs and a MySpace account can do the ringtone thing — not only create ringtones, but also sell them though MySpace. It's a new type of ringtone democracy — and it's happening now.

- ✔ **Paid music downloads:** At the time of the writing of this book, MySpace has been in talks with PayPal, an online payment gateway, about creating an all-new paid music portal on MySpace that would rival the current 800-pound gorilla of music downloads, iTunes. With 100+ million members and climbing, who says that this can't work? It's just the next big thing for MySpace. I'm sure there's more where this came from.

- ✔ **Third-party tools:** Some of the latest tools for MySpace aren't necessarily created by MySpace. Many third party software developers are creating online "widgets" that can be used within the MySpace world. Some of these things include video platforms, news feeds, and various online payment systems. The popularity of MySpace looks like it won't be slowing down anytime soon — so don't be surprised if these third-party developers continue to jump on the MySpace bandwagon.

So, whether you're a musician or just someone who want to find some great tunes on the Net, MySpace definitely rocks as the place to get your fix for all things music. As the popularity of MySpace has grown, the tools and services that the community provides only get better and better. What will MySpace come up with next? All you have to do is log on to find out.

Chapter 15

Finding Your Place on MySpace

At some point over the course of human civilization, we came to realize that there was "power in numbers." Because of that, we've spent thousands of years gathering together in a variety of ways. We gather as families, friends, and fans. We participate in churches, clubs, and companies. Although the various members of any such group may have differing levels of involvement and different responsibilities therein (janitor, accountant, sales manager, and so on), they all come together for a common interest or for the pursuit of a common goal. Life on the Internet has followed suit with the emergence of online social networking.

Though many people gather on MySpace, they come for a multitude of reasons. Not only is this a place for musicians, their fans, their fans' friends, and so on, it's increasingly the destination for a multitude of other groups who are seeking an audience. In this chapter, we find out more about how MySpace is creating tools and forums to help its millions of users not only show what they've got, but also find just the kind of fan involvement they need.

Build It and They Will Come

As membership at MySpace continues to grow, so does its ability to create and connect more specific groups of people with each other. The more people, the bigger the audience becomes — and the more specific the niches are able to become. Because of the huge numbers of diverse people, MySpace is now able to separate profiles and create specific tools and services to provide an even better user experience.

The quick appeal and adoption of music profiles definitely jumpstarted the MySpace community — and proved that it was a model for online interconnection that would resonate with people. But now, with its mainstream acceptance, there's a huge opportunity and a growing demand for places other than music-dominated sites; millions of MySpacers want to carve out their digital niches and score their daily doses of information on all sorts of creative interests. MySpace has responded to this new demand by creating new specialty-profile options — as well as some online services that are starting to make MySpace the one-stop shop for all things Web. The bigger the audience, the more new and innovative things MySpace can develop for its users. With the incredible growth MySpace is now seeing, who knows what will come next? A look at some of its more creative niches may offer a clue . . .

MySpace Filmmakers

MySpace entered into the online world at a time when video creation, distribution, and consumption is becoming easier than ever for the population at large. The world's video-distribution channels are no longer restricted to that big box in your living room and that monster-sized Cineplex that's down the street from you. With a little bit of knowledge, cash, and an Internet connection, anyone can now create videos — and potentially get them viewed by millions of people within minutes. It's the democratization of media — and MySpace has staked its claim in the middle of the revolution. If you have something to say, get it out there — the best work gets noticed, as do the people who create it.

It's a whole new age of consumer-driven video and *prosumers* — folks who use semi-pro equipment to fill the roles of both media producers and consumers. No wonder a need has sprung up for new ways to organize and make sense of this massive influx of online video to Web sites such as MySpace. Well, we can safely advise our video-producing friends not to fret. MySpace has not only noticed the need, they've actually done something about it: They've created a specialty profile specifically for filmmakers. To all the future Quentin Tarantinos and Steven Spielbergs out there, welcome — MySpace has been waiting for you.

Opportunity awaits

For as long as you can remember, the bright lights of Hollywood have been calling your name. Since you were 8 years old, you've found ways to work phrases into your everyday conversation such as, "Lets do lunch," "I'll be in my trailer," and "Don't even think of getting a scratch on my Maserati." There's already a vacant spot on your mantle — just between the Mr. T bobblehead and the aromatherapy candle — waiting for your first Academy Award.

Thanks to affordable technology, it's never been easier to get started making films. For a few hundred dollars, you can pick up a digital video camera and all the software you need to pull together that amazing story you've been aching to tell. With the further emergence of broadband Internet as a delivery system — and online video as content — technology has also made it significantly easier to get your film "seen" by the masses. The playing field is more even than ever before — it's all a matter of how you choose to take advantage of it. MySpace is ready to help get you on your way to the red carpet.

Perks of a MySpace Filmmaker profile

Ready to make your mark in the world of film? Well, first things first, and a great place to start your soon-to-be-incredibly-rich-and-famous film career is on MySpace. Just as with music, MySpace has a specialty profile that can be created specifically for filmmakers. Choosing to create a MySpace Filmmaker profile gives you access to tools and services that designed to get your filmmaking off to a flying start. A few of these include

- ✔ **Filmmaker Info:** Along with the normal information that you would include on a personal MySpace profile, a Filmmaker profile goes a few steps farther — giving you places to add information specific to filmmaking and to your videos as you bring them to (at first) the small screen. You can list your role in filmmaking, awards you've won, festivals you've attended, and more.

  The Filmmaker profile is built for those who are in the industry, so it's important that the information you add reflects that level of professionalism.

- ✔ **Screenings Calendar:** Musicians have to book live shows, and filmmakers have an equivalent: booking movie screenings. Even though MySpace gives you a way to reach and gather up an audience for your films, its true power and value show up best when you can get your fans to leave their computers and head over to a theater to check out your work. Posting your screenings — and getting them in front of your MySpace fanatics — is the first step in making your next screening standing-room-only.

- ✔ **Video Management:** The MySpace Filmmaker profile makes it really easy for you to manage all the video you're producing. With film-specific information for each film — and the capability to upload them to a video player that appears on-screen on your profile — showcasing your films has never been easier.

Creating your Filmmaker profile

Creating a Filmmaker profile is very similar to creating a personal MySpace profile — discussed in Chapter 2 — except you'll find a few differences that make this type of profile an easy-to-use platform to show off your video masterpieces. So when you're ready — take a breath, focus, and imagine yourself taking that one big step toward creating the blockbuster that's playing in the back of your mind. Then follow these steps to create your Filmmaker profile:

1. **Click the Film link at the top of the MySpace.com homepage.**

   This will take you to the MySpace Film portal — the home for all thing film.

2. **Click the Filmmaker Signup link in the main MySpace Film navigational links.**

   The Filmmaker Signup link, as shown in Figure 15-1, is the very last link on the right side of the MySpace Film navigational links. After clicking this link, you're be taken to the Filmmaker registration window.

3. **Enter in your basic account information.**

   Enter in your e-mail, username, location, date of birth, check the I Accept the Terms of Service/Privacy Policy box, and click the Sign Up button to get your registration rolling.

4. **Enter in your specific film information.**

   The next Additional Info window, shown in Figure 15-2, allows you to enter in your specific filmmaking information — such as your role in the process, your current filmmaker status, and any awards you have won. When you're done entering this information, it's displayed on your public profile. (Think of it as an instant online résumé.) Click the Continue button to keep your registration moving along.

   If you're in a hurry, you only need to select one Role and your Status. You can add the rest of the info later on if needed by editing your profile information.

5. **Upload your profile photo.**

   You know that having a great video isn't the only thing that makes you a successful filmmaker. You've got to act the part — and convincingly — to let people know who you are and what your work is all about. You can help other MySpacers paint the picture of who you really are by adding some photos of yourself to your profile — to demonstrate that you're so much more than just another warm body behind the lens. At the very least, adding a photo as your profile picture lets the other users on MySpace know that you're profile is legit. To upload a photo, click the Browse button on the Upload Photo form, find a photo or image on your local hard drive, select it, and click the Upload button. Piece of cake, right?

The Filmmaker Signup link

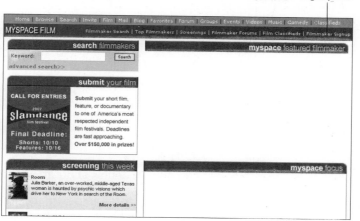

Figure 15-1:
The
Filmmaker
Signup link
is located
on the far-
right side of
the main
MySpace
Film navi-
gational
links.

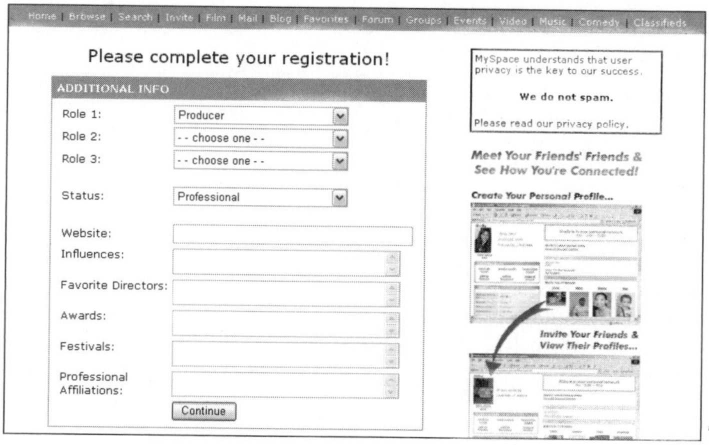

Figure 15-2:
You can
enter more
specific
filmmaking
information
into the
Additional
Info
window.

If, for some reason, you're super-impatient, you can click the Skip for
Now link at the bottom of the photo-upload form to move on the next
step without adding a photo. But make sure that you add one sometime
soon, you don't want to be "that person" without any photos, especially
if you're offering work in a visual medium.

6. Invite some of your friends to MySpace.

Ah, publicity — the filmmaker's friend. Starting modestly by generating a
little buzz may be the ticket — so why not increase your MySpace audience directly? If you happen to have some friends you think would enjoy

becoming part of the MySpace world — but they haven't made the move yet — feel free to invite them with the MySpace invitation form. If you don't feel the need to send anything out, click the Skip for Now link in the bottom-right corner of the invitation form and you'll be one more step closer to creating your profile. (Don't worry, you're almost done — you should be able to see the light at the end of the tunnel.)

7. **Upload your first film.**

   At this point, your Filmmaker profile is actually created — congratulations. You're now taken to the Manage Films window, as shown in Figure 15-3. This will be your main window for adding, deleting, and editing your film's information. If you're feeling a little frisky about keeping this MySpace train rolling, and you happen to have your first film ready to upload, go ahead! You can find out the details about how to doing the upload in the next section, "Managing your Filmmaker profile." You can always come back later to use the Manage Films window, so it's no big deal if you want to add a few films after you take a quick nap.

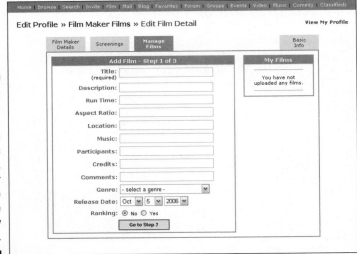

Figure 15-3:
When you get to the Manage Films window, your MySpace Film profile is officially created.

You've staked your filmmaking claim in the land of MySpace by creating an official Filmmaker profile, so now what? Well, the next step would be getting your videos up online — and to cultivate your understanding of how to make your profile start working for you. The following sections help you figure all this out — so keep on reading. You don't want to keep Hollywood waiting.

Managing your Filmmaker profile

Creating the profile and adding the films are the start, but by no means do they guarantee that anyone will take notice. MySpace delivers the audience — and it provides all sorts of tools to help you reach out to all those people — but if you fail to initiate at least some communication, you'll have to struggle to reap any rewards. Commit to taking advantage of the contacts MySpace makes available — and reach out through consistent, regular correspondence with the people who have an interest in your work. For tips on how to do that, check out Chapter 5.

After you have created your Filmmaker profile, all your film-specific options can be found by clicking the Edit Profile link. As shown in Figure 15-4, the Edit Profile link is located on your MySpace homepage, just to the right of your profile picture. These options are the main differences between a Filmmaker profile and personal profile on MySpace — and they've been created specifically to help you manage and distribute your films to your heart's content.

The Edit Profile link

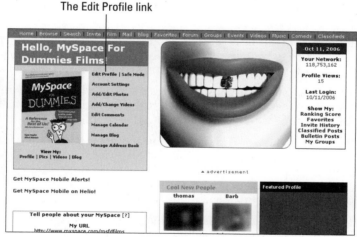

Figure 15-4: You can view and edit your filmmaking options by clicking the Edit Profile link.

There are three four main tabbed sections found on your Edit Profile window. By editing the information within each section, you can flesh out your Filmmaker profile in its most productive direction. We'll give you a closer look at each section.

Film Maker Details

The Film Maker Details tab, shown in Figure 15-5, lets you manage a majority of the text and information that will be displayed on your public filmmaker profile. There are eight fields listed under this tab that you can enter information into. To edit any of the fields, simply click the Edit link that's located under each one. The fields are as follows:

- **Roles:** This is where you can list what your role is in relation to the films being showcased on your profile page. Are you a jack-of-all-trades — multiple personalities, all talented? There are three options available, so you should be taken care of.

- **Status:** Are you a full-out pro, or are you still learning the tricks of the trade at that super-hip film school out in California? Let people know your film status by announcing yourself a Student, a Professional, or an Amateur.

- **Web Site:** Here's where you list any other sites you might have that contribute to your filmmaking. MySpace can be a great tool for sending people to already-established Web sites outside (but related to) the MySpace world. Remember, there is an entire Web out there — take advantage of it.

- **Influences:** In this field, you can enter names of the people who have inspired you to become the remarkable filmmaker that you are today. This, of course, is a digital "shout-out" to those you admire. Give 'em a holler!

- **Directors:** You can list any directors that you admire here, or if you're a director — feel free to list yourself, after all, you've earned it. There's nothing wrong with a little self-promotion, right?

- **Awards:** Let the world know just how awesome you really are by adding a few of your awards on your profile. No awards to speak of? Make up a few (Sasquatch Documentarian of the Decade, Hopscotch Grand Master, Prom Video Editing Co-Chair, and so on) and see if anyone notices. As long as your imagination is rampant and obvious, what could it hurt?

- **Festivals:** For many filmmakers, going to festivals can make or break their careers. If you're going to any festivals — or are making serious plans to go — add them in this field.

- **Professional Affiliations:** Show people just how connected you are by listing the professional organizations you belong to, and who you've worked with — or who you're currently working for — in the industry. Maybe you'll find some fellow members whom you've never met.

For most of these fields, MySpace allows you to add text to your heart's content — till the sun comes up, the cows come home, or (okay) you get it all said. You can also use HTML in many of these fields as well, so feel free to add any videos, images, and links that can help tell your story with maximum panache. Need some HTML tips? Check out the Cheat Sheet that was included with this book for a jumpstart.

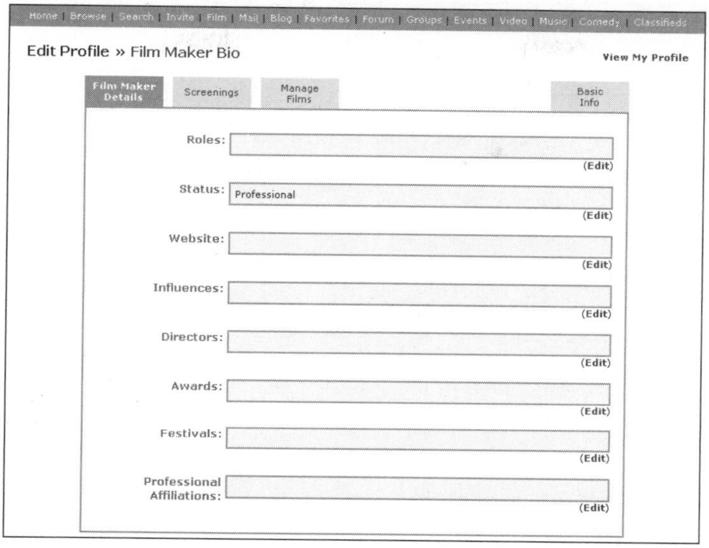

Home | Browse | Search | Invite | Film | Mail | Blog | Favorites | Forum | Groups | Events | Video | Music | Comedy | Classifieds

Edit Profile » Film Maker Bio   View My Profile

| Film Maker Details | Screenings | Manage Films | | Basic Info |

Roles: _____
(Edit)

Status: [Professional]
(Edit)

Website: _____
(Edit)

Influences: _____
(Edit)

Directors: _____
(Edit)

Awards: _____
(Edit)

Festivals: _____
(Edit)

Professional Affiliations: _____
(Edit)

Figure 15-5: The Film Maker Details tab is where you can add information that will show up on your public filmmaker profile.

Film Maker Screenings

Even with the nearly overwhelming amounts of video available online these days, lots of folks still have the desire to move away from the computers now and then — and into an actual movie theatre. (And why not? The screens are *way* bigger.) When you finally finish your next big film, you're going to want people to come check out your screenings. MySpace knows this and has created a great way to help you get your audience in the know about your upcoming events.

The Screenings tab, as shown in Figure 15-6, is where you can start adding the events that you want people to know about. To add an event, fill out all the information in the Screenings form — which includes Screening Date, Screening Time, Location, Cost, and Description. After you have it all filled out, click the Update button to save the event information.

After you add an event here, it will be listed at the bottom of the Screenings window for review and editing if needed. The event information is also displayed at the top of your public Filmmaker profile in the Upcoming Screenings box, as shown in Figure 15-7. This box will not appear unless you have entered in at least one upcoming event.

Just because the box is called Upcoming Screenings, don't feel like those are the only events you can list here. Any other parties, events, or casual get-togethers that you want your fellow MySpacers to know about can also be added here. Of course, if they're film-related, so much the better.

Figure 15-6: The Screenings tab is where you can add any event that you want to be displayed on your public filmmaker profile.

The Upcoming Screenings box

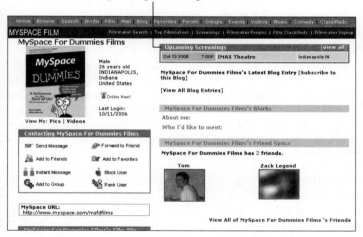

Figure 15-7: After you add an item into the Screenings window, it appears in the Upcoming Screenings section on your public filmmaker profile.

Manage Films

Considering that you have just set up your MySpace Filmmaker profile, you're probably ready to get to the part where you learn how to upload your films and other videos so you can start building your army of fans. Well, my friend, the Manage Films tab — shown in Figure 15-8 — is the section you've been waiting for. This is where the movie magic (the organizational part of it, anyway) happens.

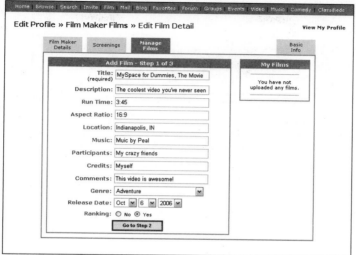

Figure 15-8:
The Manage Films tab is where you can start uploading your films and videos.

So you're finally ready for some video-uploading action, eh? To post your initial piece of motion-picture art (or that intriguing clip that showcases your potential) posted to your profile, follow these steps:

1. **Fill out all applicable film details.**

   Enter any and all the film information you can. The only required field is Title, but the more information you can add, the better. If you want the MySpacers who watch your videos to be able to rank your work, change the Rank option to Yes.

2. **Click the Go to Step 2 button to continue your video upload.**

3. **Upload your video file.**

   You should now see the video-upload form. It's the vehicle that gets your video files to MySpace. You do the upload in two stages:

   a. Click the Browse button and find your video file on your computer's local hard drive.

   b. After you find the video file you want, select it and click the Upload button to begin the upload.

Depending on your Internet connection and the size of your video file, the time that it takes to upload your file will vary. While you're uploading your file, there will be a status bar that displays the progress, as shown in Figure 15-9.

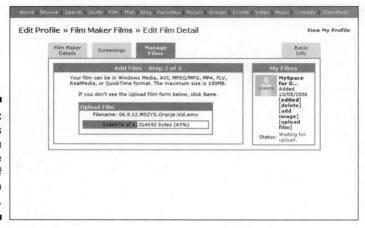

Figure 15-9:
The status
bar lets you
know the
progress of
your video
file upload.

MySpace allows for many different file formats to be uploaded to your profile. These allowed file types are RealMedia, or QuickTime format, Windows Media, AVI, MPEG, MPG, MP4, and FLV. Also, the maximum size for any single video upload is 100 MB.

4. **Upload an image for your film.**

   After your video is uploaded successfully, you will be taken directly to the Film Upload Image form. If you want to add an image that is displayed in your video player while your film is viewed, you can add one here. Simply click the Browse button and find the image you want to add. After you select the image, click Upload and the image will be attached to your newly uploaded film.

After you upload an image for your film, you will be returned to the first Manage Films window so you can add another film. Feel free to add another film at this point if you've got one ready. MySpace allows you to have four different films uploaded at the same time.

Also, more importantly, after your video files are uploaded and processed, they're loaded into the MySpace video player (shown in Figure 15-10), which appears on your public Filmmaker profile page after you've uploaded at least one video file. When your player is up and running, it's a pretty safe bet that you now have over 100 million potential fans — so the next order of business is to go find them.

The MySpace Film portal

If you decide to create a MySpace Filmmaker profile, you will automatically become part of the filmmaking community on MySpace. This means you've just joined a fast-growing group of MySpacers — any of whom could potentially become your filmmaking friends, fans, and teachers. But this also means that the more filmmakers sign up, the more competition you have as you cultivate your future audience. It's a tough world out there, but with enough work and a little bit of luck, you should be able to make your way through the clutter.

Figure 15-10: The MySpace video player appears on your public Filmmaker profile page after you upload a video file.

The MySpace Film portal, as show in Figure 15-11, is MySpace's way of creating order and organization for its massive community of filmmakers. (Coherence. What a concept.)

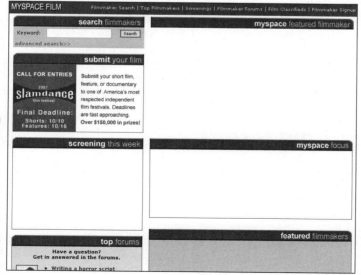

Figure 15-11: The MySpace Film portal is where you can find about all things filmmaking.

You can make your way over to the MySpace Film by clicking the Film link in the main MySpace navigation links. When you land on the portal, you'll find a few tools and services that you — whether as filmmaker or fan — should be aware of. These features can help keep you up to date on what's new in the world of film — an obvious benefit to your work. Each of these tools and services can be found by clicking the links in the main MySpace Film navigation links:

- **Filmmaker Search:** You can search MySpace for a specific filmmaker by their Role, Affiliations, and Location. This makes finding your next Screenwriter in Alabama just a few MySpace clicks away.

- **Top Filmmakers:** MySpace filmmakers are ranked by two different ways — video views and video rankings. If you want to see who's attracting all the eyeball attention on MySpace in your home state of Indiana, feel free.

- **Screenings:** Each filmmaker can enter his or her upcoming screenings and events so they're displayed on the Filmmaker profile. But there's another benefit to posting these events: They are also listed in this over-all Screenings listing on MySpace. The search results can be narrowed down by location too — which makes it a great tool for getting a line on who's doing the most dynamic things in your local film scene.

- **Filmmaker Forums:** Whether you need advice on a location to shoot (say, a scene in downtown Indianapolis) or you just want to find other people who love creating circus animations — or your interest is music video but you'd prefer holding a camera instead of a guitar — the film-maker forums can help you reach out and connect with what you're looking for.

- **Filmmaker Classifieds:** Just when you thought that camera you've had for the last five years was going to last another five, it dies on you during a critical shoot. Let the rest of the MySpace filmmakers know you're in the market for a new one by posting something in the Filmmaker Classifieds section. You'll be back up and running in no time.

MySpace Comedians

For some people, making milk shoot out of their friends' noses is a noble goal and a never-ending personal challenge. Think of the guy who's the life of the party — or that woman who's the one you want to hang out with when you need a bit of cheering up. Any time is ripe for uproarious laughter from friends and polite smiles from strangers. More than likely, this personality started early in life, and only grew as time went on. Monikers such as "class clown" seem to be thrown around freely, but some of those wacky folks truly have a gift. The world may be a stage — but now MySpace can deliver the audience.

Joining the MySpace Comedy community

Fortunately, if you're serious about not being serious, the world of MySpace Comedy is a great place to get exposure and continue to hone your craft. Whether your goal is to book some shows that are a little more prestigious than your cousin's fifth birthday party, promote your new comedy club, or earn your own late-night talk show, the key is all in getting the right exposure and building an audience (oh, yeah . . . it'll also help if you're actually funny, too).

In order to get your MySpace comedy career started, you first need to create a Comedy profile, which MySpace developed just for people just like you. Getting a Comedy profile up and running is as quick and easy as creating a personal MySpace profile — and it has a few cool things that were created specifically to help you showcase your humor to the masses. Here's a quick list:

- ✔ **Gig Management:** Keep track of your gigs and let everyone know that you host an open mic on Mondays down on Pico, or that you're headlining at the hottest new comedy club in town.

- ✔ **Comedy Focused Information:** All the information for your MySpace Comedy profile is based on your comedy experiences and influences — so anyone who lands on your space can get a good idea of what your humor is all about.

- ✔ **Video Clip Management:** It's one thing to tell people that you're funny — and it's another thing to actually be able to show them. Your MySpace Comedy profile lets you show your funniest video clips to the world. You're not camera-shy, are you?

Also, by creating your MySpace Comedy profile, you group yourself automatically with the rest of the comedians who have snagged a spot on the online community. This allows for easy connections between you and other comedians, as well as the millions of comedy fans who are out there waiting for you to make them laugh. The MySpace Comedy portal has quickly become the one-stop shop for all things funny on MySpace — and if you are a MySpace comedian, you're right in the middle of it. Who knows, if that next clip that you post gets enough views, you could find yourself moving your way up on the Top Comedians list. That will get some people's attention.

Creating your Comedy profile

Your family thinks you're funny. Your friends think you're funny. Your co-workers even think you're funny. Well, it doesn't take a genius to figure out that if all these people seem to think you've got a knack for keeping people in stitches, then there's a good chance that a majority of the MySpacers will think so too. There's only one way to find out . . .

Knock, knock. Who's there? MySpace. MySpace who? MySpace wants to laugh — so what are you waiting for? (Okay, okay. So maybe everybody *isn't* a comedian.)

Lame playground humor aside, remember: You're the comedian here. Hurry up and follow these steps so you can get your MySpace Comedy profile up and running before you have to hear another one of our jokes:

1. **Click the Comedy link on the MySpace.com homepage.**

    This will take you to the MySpace Comedy portal — be careful, it's awfully funny over there.

2. **Click the Comedian Signup link in the main MySpace Comedy navigational links.**

    The Comedian Signup link — shown in Figure 15-12 — is the very last link on the right side of the MySpace Comedy navigational links. After clicking this link, you're taken to the Comedian registration window.

The Comedian Signup link

Figure 15-12:
The Comedian Signup link is located on the far-right side of the main MySpace Comedy navigational links.

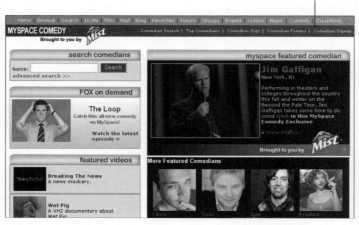

3. **Enter in your basic account information.**

    Enter in your e-mail, username, location, date of birth, check the I Accept the Terms of Service/Privacy Policy box, and click the Sign Up button to keep your future MySpace comedy career moving along. You'll be all set up before you know it.

4. **Choose your style of comedy.**

    So, what kind of comedian are you? Improv? Do you have some great impersonations of the president? After you get it all figured out, select at least one genre that you feel fits your style — and then click the Continue button.

5. Upload some photos to your profile.

You *know* you want to let people see that new sequined costume that you now wear on stage, and you just happen to have a picture. Let the world be dazzled — add a few of your latest and greatest photos of yourself here.

At the very least, you upload one photo so you have one for your profile picture. Uploading a photo is pretty painless:

a. Click the Browse button on the Upload Photo form.

b. Find a photo or image on your local hard drive.

c. Select the photo you want to display and click the Upload button.

Feel free to embrace your inner goofball, just remember what Mom always said, "if you hold your face that way for too long, it will stick that way."

After you upload your photos, your comedy profile is officially created. At this point, you can pick your MySpace home page so you can start playing with all the cool things that your new space in the MySpace world has to offer.

Although the comedy profile has some features that are specific to the comedy world, most of the communication tools — and how you use them — are the same for all MySpace users. Ready to start making a digital name for yourself? Start with the basics: Check out Part II for more information on getting connected to your fellow MySpacers.

Managing your MySpace Comedy profile

Getting your Comedy profile set up is a great first step towards phenomenal MySpace comedic stardom, but don't think that it stops there. Now that you have a place for your potential fans to go, keep 'em around awhile — create some things for them to interact with once they get there. The last thing you want is for someone to lose interest after taking the time to stop by your page — if there's nothing engaging or interesting to play with, they may be outta there. If this happens, it's likely they won't become your MySpace friend — and may never stop by again. I guess that if this happened, it would be the MySpace equivalent of hearing crickets chirping in the background during of one of your gigs, when what you want is a room full of raucous laughter. Maybe not as bad as getting hit by rotten fruit, but still not good.

That said, lets spice the place up a bit, huh? No problem. When you're looking to edit your MySpace Comedy profile, the place you always start from is the Edit Profile link on your MySpace home page. By clicking the Edit Profile link, as shown in Figure 15-13, you get wafted away to the main Edit Profile window, where you can add, edit, and delete the things on your public profile.

The Edit Profile link

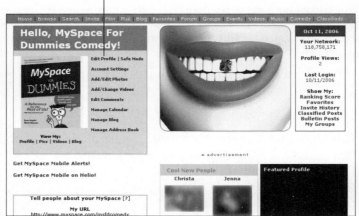

Figure 15-13:
The Edit
Profile link
is located to
the right of
your profile
image on
your
MySpace
home page.

After you find your way to the Edit Profile window, there are six tabs that
allow you to manage all your MySpace information easily.

Upcoming Gigs

This tab is where you can enter all your upcoming gigs and events that you
want all your fans to know about. You should enter in all information that you
can, such as Location, Cost, Date, Time, and Description. As shown in Figure
15-14, after you enter in a new gig, it will appear on your public profile for all
to see.

The Upcoming Gigs box

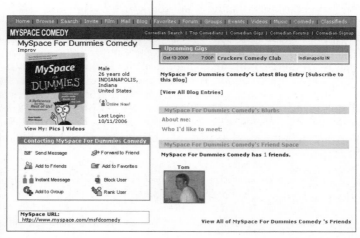

Figure 15-14:
After you
enter in a
new gig, it
will be
displayed
on your
Comedy
profile.

Career Details

Feel free to use this tab to lay it all out there about your career and how it fits into your life. The more people know about you (up to a certain point, of course), the more they can relate to you beyond the fact that you're somebody funny (we mean that in a *good* way) on the Internet.

There are eight editable fields listed under this tab that you can enter information into. To edit any of the fields, simply click the Edit link that's located under each one. The fields are as follows:

- **Headline:** This is the quote that shows up right next to your profile picture on your public profile page. If you've always wanted permission to be a wiseacre, you've got it here: Be a little witty. I dare you.

- **Bio:** I bet no one has any idea that you were raised by a herd of elephants on a tropical South Pacific Island. Tell your visitors the story — even show them a few pictures if you happen to have some. That should keep them coming back for more.

- **Members:** If you have others who join you during your comedic escapades, list them here. There's no I in TEAM, you know (though there is a "ME" if you rearrange the letters a little bit).

- **Influences:** SO many great comedians, so little time to list them. Tell the world who's to blame for making you the crazy, zany person you are today.

- **TV Appearances:** Jay Leno. Check. David Letterman. Check. Public access cable. Check. *COPS*. Check. (Wait a minute. Was that one funny?) Have you ever graced the world of mass media with your comedy? Go ahead and tell everyone how you made Conan O'Brien spit water out of his nose during your routine.

- **Film Appearances:** Many comedians dream about being seen on the big screen. If you've actually been there, you'd better tell everyone so they can be super-jealous. Oh, yeah, and see your movie.

- **Albums:** Comedians don't necessarily need to be seen — most just need to be heard. If you have a CD waiting to be bought out there somewhere, you had better let your fans know what it is — and how/where they can go buy it.

- **Website:** If you want to get your fans moving to another Web site besides your MySpace page, enter it here so they know about it.

Basic Info

Your basic info is, well, basic. This is where you can update your MySpace display name and location information. To change any of the information, just click the Edit button at the bottom of the form.

Manage Clips

When you have your own comedy profile on MySpace, there has never been a better reason (or maybe a perfect excuse) to go out and buy a video camera. The Manage Clips tab allows you to upload video clips of basically anything that you feel shows the world just how funny you really are. After you have uploaded your first few clips, they appear on your profile in an easy-to-use MySpace video viewer, as shown in Figure 15-15. Letting your fans watch your shtick, getting feedback on new material, and giving your audience behind-the-scenes access has never been easier.

Figure 15-15:
After your video clips are uploaded, the MySpace video clip player appears on your Comedy profile page.

Listing Info

This information lets people know another Web site that they can find you on as well as an option to choose what type of comedy styles you fall under. These styles, or genres, are what will categorize you on MySpace searches and listings, so make sure it's up to date and accurate.

After you have added all the info, videos, and what-not to your Comedy profile, you are now ready to entertain that future fan of yours who just happens to come across your profile. With all the great stuff you've added, there's no doubt in your mind that your visitors will be coming back for more — you even have the Friend Requests to prove it.

Basic Info (Again)

This is the second Basic Info tab and it allows you to enter more of your personal information that isn't necessarily related to comedy. These are the options that are available on a normal personal MySpace profile such as the schools that you've attended, any networking affiliations that you have, what companies you have worked for, and other personal background information.

The Beginning of MySpace Services

In the beginning, MySpace was about people connecting with people and finding out about bands they liked. Over time, the large numbers of MySpacers have made it an attractive portal for marketers, which has allowed an ever-expanding roster of services to be created. The sections that follow discuss a few of these first such opportunities, but there are many more to come!

MySpace Movies

It's safe to say that everyone likes movies — even if they don't all like the same ones. Now, you might like comedies while the next guys digs him some drama, but the bottom line is, movies rule. If you haven't noticed lately, movies aren't too cheap to produce. And for the movie to be a super-successful hit — maybe even cover its production costs (ya think?) — one thing must happen: People must go see to the theater to see it. Even today, DVD sales just can't cover the whole expense of making a movie. Well, friend, this means the huge movie-production companies need to get the word out about their next potential blockbuster — and the channel that gets the message communicated most effectively is, more and more, the online world — more specifically, MySpace.

This hankering to get the word out to a potential audience is a perfect fit with the MySpace Movies section. You want to go see cool movies, the moviemakers want you to *watch* their cool movies, and MySpace has a way to get people into the theater to see 'em. Beautiful, isn't it? The MySpace Movies portal, as shown in Figure 15-16, has now become the end-all-and-be-all place to find information about all things movie.

Some of Movie portal's features include these:

- **Show Times and Tickets:** With MySpace Movies, you don't have to leave MySpace to go dig up the show times for that next awesome film you want to see. And if you don't feel like waiting in line, there's an alternative: For most of the theatres listed, you can also buy tickets through MySpace.

- **Movie News:** Did you hear about that guy who did that one weird thing on the set of that movie in L.A.? (Boy, talk about your generic headline.) Well, if you want to know all about it, check out the Movie News section for all the latest movie-related news and of course, gossip.

✔ **New Movies:** You'll never feel out of the movie loop with the New Movies section. You can read about the movie, find show times, and watch the official movie trailers right from MySpace. So if, after all this research, you happen to catch a bad movie, it's no one's fault but your own.

✔ **Top Box Office:** MySpace makes it easy to see which movie has been bringing in all the cash the past week by posting the top ten movies in the Top Box Office section.

Figure 15-16:
You can stay updated on movies, search show times, and buy tickets by checking out the MySpace Movies portal.

MySpace Books

MySpace is fun. Reading is fundamental. What a perfect fit, eh? The MySpace Books portal, as shown in Figure 15-17, is a place where you can go to search for author information, check out the top-sellers list, and even buy a few literary works if you feel like it. Some of the other things you do can while hanging out at the MySpace books portal include these:

✔ **Feature Blogs:** Feeling like staying strictly digital when it comes to your reading habits? Blogs have quickly become very hot with many Internet readers and MySpace fuels the fire by always showcasing a featured MySpace blogger's work right on the main portal page. With a little help from MySpace, it's never been easier to get your thoughts and ideas out to the masses.

✔ **Buy Books from Amazon:** Thanks to a partnership with Amazon.com, MySpace lists several books for sale on its portal page. If you feel like you're ready to make a purchase, you're only a few clicks away from completing an order.

✔ **Reader Search:** Want to find another MySpacer who is into the same type of books you are? With the Reader Search feature, it's never been easier to pinpoint someone with interests like yours. Search away my friend, search away.

✔ **Book Groups:** The only thing better than reading a great book is talking about a great book with other people. The MySpace Book Groups allow you to easily find, connect, and interact with those who have your same taste in books.

Figure 15-17: The MySpace Books portal will help feed the bookworm in you.

MySpace Jobs

Whether you're spending it because you have to, or you're spending it because you need to, you're most likely spending cash all the time. But every dollar you spend has to come from somewhere — and unless you're a rich oil tycoon's kid or have recently hit the lottery, it usually comes in the form of a paycheck . . . from your job (or jobs). Ah, yes, that place so many of us spend a whole lot of waking hours — the always-fun J-O-B. Basically, everyone needs one — and I'm guessing that you may know a few people who are currently looking for one. Bottom line: If you don't have one, you need one — and if you've got one, you wouldn't be the only person who wants a different one. MySpace can help with that too.

You have probably heard of a million different online job searching companies that claim that they can get you into that perfect job that you've always wanted. Well, for these online job searches to survive they need people. Lots of people. MySpace currently has over 110+ million registered accounts — they must be doing something right — so who better to team up with? People need to find jobs, job search companies have job listings available, and MySpace has plenty of people who need jobs — or who may like to find new ones. MySpace Jobs to the rescue! The MySpace Jobs portal, as shown in Figure 15-18, can help the MySpacers of the world search for internships, part-time jobs, and full-time jobs. Any MySpace user can also use this portal to search by location as well. I'm sure that dream job in California is only a few clicks away.

Figure 15-18:
The MySpace Jobs portal can help you find an internship, part-time, or full-time job anywhere in the nation.

MySpace TV On Demand

With many people spending more time online, the major television networks are starting to make the leap into the online world. FOX and MySpace, both owned by Rupert Murdoch's News Corporation, have taken this next step by creating a TV On Demand portal, as seen in Figure 15-19, for many of their television shows. By simply downloading the FOX Full Throttle video player, you can be watching all the FOX television you want from the place where you already spend a majority of your time, MySpace. This is yet another way that MySpace has been the leader in the always-evolving world of media distribution. You can find your way to the On Demand TV portal by clicking the TV On Demand link in the main MySpace navigational links in the upper left-hand corner of the main MySpace home page.

Whatever it is you're into, and whatever it is you aspire to be, MySpace is working on ways to help you get there by connecting you to the people and information you need. Take a few minutes and explore the other talented individuals who have a MySpace home. You just may find the other half of your future comedic duo or an up-and-coming director that can bring your screenplay to life.

Part V
The Part of Tens

The 5th Wave — By Rich Tennant

"Amy surfs MySpace a lot, so for protection we installed several filtering programs that allow only approved sites through. Which of those ten sites are you looking at now, Amy?"

In this part . . .

Ten reasons you can't skip the Part of Tens:

- Bite-size chunks are easier to digest. Just ask the people who make fish nuggets.

- Top 10 lists are the preferred way of communicating in the world today, closely followed by text messaging and MySpace mail.

- We actually wrote these chapters in the daytime after a good night's sleep, so they might make more sense than the others.

- You've come this far . . . only a few more pages to go!!!

- We're serious about MySpace safety. So serious we talk about it again here.

- Dan Gookin, the guy who wrote the first *For Dummies* book, said he'd break our legs if we didn't include this part. We're afraid of Dan.

- The chapter on MySpace resources is like getting a list of great paint stores when you have a room that's dying to be painted purple.

- You can brag to your friends how you read *four full chapters* in under ten minutes.

- After you've "friended" all 150 million MySpace users (or however many there are by the time you get this book), you can move on to one of the other social networking sites we list . . . and start over.

- "Part of Tens" kind of sounds like our project editor's last name, Pottenger. We consider this part a tribute to him.

Chapter 16

Ten MySpace Tools for Staying Safe

*W*ith all of MySpace's highly publicized problems with adult users making illegal advances toward teenagers and stalkers using the site to find their victims, the old advice about an ounce of prevention being worth a pound of cure has never been more applicable. Taking the time to change a few settings on your MySpace profile can add a level of protection to your MySpace account that goes a long way toward keeping it free of problems. This chapter focuses on the tools MySpace has built into the site to help you keep all the Internet bad guys away from your page. In addition to the tools you'll find in this chapter — by the way, we are giving you twelve of them, not ten — consider the extra two freebies — we have some more helpful safety advice in Chapter 17.

For even more in-depth coverage on anything and everything related to safety on MySpace, check out Chapter 3.

Set Your Profile to Private

MySpace's privacy settings allow you to block your full profile from users other than the people on your Friends List. Would-be viewers who are not on your Friends List see your profile name, default photo, gender, age, city/state or region, country, your last login date, and your MySpace URL — but that's all they'll see. All other info you choose to include about yourself — your personal favorites, blog entries, and comments, whatever — won't show up. You can change privacy settings on your Change Account Settings page.

Require E-mail or Last Name to Add as a Friend

If you want to limit your Friend Requests to only the people you know in the real world, select the check box that sets that limit in the Privacy Settings screen. MySpace requires would-be friends to enter either the e-mail address or the last name you entered when signing up for the site before they'll send through a Friend Request from any user. This option is helpful if you want to keep your Friends List limited to people you already know — but don't want to take the time to review every single Friend Request you receive. This option still allows non-friends (or yet-to-be-friends) to view your basic profile.

For more information on tweaking various friend-related settings to your liking, see Chapter 4.

Approve Comments

Sometimes, despite your best efforts to keep a low profile on MySpace, your friends can blow your cover. They might leave a comment saying "WE'RE THE BEST SENIOR CLASS NORTHEAST HIGH SCHOOL HAS EVER SEEN" or "sorry to hear about your breakup, but you should have fun now that you're single again" (yikes) — and tell the world more about you than you want the world to know.

The Privacy Settings screen allows you to approve any comment your friend leaves for your profile page before it's posted. Rather than shooting the comment directly onto your page, this setting sends you a message asking you to approve or deny the comment before it posts for all to see.

The Privacy Setting screen also includes an option that limits comments on your blog entries to friends only. For more on blogging, see Chapter 6.

Limit Access to Your Blogs

Diaries have come a long way from the paper journals protected by a tiny lock and key that past generations hid under the bed. Blogs have made the art of journal writing a public exercise. Of course, you could usually break into those old diaries with a paper clip and read your sister's entries any time you wanted — but even then, they weren't viewable by millions of people at once. An online diary is as out-there and it's as visible as it gets. Keep that in mind when you decide to blog about your coworkers.

You can reclaim some privacy on your MySpace blog by choosing the privacy level of each individual post. You have four choices:

✓ **Public:** Public blog entries are readable by all MySpace users — friends, strangers, visiting Martians, everybody.

✓ **Diary:** These entries are a throwback to when you kept your writings under lock and key. They are only viewable by you — and you alone. Everybody else gets left out, because digital "locks" are impervious to even the shiniest of paper clips.

✓ **Friends:** Friends' entries are viewable only by the people on your Friends List. This is a good setting to use whenever your blog includes personal information.

✓ **Preferred List:** The Preferred List setting carves your audience down to a select few people. For example, if you want to share specific family information in your blog, you could set a Preferred List to include only your family members who use MySpace. That way, your kinfolk are the only ones viewing your entry.

Select your preferred level of privacy on the screen where you make your blog entry.

Whether you're interested in more privacy or more accessibility, you can find more information on blog settings in Chapter 6.

Keep Your Name Out of Search

The Name option on the Profile Edit screen allows you to remove your real first and last name so they aren't associated with your profile. This change keeps other users from finding you if they search your name with MySpace's search tool. You can also change your profile name to something besides your real name in the same screen.

Hide Your Photos

In much the same way your MySpace blog can be changed to a private diary, you can also turn the photos you upload to MySpace into a private album that's viewable only by you. On the Upload Your Photo page, select the Only You option under the Allow Your Photos to Be Viewable By section. The change makes your photo page accessible only through your MySpace account. The option also removes your default photo from your MySpace profile page.

Chapter 10 offers more information on specifying who gets to see your photos — and who doesn't.

Limit Your Instant Message Access

MySpace's instant messaging (IM) tools can be a handy way to drop quick notes to your friends. They can also be a pain if you find yourself getting messages from users you don't know and don't care to know. There are a couple of ways to limit your IM availability:

- ✔ **Hide Your Online Status:** MySpace lets other users know when you're on the site, presumably available to receive instant messages. Changing this option on the Change Account Setting screen blocks MySpace from reporting your online status.

- ✔ **Change Your Instant Message Privacy Settings:** The Change Account Settings screen also includes a link to your IM privacy settings. Following this link lets you select who can send you instant messages. You can choose to receive IM's from anyone, friends only, or block instant messages altogether.

For more information about customizing your instant-message settings, see Chapter 5.

Keep Your Photos out of E-mail

MySpace includes a quick link on public photo pages that allow you to e-mail links to individual photos to any e-mail address. The No Pic Forwarding option on the Privacy Settings page takes the option off your photo page so your images don't wing their way out into the e-mail world unless you send them there yourself.

It's worth noting that this option only removes the quick link for e-mailing images. People who visit your photos page can still copy your images or get the direct link to the photo and send the image out via e-mail. The only way you can keep other users completely away from your photos is to hide the page — and that's explained earlier in this chapter, in the section "Hide Your Photos."

A picture is worth a thousand words; just be sure you've got control of what yours are saying, and to whom. For more on photo settings, see Chapter 10.

Filter Group Invites

A famous comedian once quipped, "I wouldn't join any club that would have me as a member." Some MySpace groups take the opposite tack — and try to add anyone they possibly can. Usually they do that through group invites. If you want to avoid the possible guilt-by-association that might come from joining just any group, select the Friend Only Group Invites option on your Privacy Settings screen. This option makes sure only your friends can recommend group membership to you.

MySpace is all about groups, but it's also all about making your own social choices. For more on groups and settings, see Chapter 9.

Blocking Users

Sometimes people just can't take a hint. You ignore their messages, delete their comments, and set your profile to private, but they still keep bugging you. In cases like this one, it might be time to block the user. Go to the annoying user's profile page and click the Block User link, located in the box with the user's other contact links. After verifying the block, you add the user to a list that prevents them from communicating with you via MySpace. It's kind of like forwarding all your junk mail and telemarketer calls to an empty house far away from where you have to deal with them.

If the polite equivalent of "Back off!" or "In your dreams!" isn't getting the message across, Chapter 3 provides more information about blocking other MySpace users.

The Delete Key Is Your Friend

It is your space, after all. If you see something that someone has added to your page and you don't like it, kick it off your page. For example . . .

- Blog comments can be removed.
- Photo comments can be deleted.
- Friend Requests from creepy-looking strangers can be denied.
- Mail messages from people you don't know can be marked for deletion.
- You can resign from groups you've joined.

One click gets rid of profile comments you don't want on your page. Persistently pesky friends can vanish from your Friends List so you won't have to deal with their comments, bulletins, or other attempts at contact (on MySpace, anyway). And everything you put on your own page — from your photos to your blogs to your personality descriptions — can be edited or erased at any given moment. Don't think of your MySpace page as set in stone. It's a work in progress — you can make any changes necessary to get the page you want, no matter what mood you're in on any given day.

Contacting MySpace

We've been told since we were kids that nobody likes a tattletale. But as much fun as MySpace is, it isn't a playground and there aren't bullies who will be waiting for you at the curly slide. MySpace wants to hear from you when something on the site just isn't appropriate or in good taste.

Okay, you do have some countermeasures available — and MySpace encourages users to try all the tools we've mentioned in this chapter before letting them know that somebody is in violation of their policies. But when someone is in obvious violation of their terms of service, they ask that you waste no time in contacting them with that user's URL and an explanation of your complaint. They have no patience for identity theft, spam, violations of the age policy, online harassment, libel, false identities, or copyright violation, and will certainly be thankful for your helping them avoid trouble (after all, a bad apple can ruin the whole bunch). You can get links to MySpace's customer-service contact page by clicking the Help link at the top of your profile page.

We do want to echo one point that MySpace makes to would-be customer service users: If a MySpace user threatens you in any way, not only should you let MySpace know, but you should also contact your local law-enforcement officials. Just because a threat isn't made in a physical or face-to-face confrontation certainly doesn't make it any less serious.

Chapter 17

Ten Ways to Keep Away from MySpace Bad Guys

*W*e mentioned — way back in the first chapter — that MySpace is a reflection of the real world. As such, when you use MySpace, you need to apply a lot of the same rules for getting by that you use in your everyday life. This chapter should serve as a reminder of all those little life lessons that also work on MySpace.

Okay, we'll probably sound very parental here, warning you to look both ways before you cross the street. We may even sound like one of those hokey public-service commercials. No biggie. We figure MySpace can be a fun place or a dangerous place — and applying a little common sense can make all the difference. Consider this chapter your jump start on MySpace street smarts.

Don't Take MySpace to the Real World

MySpace was established to let bands reach their audiences and expand their fan bases. Since then, it's evolved into a place that's not just for bands and their screaming throngs (hey, daydreams are free) — it's the place for everyone: "the place for friends," as they say. Through MySpace, people make contact not only with their current friends, but also with new people who share similar interests. We enjoy using the site for that purpose — and we've made some good friendships online that way, with people we would never have even met if it weren't for MySpace.

But MySpace — like the whole Internet — grew out of the real world. It has all the human potentials, both good and bad. So we think three overall security tips are worth a quick review, even if they seem a little obvious at first. (Some people just haven't figured them out yet. Do them a favor: Show them this page.)

So here are our the *MySpace For Dummies* Big Three All-Star Don'ts:

- ✔ Don't set up private meetings to meet people you just happen to encounter on MySpace.
- ✔ Don't share any information that might allow people you meet on MySpace to track you down via other means. (Translation: Don't give out personal access information like your phone number or home address.)
- ✔ Don't ever post any sort of personal financial or identification information on MySpace — for instance, the Social Security, credit card, or bank account numbers that scam artists and identity thieves are always looking for.

Our goal with all these security tips isn't to turn you paranoid (not *too* paranoid, anyway). It's just to make sure you don't share anything on MySpace that might hurt or endanger you in the real world. The more you keep the real world separate from MySpace, the less chance you have of running afoul of safety issues.

Getting messages from people you don't know is almost inevitable on MySpace. Remember that ignoring these messages is always an option. Most of the time, users who don't hear back from you simply go away. Persistent message senders can be blocked or reported to MySpace — and you have every right to do that at the mere tinge of "creepy" or "crazy."

Don't Talk to Strangers

Sometimes the old advice is the best advice. When you get a mail message or IM from a MySpace user you don't know, follow up — discreetly — by clicking the sender's profile and poking around that page a bit. If it doesn't look like anyone you know, ignore the message and delete it. If it's really one of your friends hiding behind an anonymous profile, that person will write you back to reveal his or her true identity eventually. Otherwise, keep your contact to your friends.

Don't Use Your Real Name

You can set your profile name to be anything you want. If privacy is a concern of yours, avoid using your real name or a known nickname in your profile. Opt for something that reflects one of your interests, like the name of your favorite sports team or a character from a movie, or something a little cryptic and mysterious. Anything that makes it difficult to track you down in the real world will work.

Don't Post Contact Information

Because contact information is so easy for the wrong people to abuse, MySpace's Terms of Service actually *prohibit* posting contact information on your profile page. So spare yourself some spam and creep-out contacts; don't go putting up your address, telephone number, or home e-mail address. You can even go a step farther and remove your city location (via the Edit Profile link on your home page) or take down any current school information you've linked to your account.

Don't Leave Unwanted Clues

You can take lots of precautions to keep your real name off MySpace, your contact information unshared, and your profile blocked from everyone except your friends. But you can also undermine every one of these safety steps by leaving unwanted clues on your profile. You might name your school in a blog entry or mention the name of your favorite dance club in a caption on your photo page. Take a look at any content you want to post to your MySpace page for clues like these that could sabotage your efforts to keep your profile private.

On the same note, don't say or do anything on MySpace to reveal the identity of — or personal information about — any of your friends if they haven't already said it there themselves. If they want the world to know, they can say it first, and probably should (if anybody's going to say it). After all, you don't want them revealing your secrets, so don't reveal theirs. Mutual confidentiality is a great way to stay friends.

Don't Post Anything You Don't Want Your Mother to See

The information you put on your profile page could mean the difference between getting a lot of messages from strangers and getting none. Choosing a profile picture of yourself in your bikini or your muscle-baring workout clothes and adding a headline that reads "SEXY, SINGLE, AND LOOKING" is going to attract more users trolling for dates (or something else) than a profile with a subtler photo and headline.

Of course, if you're of legal age and you *are* indeed looking for someone to start a relationship with, by all means send out such a message on MySpace. Just be sure to not add in any personal information that would reveal more about how to contact you *outside* MySpace. The idea is to avoid any offline encounters you don't plan yourself.

Also keep in mind that MySpace is a public forum where co-workers, would-be employers, teachers, and professors, and others can (and will) see what you post. It's always a good idea to keep these audiences — and Murphy's Law — in mind. That way, if they stumble across something you wrote, you've already done your best to make sure you're not sending signals that could mess up your offline life.

Play Nice with Others

The world of anonymous posting on Internet forums and message boards has led to a recently discovered condition called "Internet muscles." It's a familiar malady: Talk is cheap; anonymous talk is big *and* cheap — sometimes a lot bigger than who's doing the talking. To certain individuals, the anonymity that the online world affords is like an invitation to develop aggressive and threatening attitudes they wouldn't get away with in the real world without the brawn to back up their behavior.

You can see bouts of Internet muscles flare up on MySpace from time to time, as some people treat the site as an opportunity to start arguments and leave nasty comments for other users. Trust us, nothing good ever came out of Internet fighting (unless you really enjoy bouts of high blood pressure). Go for the Delete key or the Block User option when someone gets under your skin. Firing back might lead to offline issues that aren't worth dealing with. After you've taken care of business, log off MySpace, count to 100, and talk to your *real* friends — either in the real world or when you're back online. Why not step aside for awhile and go grab a cup of coffee?

Don't Share Your Account

If you have a personal account, keep it personal. Here are three ways to do that:

- ✔ Don't let others jump on and send messages or leave comments under your account that you might have to explain later.

- ✔ Don't share your password with someone else. It's supposed to be a secret — your secret.

- ✔ If someone figures out your password and logs on to your account, use your Account Settings screen to change the password to something new or just cancel the account and create a new one.

Always Sign Out

Whenever you finish using MySpace, your last step should always be to click the Sign Out link at the top of page to end your session. If you don't, and your computer stays on, you're still signed on. Staying signed on could give the next person to sit down at the computer full access to your MySpace account.

Be especially careful not to forget this step if you use a public terminal to access MySpace.

Use a Separate E-mail Address

Although it's nearly impossible for anyone to get access to the e-mail address associated with your MySpace account, you can give it a little extra protection — as a good final line of security — by using a separate e-mail account for all your MySpace activity. This option is especially useful if you have a school or business e-mail address you want to use, but which might reveal info you don't want to share about yourself if it's discovered as your link to MySpace. There are a lot of options for getting free e-mail accounts on the Internet these days. See Chapter 2 for details on a few free e-mail options.

Chapter 18

Ten MySpace Resources

Your new MySpace page is like a new house. Chances are, when you move into a new house, the rooms are empty and the walls are white and bare. It's up to you to add the color and decorations to make it your own.

Though MySpace is highly customizable, most of the tools for dressing up a MySpace page are actually not provided by MySpace. A whole new class of online tools has popped up to help MySpace users make their pages unique. (Gee — ya think this thing is catching on?) This chapter points you toward a few of the top sites for getting your MySpace page above board and winning you positive comments from hordes of admiring visitors.

Thomas' Myspace Editor

This popular MySpace editorial tool generates a unique page of programming code you can drop into your MySpace page to give it your own look. Simple drop-down menus let you set the color and image on your background, the size and color of your text fonts, the borders of your page tables, and color of your scrollbars. Once you have your code, just copy it and drop it into the About Me section of your profile or the bio on your band site to create a one-of-a-kind look to your MySpace page. Generate your code — and your look — at www.strikefile.com/myspace.

MySpace Toolbox

MySpace Toolbox, found at http://myspacetoolbox.com, provides a profile editor that's similar to Thomas' Myspace Editor, except it takes the tools a step farther — into the realm of pre-designed layouts and ready-to-load goodies such as backgrounds, images, and videos by popular musical artists. You can also customize your favorite music, movie, and book lists with images to replace the text. Do watch out for the advertising links on this site, though. Sometimes they lean toward the adult side, though there aren't any related images lurking around to worry about.

Glitter Graphics

Leaving a sparkling, pastel message in your friends' comments columns seems to be the current rage on MySpace. Glitter Graphics, located at www.glittergraphics.us, provides a generator you can use to create your own glittery messages that are sure to catch any visitor's eye. The site also features tools for creating blog and profile surveys, as well as eye candy (scrolling images and graphics).

Tools For MySpace

Tools For MySpace features a page layout editor. (Yeah, we know — every site we've mentioned up to this point has a page-layout editor and we've probably only touched 0.1% of the Web sites out there that feature a one of those. Embarrassment of riches, okay?) This site, online at www.toolsformyspace.com, offers up a few other fun tools — including code for adding games to your page, a customizer for your Contact Table, and page translator that alters your page to another language or into slang. Our favorite tool, though, is the customized box that lets visitors know when you're in their extended network.

GIMP

GIMP (also known as "*the* GIMP") is the shortened name for the GNU Image Manipulation Program. With a name like that, we'd prefer it be simply called GIMP as well. In simpler terms, GIMP is image-editing software you can use to get your photos ready for MySpace. The software is on a par with professional image editors such as Adobe Photoshop — and is completely free. The software is available for the Windows, Mac, and Unix (so you know it'll work on Linux) computing platforms. You can get your own copy of GIMP at www.gimp.org.

Windows Movie Maker

MySpace provides a place for you to upload your personal videos to share with other MySpace users. Before you upload your video, though, you might want to edit it down to the best parts or add titles and credits. Windows Movie Maker is a free application that comes with Windows XP; it includes tools for editing clips, adding sound and text to video, and saving your finished piece as a Web-ready file. Get more info on using Windows Movie Maker at www.microsoft.com/moviemaker.

iMovie

Windows Movie Maker is a Microsoft-created product, so it shouldn't be too surprising that the software only works on a Windows PC. If you have a Mac, look for the latest release of iMovie to accomplish the same tasks. It's not a free product, but it's part of Apple's iLife suite of products — and that includes tools for photo editing and creating music, Web sites, and DVDs. Go to www.apple.com/ilife for details.

Audacity

Between all the music files being passed around and all the podcasts being created and posted to the Internet, the online world has become the top platform for sharing sound. Audacity puts the power of a sound recorder and editor on your computer. This free software, downloadable at http://audacity.soundforge.net, provides the software for turning your PC or Mac (or Linux machine if you're really geeky and proud of it) into a recording studio. If you're in a band, you can use the software to convert your song files into formats ready for upload to MySpace. Wannabe podcasters can also record their shows with Audacity.

It's worth noting that Audacity is only the software piece of turning your computer into a recording studio. If you want to start recording on your computer, you're going to need a few other tools. If you're ready to take that step, we recommend you take a look at *PC Recording Studios For Dummies* by Jeff Strong. If you want to launch a podcast, grab a copy of *Podcasting For Dummies* by Tee Morris and Evo Terra.

Quizilla

What better way to explain who you are to the MySpace universe than by sharing the results of an off-the-wall quiz created by a bored Web wanderer? (Works for us.) Okay, that might be a cynical way of looking at Quizilla, the site where people can create quizzes designed to give you insight into your personality. Once you get your quiz results, you can generate some code that you can paste into MySpace so you can share the new insight with your MySpace friends. (Hey, we just found out the obsolete technology our personality most resembles is Gregg shorthand!) Get in on the fun at `http://quizilla.com`. This site has become so popular that is was recently purchased by MTV Networks — look for changes on the horizon!

Spell Check

Okay, you don't have to go ransacking the Internet for this one. But seriously, would it kill you to run all the stuff you type into MySpace through spell check just once before you put it online for the world to see? Maybe proof-read it really quickly?

Sorry, it's just a pet peeve of ours . . . we *are* authors, you know.

Chapter 19

Ten Other Social Networking Sites

Although it's now the best known, MySpace wasn't actually the first social-networking Web site. Of course, given its popularity — and the race among Web sites to become the "next MySpace" — you can bet MySpace won't be the last of its kind, either. In fact, the species seems to be multiplying. Whether they came before or after the launch of MySpace, other social-networking sites offer their own spins on the idea of linking up online. How many different networks users actually want to participate in at the same time is yet to be seen, but there are certainly going to be a lot of options for those willing to commit to more than one. There are even social-networking sites for your pets!

Friendster

Napster may have triggered a "-ster" craze in Web site names a few years ago, but Friendster was one of the first widely used sites dedicated to social networking. It launched in 2002, and was the leader in the field for a couple years until MySpace's music-focused approach got really popular and moved to the front of the pack. Friendster offers many of the same profile-creation options as MySpace — including extensive biographical information, messaging with friends, music and video posting, and blogs. MySpace got the upper hand on Friendster by being more open to allowing band, promotional, and parody accounts. Friendster has stayed in the social-networking game, though — and currently claims to be the online home to nearly 30 million users. You can visit at www.friendster.com.

Facebook

Facebooks are the printed books traditionally given to incoming college freshmen, showing photos of other students and members of the campus faculty and staff. In 2004, a Harvard student applied the idea to a Web site and `www.facebook.com` was born. The site is primarily known as a social network for college students to connect with other students on their campuses. Facebook has 100% penetration in U.S. colleges and one survey reported that 85% of the students who attend colleges covered by Facebook have a profile on the site.

The site added profiles for users in high schools, the military, and certain corporations as it grew. In 2006, Facebook finally opened itself to members who weren't affiliated with schools or member businesses — but its origins are still its greatest strength. With this site's strong ties to the tech-savvy college-student community, some Internet watchers believe Facebook has the best chance of challenging MySpace's dominance in this field.

Classmates.com

With over a decade online, Classmates.com is the old man of the online social networking world. Classmates.com built on the idea of extending existing offline social networks into the online world by creating a site to keep people in touch with their high school and college classmates. Like most networking sites, individuals can sign up and create a profile sharing basic personal information. Classmates.com groups user profiles by school or work affiliations.

Classmates.com differs from some networks by offering a fee-based membership level that allows users to see other members' full profiles, initiate contact with other members, or form groups for event planning. Basic membership at the site is free, however — and Classmates.com claims over 40 million active members. If you wonder how many of those might have gone to your old school, you can check 'em out at `www.classmates.com`.

Reunion.com

Similar to Classmates.com, Reunion.com works to network users with people they've known in the past and might have lost touch with. The site started as a merger between two alumni networking sites (similar to Classmates.com). Since then, Reunion.com has expanded to offer services that focus on linking you up with individuals who might be searching for you through the site.

Reunion.com also offers a fee-based premium membership that offers messaging and full profile-viewing privileges. Premium membership also delivers the opportunity to see which other members have been searching for your name. Full details on the site are at www.reunion.com.

Bebo

Found at www.bebo.com, Bebo is one of the fastest-growing online social-networking options. It has had 22 million users sign up — in its first year of existence. Along with the usual photo, blog, profile, video, and comment posting options, Bebo also adds in self-created polls and quizzes to your Bebo pages.

One of the more interesting tools Bebo calls their own is the whiteboard — a feature that lets other users draw a picture to be posted on your page. The site is especially popular in Ireland, where it ranked as the country's second most popular Web site.

Xanga

The blog is the star at www.xanga.com. Xanga pages put the users' blogs front and center. Fee-based premium memberships expand the storage space on your account and open up your page to customizing via pre-designed layouts — but even non-paying members can update the do-it-yourself way by using HTML code.

Networking on the site happens as users join blogrings — yep, the blogs come linked as rings (no, you can't put your car keys on them) — leave comments about particular blog entries, or subscribe to other users' blogs to stay up to date on their entries.

Orkut

The vast growth of Google has landed the tech powerhouse in almost every field. So it's no shock that Google has its own social-networking site. Orkut, found at www.orkut.com, launched with little fanfare in early 2004 — but these days, it's grown to over 28 million users.

Orkut takes a unique approach in its growth: Membership is by invitation only. The Orkut sign-up page claims the approach assures that "we won't grow too large too quickly and everyone will have at least one person to vouch for them." (Of course, maybe this invitation-only thing carries enough "exclusive" cachet to make *everybody* want in. Pretty clever, those marketing departments.)

Orkut is especially popular in Brazil. The South American nation accounts for over half of Orkut's users.

Flickr

Photo-sharing site Flickr, which is owned by search giant Yahoo!, makes the cut as a social-networking site as well, thanks to its approach that provides public viewing for photos posted on the site. Flickr users create photo albums on their accounts, and that's where they store and share personal photos with other users (or with the public at large). The site gets a leg up on other photo-storage sites by allowing users to tag their photos with keywords — which makes the images a lot easier to search. Users can also set albums as private if they wish. Flip through some Flickr albums at www.flickr.com.

YouTube

This is not your grandparents' — or even your parents' — TV. Here — through the magic of the Internet — the viewers get to provide the content. YouTube, which was acquired by Google for $1.65 billion in October of 2006, jumped out of the gate and quickly established itself as the premiere community for sharing video clips and quickly became a part of the pop culture. The site is adding accounts and viewers at a rate rivaled only by MySpace, as more people catch on to the often-hilarious content shared on the site.

Even traditional media outlets like the television industry and record labels have warmed to YouTube, despite their qualms about the redistribution of their content. Initial attacks on the site — based on worries over copyright violation — have changed to acceptance. (After all, the site offers additional exposure to network broadcasts, music-video plays, and even favorite advertisements! Sweet.) Tune in at www.youtube.com to catch the latest clips.

Dogster and Catster

People who adore their pets want them in every aspect of their lives. Our canine and feline companions can now join the online social-networking revolution via their owners — who have those handy opposable thumbs for using the computer — at Dogster (www.dogster.com) and Catster (www.catster.com).

Owners establish profiles for their pets that include photos, bios, nicknames, pet peeves (sorry about that), favorite toys, and favorite tricks for dogs (never a species known for tricks, cats just share their favorite napping spots). Of course, the dogs and cats can sign on friends to their pages and share messages with their fellow four-legged companions. And — naturally — both sites have space where pets can blog the details of their day.

Index

● *C* ●

● **Z** ●